# Unleashed Fury

New Directions in the Human-Animal Bond
Alan M. Beck, series editor

# Unleashed Fury

## The Political Struggle for Dog-friendly Parks

Julie Walsh

Purdue University Press
West Lafayette, Indiana

Library of Congress Cataloging-in-Publication Data

Walsh, Julie M., 1962-
  Unleashed fury : the political struggle for dog-friendly parks / Julie Walsh.
      p. cm. -- (New directions in the human-animal bond)
  Includes bibliographical references and index.
  ISBN 978-1-55753-575-7
  1. Dogs--Law and legislation--Political aspects--United States. I. Title.
  KF390.5.D6W35 2011
  346.7304'7--dc22
                                        2010017992

In memory of Plato (7/20/89–1/15/02),
Cabot (3/14/02–5/9/09), and their
many canine friends who have
gone to their final rest

# Contents

# Acknowledgments

There are so many to thank! This project was not exactly a mainstream one in the discipline of political science, and I benefitted enormously from the support of sympathetic colleagues and friends. At American International College, several colleagues, past and present, provided useful advice and moral support. Many thanks to Robin Varnum, Tom Maulucci, Fred Sard, Art Wilkins, Kim Hudson, Josette Henschel, Wes Renfro, Vickie Hess, Alan Cottrell, Kathleen Angco-Vieweg, and Joe Ramondetta. I had great mentors at the University of Connecticut—Howard Reiter, Rich Hiskes, and Kent Newmyer—who taught me to think outside of the box and to whom I am forever grateful. *None* of these people *necessarily shares my views about dogs and leashing*, a fact that is true for all those humans I thank below as well.

Special thanks are owed to Dr. Alan Beck at Purdue University for his willingness to entertain this topic and his helpful commentary. It was enormously valuable to have such an expert on the human-animal bond review this work. Many thanks to Rebecca Corbin, Katherine Purple, and all at Purdue University Press who have been so helpful in this process.

I am grateful as well to all of those people, on both sides of this issue, who spoke to me about their experiences or answered my written questions. Special thanks to Ken Ayers, Marc Bekoff, Linda McKay, and Karin Hu who alerted me to studies in this area.

I owe particular gratitude to an incredible group of friends, whom I met while walking my dogs. With them, I share not only a love of animals, but a great bond. Their friendship has been on full display daily or weekly during our many walks when we have appreciated one another, our dogs, and the beauty of nature. That experience provided some of the motivation to write this book. One of these friends, Vic Neumann, is an exceptionally talented

*Cabot with Devin in background, courtesy of Vic Neumann.*

photographer who is kind enough to take and share photographs of our dogs. One of those pictures is included in the acknowledgments section. Thank you to Vic and all of my dog-walking friends: Ross Shapiro, Val Mendizabal, Barb Ferguson, Joanne Pigott, Igor and Marina Knelev, Lilly Feldman, Deb Percival, Charry Salmon, Dan Tamkin, Peter Cooperman, Roger Giadone, Liz Vitale, Louis Kiefer, Sheryl Horowitz-Kiefer, Pat Ryiz, Mary Bannon, Jay Lichtmann, Marilyn Rotondo, Fran Macoomb, Becky Labombard, Lisa Roellig, Susan Berlin, Carol Galbraith, Sandi Cone-Foley, Thomas Foran, and Deb Feigenbaum.

My thanks extend to my canine friends too. I dedicated this book to two very special dogs, Plato and Cabot, and their many friends who have gone to their final rest. It seemed quite fitting to dedicate this book to dogs, all of whom enjoyed off-leash play. Plato, a Dalmatian, had an incredible zest for life, which she confronted each day with exuberance and joy. It was truly a beautiful site to watch her run, something she did often. Mistaking herself for a Labrador, she loved the water as well, particularly the act of jumping into it. Although Plato was shy, she was incredibly bonded with my husband and me and managed to share her love with a few other close friends, particularly humans Sukie Zeeve and Louise Martin and her canine buddy, the late and beloved Rupert. Very much an individual, Plato had her "issues," such as a fear of squeaking toys, and even eating out of a bowl. We loved her for the beautiful individual that she was and miss her greatly.

Cabot, who would *never* have been able to understand a fear of squeaking toys, had a much larger circle of friends. When she died very suddenly and unexpectedly, many people cried for her, not just me. My dog-walking friends overwhelmed me with their generosity of spirit and outpouring of love. It is no wonder that people cried for Cabot, as she loved everyone, both dogs and people. She was always happy, almost smiling. I recall leaving her for a few days when she was young with a woman who took dogs into her home. When I returned to pick her up, the woman, looking a bit tired, said in so many words, "She just can't wait to get her paws on the other dogs! She wants to play with all of them." She then asked me about getting her training. In fact, Cabot proceeded to do a lot of training—of me, whom she had wrapped around her paw; my husband Mike, who purchased a step to make it easier for her to get on the bed; my brother-in-law George, who brought her bones cut just so she could get the marrow out; and even my friends, especially Ross, who was taught to give her cookies at every turn in the walk. (His late and beloved dog Roxy trained me similarly.) Cabot had a passion for squeaking rubber toys and would take these, some of which she had "borrowed" from other dogs, into the water and at times, drown them by mistake. She would then spend *a lot* of time obsessively looking for them. Once, the year before she died, she lost one in a river and just would not give up. Ultimately, I had to fish out this beautiful, exhausted, flat-coated retriever. That day I felt more love for her than ever, and later I silently sat with her as she slept. That was Cabot, a big personality and a true love. Life will never be the same without her.

I am also deeply indebted to the human members of my family. Mike, my husband, has been incredibly supportive throughout all of my undertakings. Mike's family and my brothers, sister, and their spouses and children have all been supportive of me as well. They have followed the progress of this book, which has been many years in the making, and have encouraged me along the way. Special thanks to Jim, Beth, John, Joan, Joe and Barb McGivern, Mary and George Valentine, and Mary Walsh. Thanks too to our two dogs, Devin (a.k.a., "such a good boy" and also a love), and our pup, Sadie, who brought joy back to us in the aftermath of Cabot's death.

# Chapter I

## Why are Dog Walkers so Mad?

In town and city council meetings all over the United States, citizens have been debating leash laws for dogs with an intensity usually reserved for such hot-button issues as abortion or gun rights. As with those issues, positions are passionately held, opponents are often demonized, and compromises appear difficult to obtain. Typically, dog walkers far outnumber leashing advocates at these meetings, and it is their fury that the media highlights. To the casual observer, dog walkers seem to have lost perspective and to be inexplicably furious. What the casual observer does not know, however, is the story behind that anger.

At parks across the country, it has become commonplace for dog owners to be scolded, ticketed, and in some rare cases, even arrested for walking their dogs off-leash in places that had either allowed or tolerated that activity before. It was just such an arrest in San Francisco that motivated many people to join organized groups to advocate for the interests of dog walkers in 1997. Michelle Parris, described as "the Mother Teresa" of the dog community, had founded and ran an organization called "Grateful Dogs Rescue," which rescued and trained dogs with special needs, either behavioral or medical. Fostering such dogs until they were placed in appropriate homes, Parris prevented them from probable death. To make money, Parris ran a dog day care service, Doggie Desires. For the last twenty-five years, she had taken these dogs for a walk to a field in San Francisco with no problems. On April 8, 1997, she let her two dogs and her two clients' dogs, all "mostly miniature or elderly … [and] well behaved," out to play at this location and was confronted by law enforcement.[1]

In response, Parris declined to show her license, packed her dogs in the car, and left. According to the park ranger, Parris was confrontational, allegedly

1

saying, "You're the bitch that's been harassing everyone."[2] Parris maintained that the ranger would not identify herself, and as a result, she decided to leave. On her way out, driving at approximately twenty miles per hour, she was surrounded by four official cars and arrested. To dog walkers, this was the behavior of an authoritarian government—hauling an unarmed woman away for walking dogs off-leash. The federal government formally charged Parris with two misdemeanors, for allowing her dogs to run off-leash in forbidden areas and for preventing a park ranger from doing her job. While prosecutors dropped the former charge, they tried Parris on the latter one. As we will later see, that trial, which bordered on farce at times, galvanized dog walkers all the more.

While such arrests are unusual, ticketing has become commonplace. Increasingly, dog walkers are witnessing the criminalization of a treasured part of their daily routine. Making matters worse, the media has at times trivialized and ridiculed the impassioned response of dog walkers. Compared to concerns about terrorism, global warming, health care, and a plethora of other issues, leash laws can indeed seem trivial. Yet recreational interests are important to people and in normal times, ensure their psychological and physical health. Consider the attention given to sports at all governmental levels and on newscasts. Any attempt to eliminate a sport would be met with opposition. For a substantial minority, off-leash dog walking is their "sport" or recreational interest.

In fact, for dog owners, we will soon see, walking their dogs is much more than a sport. It is an essential part of providing adequate care for someone they love, their dog. As we will discover, the most popular breeds of dogs today are ones that require substantial amounts of exercise and socialization with other dogs. It is cruel to deny these dogs activities, such as running and swimming, for which they were bred. When confronted with newly enforced bans on these activities, owners have demanded explanations from authorities. Unfortunately, those explanations have further frustrated dog walkers because they typically fly in the face of scientific evidence.

## THE SCAPEGOATING OF DOGS

Dogs, according to some governmental explanations, are at best a nuisance, and at worst a danger to society. They are allegedly responsible for the bacterial pollution of waterways and the extinction or near extinction of several species of wildlife. Further, they are a danger to the physical safety of humans, particularly children. The problem is that research does not support these conclusions, especially when properly focused on the pertinent issue at hand, namely, the impact of a *supervised*, off-leash dog.

Several studies have documented the harmful effects caused by feral and free-roaming dogs, but far fewer studies have examined the effects of recreational walking with dogs, leashed or unleashed, on the environment and other species. The results of those studies, in their totality, do not justify the blanket exclusion or leashing of dogs. To be sure, there are a few studies that found instances of dogs harming or otherwise causing problems for wildlife by introducing diseases, such as parvovirus.[3] That latter risk, of course, can be minimized via requirements for vaccinations. On the other side, there are studies that found no impact of dogs on wildlife patterns at all. For example, Forrest and Cassady St. Clair concluded, "Designation of sites for dogs to be on- or off-leash had no measurable effect on the diversity or abundance of birds and small mammals within the sites that we surveyed in the Edmonton River Valley."[4] Several additional studies found an impact on the flushing patterns of bird species and the use of trail areas by small mammals, such as squirrels and rabbits. For example, Lenth et al., in their study of Boulder County, concluded that mule deer, prairie dogs, and small mammals "exhibited reduced levels of activity in proximity to trails in areas with dogs."[5] Yet there is not a consensus that such impacts are injurious to those species that have modified their behaviors. As Gill et al. explain, "From a conservation perspective, human disturbance of wildlife is important only if it affects survival or fecundity and hence causes a population to decline."[6] There is simply not sufficient evidence upon which to charge dogs with causing wildlife populations to decline. In areas with heavy human and canine usage, it is, in fact, likely that other species have adapted to those patterns.[7] Just as the introduction of dogs and humans to a remote area could be disruptive to wildlife patterns, the *removal* of dogs and humans from heavy-use areas could be equally disruptive to some species.

Dog attacks of humans are another count in the indictment of off-leash play. Dog bites are common. Reminding people of this fact, Beck and Katcher write, "almost everyone knows the quote of John B. Bogart, city editor of the New York *Sun*: 'When a dog bites a man, that is not news, because it happens so often. But if a man bites a dog, that is news.'"[8] The data indicate, however, that the majority of dog bites occur on the dog owners' property, while the bulk of other incidents involve leashed and unsupervised, free-roaming dogs. For example, in New York City, the most populated urban setting in the country, the Department of Health found that only 2.3 and 2.2 percent of all dog bites in 2004 and 2005, respectively, occurred in public parks. Even then, the data do not specify whether the dog was leashed or not. Based on these findings, the Department of Health recommended an amendment to its code so as to allow off-leash play in public parks for certain hours.[9] The less common but horrific attacks in which a human is killed typically occur "in or around the house of the victim" and "[m]ore than half . . . involve dogs owned by the victim's family, and most of the other cases involve dogs of neighbors, friends, baby-sitters, or other acquaintances, meaning the animal is known to the victim."[10] What is more, experts agree that exercise and socialization *reduce* aggression in dogs. It is not unreasonable to conclude, then, that off-leash areas have the potential to lessen the number of bites on private property, where they are most common.

Finally, dogs are cited as polluters. Leash advocates at times merge the poop issue with the leashing one even though leashed dogs also create waste. To be sure, dog feces left un-scooped in public parks presents serious health risks. As Brandow documented in his analysis and history of New York City's poop scoop law, this issue nonetheless has the capability of arousing bitter divisions in the citizenry. As he explains, meetings over this issue in the 1970s "were characterized by shouting, merciless heckling of speakers, and borderline violence."[11] Dog owners sniffed a plot to ban dogs from the city, while others who exaggerated the health risks of dogs to humans wanted their expulsion. Both groups raised the stakes and made the issue much more threatening than it was in reality. As it turned out, New York's poop-scoop law became a model for other cities and helped to reconcile dogs with urban life. In that time period, however, the National League of Cities listed dog issues as the number-one concern about which mayors and city council members received mail.[12] Given that history, the marriage of this issue with leashing concerns is particularly volatile. It would seem wiser to disentangle this issue from the leashing one and to require owners to pick up after their dogs, whether leashed or not.

It is worth noting that even on this legitimate issue, dogs are sometimes assigned more blame than they deserve. For example, in Arlington County, Virginia, officials threatened to close off-leash sites in the 1990s because of water quality issues in the Four Mile Run watershed. Pro-leash advocates fingered dogs as the primary contributors to fecal coliform in the water. Judy Green, who was president of Arlington Dogs at the time, remarked, "Too often, particularly with the environmental issue, they are quick to blame dogs."[13] An actual study later found that dogs did indeed contribute fecal coliform to the water area, but not nearly as much as humans and waterfowl.[14] It is that type of exaggerated complaint, often made without any supporting evidence, that especially goads dog walkers.

## WHY DOG WALKERS CARE SO MUCH

In making all of these accusations, government officials do not seem to anticipate the intensity of reaction that they trigger from a large number of dog owners. This leashing issue hits a nerve because it is so emotionally important to them, grounded, as it is, first and foremost in a love for their dogs. To be sure, there are a small percentage of fanatics on each side of leash disputes. Describing them, Mahtesian writes,

> At one extreme, there are individuals . . . who resist any restraint on ownership. . . . The other fringe is inhabited by the pet-haters—such as . . . the individual suspected by Chicago police of poisoning dogs in the Rogers Park neighborhood.[15]

There is no denying the existence of such people, but they alone did not make this issue so volatile. On the contrary, the issue seems to generate emotional intensity in large numbers of non-fanatical people. As Serpell explains,

> People's opinions about the domestic dog have a tendency to veer towards extremes. For an increasingly large sector of the population, the dog is now perceived as a dangerous and dirty animal with few redeeming qualities . . . a veritable menace to society. . . .
>
> At the other end of the spectrum, an even larger constituency of dog lovers exists for whom this animal has become the archetype of affectionate fidelity and unconditional love. To members of this group, dogs are more human than animal.[16]

Despite the presence of these strong feelings, most people do not behave in criminal or conspicuous ways. They do, however, pay close attention to issues affecting their dogs and care deeply about the outcomes.

### The Power of Love

To understand the intensity with which the anti-leash side approaches the issue, one must first recognize, whether in agreement with such feelings or not, the depth of the bond between humans and dogs. As Serpell notes, "The dog-human relationship is arguably the closest we humans can ever get to establishing a dialogue with another sentient life-form."[17] This relationship began toward the end of the last Ice Age when humans were hunting and gathering. At that time, it is theorized that bands of wolves followed humans to feed on the latter's refuse and carcasses. As some wolves became dependent on the humans, it is speculated that they also provided a useful service in scaring other predators away. When people began to settle in permanent communities, they, in turn, influenced the development of the domestic dog via selective breeding. A recent study traces the origins of this domestication to the Middle East about 10,000 years ago, but larger numbers of dog remains from many parts of the world are dated 7,000 to 9,000 years back.[18] The dog was the first domesticated species. The human-canine relationship, then, clearly has an extensive history.

Humans have long been able to communicate with dogs to develop working relationships, as dogs historically have assisted humans in hunting, herding, security, and many other tasks. While some still use dogs for hunting and other work-related tasks, such as search and rescue, companionship is now often a more important or even sole function of dogs.[19] In all cases, the individual human and individual dog establish a relationship. As Hart explains, dogs "develop specific attachments for individuals, and remain near or in physical contact with their owners as if attached by an invisible cord."[20] They communicate with humans without speech but with great expression. Masson argues that "the reason why humans and dogs have such an intense relationship is that there is a mutual ability to understand one another's emotional responses."[21] Dogs express their emotions in ways that people understand instantly and signal love, affection, and forgiveness as a matter of course. Describing this canine propensity best, Masson writes,

> Dogs register no need to theorize about love . . . , they just show it. And show it and show it and show it. I am continually amazed at my dogs' ability to love so unconditionally and without ambivalence. . . . The capacity for love in the dog is so pronounced, so developed that it is almost like another sense or another organ. It might well be termed hyperlove, and it is bestowed upon all humans who live closely with a dog.[22]

Humans experience great pleasure from this relationship, as the dog provides them with an openly expressed love free from any criticism. As Sanders explains, humans are thus prompted "to feel strong emotional ties to their dogs."[23] Most, in other words, return the love. They play with and pet their dogs, talk to them, and bond with them on a deeply emotional level.

Statistics and studies demonstrate the importance of this loving relationship with humans. Indeed, dogs are often accorded the status of family member, a level of relationship that typically engenders the strongest emotional ties. While survey results vary somewhat, Sanders cites studies in which 70 to 99 percent of respondents defined their companion animals as members of the family. Over half, exactly 53.5 percent, identified their dog as a family member in the American Veterinary Medical Association's 2006 study.[24] A full one-third, according to two studies cited by Hart, ranked their dogs' importance *on par* with other human members of the family. According to Beck and Katcher, psychological tests often indicate that pets are "preferred family members, the ones we feel closest to."[25] Indeed, in one study, 69 percent claimed to give as much attention to their dogs as to their children. Evincing this fact, more than six million people report that they are as attached to their dog as they are to their children. It is no surprise, then, that people include their dogs in the rituals, celebrations, and routines that comprise their social life. Surveys show that roughly 90 percent of dog owners give birthday or holiday gifts to their dogs, 37 percent talk to them on the phone, and 17 percent carry pictures of them in their wallets.[26] Suffice it to say, millions love their dogs and assign their relationships with them high priority.

According to one survey, "93 percent of pet owners would risk their lives to save their animal."[27] Not surprisingly, then, people are willing to spend a great deal of money to care for their pets. In 2007, nationwide spending on pets, including food and medical care, was estimated to be $41 billion.[28] As Anderson observes, "We shower our companion animals with gourmet and organic foods, spa treatments, state-of-the-art medical care, luxurious vacations, and financial security."[29] As a result of human lifestyles and work schedules, dogs are in need of walking services and toys to occupy their time. Given their status as family members in so many cases, people want to provide them with healthy foods and to prolong their lives as long as possible. Veterinary care has risen to the latter challenge. According to Schaffer, "In 1980, . . . there were 1,981 specialists who held board certifications from twelve specialty professional organizations. By 2007 there were almost 9,000, and the number of recognized specialties had grown to twenty."[30] Because the overwhelming percentage of dogs now live inside the home, their cleanliness is also important to people, and there are myriad grooming services to accommodate that need. Indeed, 47 percent of pet owners reported that their pets slept with them in bed.[31] All of these behaviors are indicative of the love that people feel for their dogs.

## The Human Benefits

While non-pet owners might scoff at people's willingness to sacrifice their money and time for their pets, humans, the evidence shows, are often well served from these relationships with dogs and other pets. Some studies indicate that relationships with dogs foster social affiliation and self-esteem in humans. Dogs invite humans to be more extroverted. In his study of a London park, Messent found that those with dogs were more likely to converse with strangers. Because social contact nurtures self-esteem in people, Hart considers this socializing effect of dog companionship to be among the "most important indirect benefits for people."[32] This benefit has proven especially significant for children and elderly adults, especially children without siblings and elderly people who live alone. According to studies cited by Bekoff, Croatian children who lived with dogs were more empathic and socially oriented than those who did not live with dogs. American university students who had lived with dogs or cats were found to be more self-confident as well.[33] Other studies have noted that contact with animals might help to develop communication skills in young children.[34] In the case of elderly people, one study documented that bereaved persons with pets were less likely to experience depression and a deterioration of health in the immediate aftermath of spousal loss. "For years," according to Anderson, "considerable research on human-animal interactions (HAI) has shown that animals, dogs in particular, can ameliorate the effects of potentially stressful life events, such as divorce and grief; reduce levels of anxiety, loneliness, and depression; and enhance feelings of autonomy, competence, and self-esteem."[35]

Studies have documented physical and physiological benefits from the presence of dogs as well. For example, among other benefits, dogs have been found to increase post-coronary survival rates and reduce blood pressure.[36] In their studies, Beck and Katcher found that the sight of pets reduced stress levels. Unlike speaking to people, talking to animals also reduced stress and blood pressure. These studies have been confirmed "over and over again" and additional studies found, not surprisingly, that a "subject's own dog reduced stress more effectively than a strange dog."[37] The sight of a dog can induce a state of reverie, which can have the same effect as meditation and relax people enough to reduce blood pressure. However, Beck and Katcher stipulate that other animals and natural scenes can induce this effect as well.[38] In a recent review of findings in this area, they cite the need for additional and more focused research to resolve inconsistencies in the literature, but conclude that there is solid evidence of significant health benefits and positive influences on "transient physiological states, morale, and feelings of self-worth" from animal interactions. They are careful to note that not all populations are beneficially impacted from animal interactions, and further studies need to identify such populations.[39]

With training, dogs can contribute even more to the well-being of persons. They have long been used to assist the blind and disabled. More recently, dogs have been trained to detect oncoming seizures and some forms of cancer. Even for those who have dogs solely as companion animals, Hart highlights the simple benefit of the facilitation of exercise on the part of humans, which also contributes to good health. Given the epidemic of obesity in the United

States, the facilitation of exercise is no small matter.[40] Focusing on the benefits found in multiple studies, Hart concludes, "People who enjoy close relationships with their dogs appear to be buffered against many of the vicissitudes of life. Increasing documentation shows that stresses have less impact and that general health is more stable for dog owners than non-owners."[41]

These beneficial relationships with dogs are all the more valuable given the decline of community and the often troubled state of human relationships. As Sanders explains, "In a society in which everyday interaction is typically secondary, fleeting, noninvolving, and instrumental, many of us experience a lack of social connectedness and intimacy. . . . [P]eople often turn to companion animals as sources of these positive experiences."[42] Dogs, in particular, compensate with an obvious display of their emotions. Watching their antics and play, dog owners find it impossible not to catch their spirit. They develop an intrinsic appreciation not only for them, but for life itself. In Bekoff's words, "When animals play we can feel their deep joy. Play is contagious, and other animals [including humans] feel the joy and glee as well. . . . [T]he inherent joy and serenity in play often spreads to anyone who is watching."[43] Humans therefore derive great joy from watching off-leash play. Additionally, that experience often creates a bonding experience among the human observers.

Repeatedly in leash disputes across the country, dog walkers emphasize the significance of the social connections formed with other dog walkers. Communities are indeed born in these public spaces. While they might start from the contagion of play and a common interest in dogs, the friendships soon expand. Describing the social process at one off-leash area in Fairfax County, Virginia, Battiata writes, "people learned the dogs' names, then one another's. Birthdays were celebrated. There were picnics in July. Outdoor Christmas parties. A phone directory was compiled. . . . People got attached to the place. It was a kind of victory over the anonymity and transience of life in a commuter suburb."[44] In short, people in these communities come to know one another, not just as functionaries, but as human beings. As Steve Temmermand, the division chief for Arlington, Virginia, Department of Parks, Recreation and Cultural Resources, explains, "We realized a long time ago that these parks weren't about the dogs so much but about people coming together and building communities. There are potluck supper clubs, book clubs, people exchange movies, all kinds of stuff. It's an entire social network. People have met their boyfriends, girlfriends, and spouses at these parks."[45] People report experiences of true friendship in these places, whether it is in the form of a sympathetic ear, a response to a pet's death, or a willingness to do a favor in time of need. Strikingly, these communities sometimes cross class lines as well, something that is increasingly unlikely in other organizational memberships. In a world of suburban sprawl and class homogeneity, these informal communities are quite rare and therefore very valuable to their participants.

Indeed, increasing numbers of people are less likely to have attachments, such as those to family, which would offset the anonymity of urban and suburban life. For example, the proportion of adults living alone roughly doubled between 1977 to 1978 and 1998 to 1999, a trend explained in part by the number of widows who live alone and were more likely to live with family members in times past.[46] Additionally, there has been a rise in the proportion of unmarried adults, a fact that contributes to the trend. By 2000, for example, one third of men and one fourth of women over fifteen had never married, percentages that represented a historically high level.[47] Couples also have fewer children and more are childless.[48] Surely, at least a proportion of these individuals, couples, and small families would appreciate any and all communal relationships of value, inclusive of dog-walking groups.

Importantly, such demographic groups are also more likely to have a strong connection with their pets. The percentage of people who identify their dog as a family member drops below 50 percent in four-person households. There is an almost 20-point drop in this percentage from two-person households, where 60.5 percent consider their dog a family member, to five-plus-person households, where only 41.7 percent do.[49] Studies also demonstrate that attachment to pets is highest among people living alone and among couples who do not have children living at home. Dogs, according to yet another study, have been found to accommodate the needs of widowed, separated, and divorced people more so than others.[50] Because of the increasing numbers in these demographic categories, the human benefits of dog ownership have become more pronounced and widespread.

## The Stakes of Leashing Controversies

When authorities threaten to enforce leash laws, they are unknowingly attacking both these attachments with dogs *and* human communities. Threatened with such loss and concerned about meeting their dog's exercise needs, people respond with intensity. Valuing both relationships with their dogs and other dog walkers, they are defensive. In fact, the loss of public space to exercise dogs ultimately threatens the ability of many people to have dogs or much more importantly, to care appropriately for their particular dog. For those who live in condominiums or apartments with no yard, off-leash areas are necessary for most sporting and other medium and large breeds. There is no yard to fence. For these people, the enforcement of leash laws, then, is exceptionally threatening.

When such people plead their case to authorities, they are sometimes told implicitly or even explicitly that the onus is on the dog owner to provide space to exercise his or her dog. Arguably symptomatic of the radical individualism rampant in today's society, this attitude completely privatizes dog ownership. If someone owns a dog, he or she must own enough land to exercise the dog properly.[51] According to this line of thinking, why should non-dog owners have to accommodate the needs of those who choose to have dogs? Of course, this logic also questions why childless people have to subsidize schools, why the young should pay taxes to support the elderly, and why any group is deserving of the support of non-members. It is, in other words, a radically individualist philosophy that denies the very idea of a common good. This philosophy tends to yield better results for those with resources, but people of moderate means sometimes embrace it as well. It provides the philosophical grounding for communities of only the retired or other gated and homogeneous enclaves. In contemporary American society, with its increasingly defined class divisions, this approach to dog ownership arguably would yield one of two results. Those with fewer resources would be denied the opportunity to experience dog ownership, with all the emotional riches that the experience provides, or their inadequately exercised dogs would behave poorly, a reality that would lead to more dogs in shelters, more dog bites, and other negative results. As it is, according to one study, almost 64 percent of all dogs obtained as puppies in the United States are given up within one year of acquisition.[52]

Currently, dogs are possessed by people in all income brackets, though the lowest rates of ownership are found among those making under $20,000. Even in that group, approximately 30 percent owned dogs in 2001. In that same year, which, we will later see, was an important one for dog owners in San Francisco, the percentage of households with dogs ranged from 33.9 to 40.5 percent in those income brackets above $20,000. Ownership rates increased for all income brackets by 2006, with a range of 30.7 to 42.8 percent.[53] Clearly, great numbers of people would be impacted by policies that completely privatized dog ownership. When some authorities and pro-leash forces advocate this option of privatization, they most likely do not recognize how threatening it is to those without yards. Even to those with adequate resources, this suggestion is insulting. Likening it to smoking, Battiata writes,

Dog owners have become the new smokers. . . .

Once free to smoke (run their dogs) wherever they pleased, smokers (dog owners) are now consigned to furtive puffing (off-leash exercise) in small alcoves, posted paddocks and other ghettos.

> Dog ownership, once a barometer of confidence and cool . . . now carries with it the faint but undeniable whiff of weakness, a presumption of a moral flaw.[54]

If that is the inference, then an intense response to calls for privatization should not be all that surprising.

The other problem with privatizing dog ownership is its utter incompatibility with the social nature of dogs. As Marshall Thomas and others have documented, dogs require contact with other dogs. She chronicled the travels of her dogs, all sans leash and supervision, in Cambridge, Massachusetts, and concluded that their sole goal was interaction with other dogs. Additionally, describing the relations among the dogs themselves, Marshall Thomas again emphasized the significance of social interaction in a dog's life.[55] Perhaps more is not known than known about the social relationships of dogs. As Bradshaw and Nott explain, the "social systems of carnivores are highly flexible, even within species, and . . . they often depend on ecological factors, such as availability and distribution of food." Equipped with auditory, visual, and olfactory means of communication, dogs can establish several types of social systems. Bradshaw and Nott caution as well that there are important differences with wolves, as human selection in breeding has made certain visual signals, such as ears, less communicative.[56] While the specifics vary among breeds and from one situation to another, however, it is clear that the dog is a highly social animal. Anecdotal evidence of separation anxiety in dogs is yet additional proof of this fact. For dog lovers, laws that prevent dogs from fulfilling something so basic to their nature would be objectionable. If there is any sense of vicarious living here, maybe humans are delighting in their dogs' natural sense of community all the more given the sorry state of their own.

## CONCLUSION

In sum, the impassioned response among anti-leash advocates is grounded primarily in love for their dogs. Play is a social necessity for dogs and obviously brings them great joy. Those humans who love them consider it cruel to deny them this activity. Having partaken in the joy of play, many people are addicted to it as well. Its observance brings *them* happiness. Additionally, people are passionate about the human friendships and communities that have developed in these spaces. While in some sense "new," these communities of dog walkers are ironically traditional in that they are tied to a geographical place and are face-to-face. When authorities threaten to drive dog walkers from these special places via leash laws, people respond with intensity.

# Chapter II

## What is Behind the Sudden Clamor for Leash Laws?

Leash laws are a relatively recent phenomenon. In most places, they did not appear on the books until the second half of the twentieth century. Further still, it was not until the late 1980s and early 1990s that these laws were seriously enforced on a wide scale. That enforcement is what precipitated so much controversy. To be sure, laws prohibiting roaming dogs date back to the late nineteenth and early twentieth centuries in the United States. Grounded in fears of rabies in an age before vaccinations, those laws focused on the unsupervised, free-roaming dog who could also annoy people by tipping their garbage cans and defecating on their lawns. These statutes, however, did not specifically require leashing of supervised and licensed dogs. Those laws came later. With some exceptions, the specifics of these leash laws are legislated at the local level. As a result, there is, of course, great variation in their origins, purposes, and details.[1] That diversity makes the simultaneous emergence of controversies in widely scattered parts of the country all the more worthy of an explanation.

### A CHANGING SOCIAL CONTEXT

Why then did authorities across the country begin to enforce leash laws at this common juncture in American history and trigger the ire of dog walkers? While particular factors always figure into a comprehensive explanation for any one controversy, there were common forces and factors at play nationally. Increases in population density and a rise in the percentage of people who engage in outdoor recreation have created more potential users of public space. Dogs have increased their numbers as well, and we will see, are likely to have substantial exercise needs. Unfortunately, open public spaces reserved for recreational use are shrinking, not expanding, to meet these demands. When the inevitable conflicts over land use emerge, the competitors are not likely to know one another in any other context. As scholars have documented, communal structures and mores have declined considerably since the 1970s. As a result, such competitors are less likely to resolve conflicts among themselves and more likely to call upon authorities.

## Sprawl

Public spaces have shrunk for a number of reasons, but "suburban sprawl" seems to be the most common explanation. Suburban sprawl is characterized by a developmental model that consists of five components, each of which is segregated from one another. First and most importantly, scholars identify housing subdivisions as the primary component of sprawl. Next are shopping centers and office parks, which typically consist of large box buildings that are surrounded by parking lots. Public buildings, such as schools and town halls, are a component of sprawl as well, as they often are not located in residential neighborhoods and are also surrounded by parking lots. Finally, sprawl consists of miles of paved roadways, which are essential to connect the other four components. As Duany et al. observe, "Since each piece of suburbia serves only one type of activity, and since daily life involves a wide variety of activities, the residents of suburbia spend an unprecedented amount of time and money moving from one place to the next."[2] Perhaps this fact explains why the vehicle population has grown six times faster than the human one since 1969. As of 2000, there were approximately 190 million licensed drivers and over 200 million registered vehicles. Since 1996, the number of registered vehicles has surpassed the driving age population.[3]

There is no agreement over the causes of sprawl. Although population growth contributes to the phenomenon, public policies, such as single-use zoning, mortgage incentives, interstate highways, and neglect of mass transit, bear responsibility as well. Whatever its causes, the consequences of sprawl are apparent. Open spaces are shrinking. Between 1960 and 1990, the amount of developed land in metropolitan areas more than doubled. In rural areas, almost twenty million acres of land were lost to development between 1970 and 1990.[4] In Arlington County, Virginia, a site of a leash dispute, more than 97 percent of the land is developed. If that county wants to create green space, according to Battiata, it must "buy buildings and tear them down."[5] Shrinking areas of public space, a clear consequence of sprawl, invite greater competition over their use.

## Decline of Community

This loss of public space arguably detracts from communal development and the formation of any bonds among the citizenry as well. Without physical spaces to meet, it is difficult to build community. Putnam argues further that "each additional ten minutes in daily commuting time cuts involvement in community affairs by ten percent."[6] Sprawl inevitably increases commuting time, not only to work, but to other activities too, a reality that is likely to make large numbers of citizens virtual strangers to one another. In his seminal work, *Bowling Alone*, Putnam additionally notes, "more than a third of America's civic infrastructure simply evaporated between the mid-1970s and the mid-1990s. . . . Thirty-two million fewer American adults were involved in community affairs in the mid-1990s than would have been involved at the proportional rate of two decades earlier."[7] Studying rates of involvement in politics, secular community-based organizations, the workplace, and religion, Putnam concludes that the "classic institutions of American civic life . . . have been 'hollowed out.'"[8]

To make matters worse, the decline in membership in formal organizations has impacted informal patterns of behavior. For example, people entertained guests at home 45 percent less in the 1990s than in the 1970s.[9] Face-to-face interaction with neighbors and other citizens is increasingly rare or at least, not as common as it once was. Likewise, Pipher reports that 72 percent of Americans did not know their neighbors by 1990. Compared to 1970, the number who claimed that they spent no time with neighbors doubled.[10] Summarizing these behavioral changes, Putnam writes, "We spend less time in conversation over meals, we exchange visits less often, we engage less often in leisure activities that encourage casual social interaction. . . . We know our neighbors less well, and we see old friends less often."[11] Such mores result in a world of anonymity. As Pipher has explained, people come to know each other in this world not as human beings, but as functionaries. People encounter one another as worker, clerk, teacher, accountant, or as cast in any other role, and they have no idea about that person's family life, background, or other interests.[12] It is therefore easy to condemn someone in the performance of a given role when there is no knowledge about that individual's life, which could include a sick child or multiple jobs.

In his explanation of the decline of communal life, Putnam argued that work, sprawl, television, and generational change were all important contributory factors. Behind generational change, he identified television as contributing the most to the breakdown in community life. Television privatizes leisure time and isolates people. As Pipher puts it, "People spend more time watching music videos but less time making music with each other."[13] Medved goes further to claim that television promotes impatience, self-pity, and superficiality. Advertisements nurture desires in search of immediate gratification, while characters and their lifestyles invite negative assessments of our own lives.[14] Television not only acts as a substitute for more social forms of entertainment, then, but also reinforces an ideology of radical individualism. It encourages people to focus on the satisfaction of their own desires and implies that said satisfaction is easily attainable and will result in happiness. Conversely, it divests individuals of all responsibilities and obligations to others, as every person is on his or her own. It is the perfect complement to an anonymous world. The Internet potentially exacerbates this human isolation, as e-mail can reduce both face-to-face interactions and telephone conversations. Additionally, computers have standardized interactions with bankers, accountants, social workers, and even educators, making any personal relationship with these workers less likely. Consider that college courses can be taken online and investment brokers can rely upon computer programs to advise clients. Everyday encounters with workers are limited as well, as a trip to the grocery store self-checkout reminds us. Computers have thus contributed to less frequent and more anonymous human interactions.[15]

To be sure, as Pipher highlights, anonymity has its advantages. In the small-town community of the past, privacy was not exactly celebrated. People knew each other's business and secrets. Yet there is a certain coldness to social interactions that deny the complexity of one's full humanity. Can parents shed worries about their children at the workplace door? Is there such a stark dichotomy between the private and public worlds? Whether there is or not, the social structure sometimes demands that people act as though there is. In such a world, it is easy to understand how dog walkers and other park users can at times demonize one another. Neither is likely to have any knowledge of the other's humanity, the sources of stress and joy in one another's lives. They are strangers. What is more, people are accustomed to dealing with one another only one dimension at a time and thus confront competitors for the use of public space as just that, competitors and not human beings.

Additionally, people's leisure activities have changed since the 1970s. There has been a shift from social activities, such as bowling and card games, to more individual and family ones, particularly outdoors. More men and women are now likely to engage in various forms of physical exercise, including hiking, jogging, and biking.[16] Even in cities, gentrification has lured more upper-income people who are likely to seek outdoor recreational opportunities.

While these activities make for a healthier lifestyle, they do little to build community and of course, result in greater numbers of competitors for open space.

## Population Changes

There are, in fact, many more such "competitors" now. Tripling its population since 1900, the United States counted 281 million people in its 2000 census. Furthermore, the growth of 32.7 million people in the 1990s represented the largest numerical increase of any decade in American history. In 2000, seven states surpassed the mark of 10 million people, a milestone no state had reached in 1900. California, which perhaps not coincidentally claims to be the birthplace of dog parks, has the most people, 33.9 million. California's population increase in the twentieth century totaled more than the combined increase of twenty-seven states.[17] Population density tripled as well in the last century, jumping from 26 people per square mile of land area in 1900 to 80 people per square mile in 2000. There are, of course, important regional differences here, as the Northeast has the highest population density with 330 people per square mile, and the West has the lowest with only 36 people per square mile. Increasingly, the US population has become more metropolitan as well. In 2000, 80 percent of the US population lived in a metropolitan area, with one third of the population in metropolitan areas with 5 million or more residents. In 1900, only 28 percent lived in a metropolitan area at all. Indeed, all fifty states had at least a portion of their population living in metropolitan areas by 1980.[18] Suburbanization accounts for almost all of this increase. Clearly, at century's end, people were living in closer proximity to each other and in greater numbers. Added, then, to shrinking public space is the ingredient of more people who are less likely to know one another, a recipe sure to guarantee conflict.

**Table I.** States and population density per square mile.

| People per square mile | 2000<br># of states | 1950<br># of states | 1900<br># of states |
|---|---|---|---|
| 200+ | 12 | 7 | 3 |
| 75-199 | 17 | 10 | 7 |
| 25-74 | 12 | 19 | 18 |
| Less than 25 | 9 | 14 | 22 |

Source: Frank Hobbs and Nicole Stoops, US Census Bureau, Census 2000 Special Reports, Series CENSR-4, *Demographic Trends in the Twentieth Century* (Washington, DC: US Government Printing Office, 2002), 36.

For consistency, Hawaii and Alaska are included in all three years.

**Table II.** Total population per state.

| Total Population | 2000<br># of states | 1950<br># of states | 1900<br># of states |
|---|---|---|---|
| 10 million + | 7 | 3 | 0 |
| 5 million-9,999,999 | 13 | 4 | 2 |
| 1 million-4,999,999 | 23 | 27 | 25 |
| 999,999 or under | 7 | 16 | 23 |

Source: Frank Hobbs and Nicole Stoops, US Census Bureau, Census 2000 Special Reports, Series CENSR-4, *Demographic Trends in the Twentieth Century* (Washington, DC: US Government Printing Office, 2002), 27.

For consistency, Hawaii and Alaska are included in all three years.

Humans are not the only ones multiplying either. There are approximately 74 million dogs, with about 10 million more households owning dogs than did a decade ago.[19] Not only are there more dog owners and dogs, but both have changed somewhat in kind. People now have bigger dogs, with the Labrador retriever the most popular breed. From 2006 through 2008, the Yorkshire terrier placed second among most popular breeds, a fact indicative of the rising popularity of small breeds. While such breeds represented only 18 percent of American Kennel Club (AKC) registrations in the 1940s, they are now up to 29 percent. Yet the third and fourth most popular breeds from 2006 through 2008 were large ones, the German shepherd and golden retriever. Indeed, such breeds make up the largest share of the AKC registry, 45 percent. In the years of most significance to the case studies in San Francisco and Connecticut that will be cited later, large breeds claimed the top places in the AKC registry. Their popularity seems to have come at the expense of medium-sized breeds, such as spaniels, who have declined in popularity since the 1950s. Of perhaps more significance for this study, dogs who require substantial amounts of exercise comprise nearly half of the registry today compared to just 35 percent in 1915. For example, highly popular Labradors "are active and sociable dogs," who "need daily exercise, preferably in the form of retrieving and swimming."[20] Low activity breeds account for only seven percent of registrations.[21] The most popular breeds, then, need places to exercise. Given that dog owners too are now more likely to live in urban and suburban environments, this is a constituency that will be in search of public space.

## Summary

Together, all of these developments have led to disagreements over the use of open space. Since leash laws were already on the books in many places, it was predictable that competing users would call for their enforcement. The

**Table III.** The top five most popular breeds.

|  | 1996 | 2001 | 2008 |
|---|---|---|---|
| Breed | Rank | Rank | Rank |
| Labrador retriever | 1 | 1 | 1 |
| Rottweiler | 2 | n/a | n/a |
| German shepherd | 3 | 3 | 3 |
| Golden retriever | 4 | 2 | 4 |
| Beagle | 5 | 5 | 5 |
| Dachshund | n/a | 4 | n/a |
| Yorkshire terrier | n/a | n/a | 2 |

Source: American Kennel Club

decline of community leads to reliance on law enforcement as well because it is less likely that a complainant would deal with a perfect stranger to reach some sort of accommodation for competing uses. Instead, the demand was for enforcement of leash laws, and that is what happened in areas across the country. Those calling for this enforcement, while usually fewer in number, are every bit as passionate in their advocacy as dog walkers.

## EXPLAINING THE PASSION OF LEASH ADVOCATES

Pro-leash forces, like dog walkers, cherish whatever forms of relationships and activities that they have found as safe havens in this anonymous society. From their perspective, dog owners threaten their solace and therefore are infringing upon their rights. Of course, there are myriad explanations for their intense reaction to this issue, just as there are for anti-leash advocates. One explanation, which would certainly not apply to all leash advocates, goes to the very nature of the human conception of self.

### Humans versus Animals

Arguably, the dogs' closeness to humans has the potential to evoke strong feelings of rejection, just as it does to provoke love. Noting that human societies have been surprisingly ambivalent toward dogs, Serpell cites examples of places where dogs are eaten and/or treated as outcasts. Even in societies that allegedly value dogs, some dogs are the victims of cruel and yet legal experiments. For many, the dog poses a threat to the barrier between humans and animals, which is posited in both Western philosophy and religion. "As the Yurok Indians recognized," Serpell explains, "the real danger posed by the domestic dog is that its friendship threatens to dissolve or undermine the psychological barrier that distinguishes human from animal. . . . [T]he dog unwittingly represents the thin end of the wedge; a demanding and insistent reminder of the feelings, interests and moral claims not only of dogs, but of animals in general."[22] To preserve that dichotomy and thereby deny that humans are animals, some perhaps unconsciously reason that dogs must be placed squarely in the "animal" column. Therefore, they deserve no better treatment than any other animal, including the ones commonly eaten. To speak about their relationships with humans or their needs for socialization and play is to speak nonsense.

It was Enlightenment philosophers, particularly Descartes writing in the early seventeenth century, who propounded this view. Prior to the Enlightenment, in feudal times, animals and humans were said to have places on the Great Chain of Being, with God at the top. In that older worldview, there was a sacred component to all of God's creation. People had duties to those humans and to God above them and obligations to those below them. Even then, as Wise explains, "[i]t wasn't just that nonhuman animals occupied lower rungs, but that we differed so fundamentally that we were incomparable. Nonhumans were literally made for us."[23] The Enlightenment ushered in an age of reason and asserted that men (and just men at this time) had universal rights. It was in fact the ability to reason that entitled men to rights. In contrast, per Descartes, because animals could not speak, they could not think, experience emotion, or possess a soul. They were "mindless machines."[24] His assumption legitimized a form of science that objectified and de-sanctified nature, inclusive of its animals, and therefore assigned it only an instrumental value. In other words, consistently with the older mentality, nature and animals were for human use, simply means to pursue human ends. In this paradigm, it was unthinkable to have a relationship of intrinsic value with an animal.

Western religion for the most part compounded this dichotomy via its claim of a unique relationship between humans and God. Consider, for example, the still-heated debates about creationism versus evolution. Darwin, of course, argued that species were separated more by degrees than by kinds. Like humans, other animals can think and feel. For those who insist upon a sharp demarcation between human and animal, evolutionary theory is problematic. Certain denominations of Christianity, which exert considerable influence in the United States, categorically reject evolutionary theory and as a result, emphasize human uniqueness. Many practitioners of those denominations therefore are likely to find arguments about human and animal similarities insulting to their religious beliefs.

Contemporary society, with all its modern conveniences, might nurture this dichotomy between human and animal as well. Suburbanization, the electronic revolution, and the availability of goods tend to breed detachment from nature. About society in the 1990s, Pipher writes,

> Most children gain their knowledge of the natural world vicariously. In the history of the world, this distance from the natural world is a new phenomenon. . . . Even a generation ago . . . [f]amilies visited farms on a regular basis. Children saw cows being milked, pigs fed, chickens plucked, grain planted . . .[25]

Nowadays, as she highlights, children are much more likely to be able to identify the brand names of cereals than the trees, plants, or birds on their street. The supermarket offers any type of food anytime of the year, a reality that for all its benefits, further erodes a sense of nature's rhythms and any awareness of our own omnivorous nature. Nowadays, as Beck and Katcher highlight, "a very large part of the population" is "excluded from contact and care of living things other than their own children."[26] Consequently, modern society has hidden our dependence on nature and reduced our awareness of animals, who can then easily be defined as "other."

According to this line of thinking, humans are assumed to be completely different from animals, who are uncivilized, savage, and dirty. Humans, in contrast, are civilized, virtuous, and sanitary. Incredibly, even in their fantasies, humans depict themselves as potential victims of other alien species, when all prior dealings with alternative species on this planet would indicate that humans are more likely to be aggressors. Perhaps such fantasies tap into the fear that a more intelligent species will do to us precisely what we have done to less intelligent species on earth. At any rate, evidence of human misbehavior, toward each other and other species, abounds to the point of being commonplace. It is difficult to conclude that humans are civilized and virtuous after a nightly newscast.

When confronted with such evidence, some label these offensive humans as "animalistic" and therefore not human. In his outstanding account of the war in Bosnia, Maass argues that human savagery lies closer to the surface in all societies than any would care to admit. After noting the sophistication and decent standard of living in Yugoslavia before the war, he documented how quickly and easily the bonds of civilization were destroyed. Tellingly, he described the murderous behavior of humans as evidence of the "wild beast" within and intimated that the breakdown of society quickly exposes us to be animals. He writes,

> We have an easy time thinking of animals as animals in part because they smell like animals. That's a difference between us and them. But what are

you supposed to think when you find a group of humans who smell no better than cows, even worse? It reminds you that humans are animals, with the ability to stink like pigs, and kill like wolves.[27]

Perhaps a fear of such human potentiality invites a denial of its existence. Because the dog, as Serpell states, exposes human likeness to other animals, that might be an unwanted reminder for some of our carnivorous and predatory potential. Instead of celebrating the positive emotions in other animals, such as love, some fear the corollary implication about themselves. Even worse, from this perspective, dog lovers emphasize canine and human similarity and therefore would be particularly goading to those with this view or those who want a sharp demarcation between humans and animals.

## Fears and Resentments

To be sure, not all proponents of leashes have disdain for animals in general or dogs in particular. There are other explanations for intense reactions. Elderly people, for example, have legitimate fears of injury should an untrained dog jump on them excitedly. If off-leash parks require their expulsion or limit their hours of access, they too might react with outrage. Parents might similarly fear that their young children could be knocked down and injured by loose dogs. Concerned about sanitation and the dangers of un-scooped waste, parents might want the removal of dogs from any areas where their children play. Select members of these groups, the elderly and parents, classify dogs as a threat to the physical well-being of themselves and their children. Probably lacking knowledge about the importance of off-leash walking to dog owners, these groups might support leash laws at all times and places since that solution would rectify their concerns easily and completely.

Consider also that pro-leash advocates are not included in the community of dog walkers. Those communities form around common interests and shared activities, not geographical proximity. Given the increasing rarity of multiuse, off-leash areas, people travel considerable miles to visit them. If an opponent lives in close proximity to an off-leash area, claims of "community" bonds might be especially galling. Who are strangers, outsiders no less, to come into the neighborhood and form a tight-knit community at the local park that does not include someone who lives nearby? Furthermore, the claim seems ridiculous given that some have lived in this area a long time and have never experienced any "community" bonds. Not having experienced the connections that come from this type of community, opponents are prone to discount its importance or possibly resent it. Alternatively, some leash advocates might be connected to healthy communities in the forms of churches, schools, and/or their children's sports and other activities. As a result of their *lack* of isolation, they might be less likely to understand the void filled by dogs and communities of walkers.

Opponents too deal with traffic, lengthy commutes, and the stresses of contemporary society. While the number of work hours has remained relatively constant since 1980, the number of women who work outside the home has increased. Fewer than one out of three women did so in the 1950s, compared to two out of three in the 1990s. As a result of that and other factors, the Organisation for Economic Co-operation and Development reports that "families may . . . face a 'time squeeze,' especially when young children or other persons requiring personal care are present in the home."[28] In other words, there is less time to spend with children in leisurely activities. Parents drive their children around the suburban sprawl centers and are more likely to be involved in their activities. In short, we all live in a hyper-stressful, over-scheduled world. Imagine a parent who has worked a long day and driven his or her children around town, finally arriving at a local park for a bike ride or to fish, for example. The last thing such an individual would want to confront is competition over the use of that park. That parent would want access to that park when convenient for him or her, as such free time is rare. If the child was too frightened to go because of loose dogs, it is easy to see how the child's parents would react angrily to their presence. In the parents' eyes, it would be a conflict between the dogs' use of the space and their own child's. That, from their perspective, is non-negotiable and to expect otherwise is irrational.

While dogs can bite, as previously explained, the media has helped to stoke people's fears here as well. Highly unusual cases are spotlighted, with the implication that any dog could do this to any person. In the late 1990s, in the aftermath of school shootings, a similar portrait was painted of American teens. While there is no overstating the tragedies that resulted from the actions of a few teens or in the cases of vicious dog attacks, it is as ludicrous to invite a general fear of all dogs as it is to invite one of all teens. The media highlight the sensational or the extraordinary too often without placing such information in context.[29] They neglect to explain that the overwhelming majority of bites occur on private property, not in public parks. As a result, more people these days are probably inclined to think of worst-case scenarios, not just with dogs, but in all contexts. What if a dog is vicious? Should you play it safe and keep away from all dogs? Given that you are also unlikely to know the dog's keeper, you might just think he or she fits the bill of the sociopath described in the story before the dog case. Suffice it to say that the loss of community has not only made us strangers to one another, but has made all dogs strangers to non-dog owners. Couple that with the media's coverage and you begin to understand people's wariness.

## Love of Animals

To be sure, some leash advocates love dogs and even own them. They might have small dogs, who do not need the same space to exercise, or dogs who do not socialize well with others. They too compete for public space and are sometimes among the most vociferous opponents of off-leash areas, as they are just as likely to share a strong bond with their dogs and to consider off-leash advocates threatening to their dog's well-being or safety. For that reason, they respond emotionally as well.

There are also leash proponents who seek to protect wildlife and nature from the domestic dog, whom they consider a threat. Far from embracing a dichotomy between humans and animals, such individuals are likely to emphasize connections among various species and plants. Dogs, in this view, disrupt the balance or ecosystem because, as a domestic species, they are foreign to the natural environment. Some with this view are concerned with the sustainability of ecosystems and fight for leash restrictions to ensure that goal. Others clearly have a passion for certain species of wildlife, birds for example, and defend their interests as passionately as pet owners. Given that passion, these defenders are alarmed by the potential for dogs to bring harm to wildlife. As a result, they emphasize those studies that demonstrate risk factors to wildlife from the presence of dogs, whether via the transmission of diseases, such as canine distemper, rabies, and parvovirus, or harassment. From this perspective, if the behavior of even a few dogs might harm wildlife, then all dogs should be leashed or perhaps excluded from the area to eliminate that chance. They are persuaded by those studies, earlier discussed, that highlight an impact on foraging and flushing patterns of wildlife and consider such effects harmful. For all of these constituencies, dog owners, naturalists, and wildlife defenders, motivation might come from their love of animals and nature as well as their fear that dogs will harm the objects of their love. In leash disputes, they sometimes make political alliances with those who disdain or fear dogs and/or those who just find them annoying.

## CONCLUSION

It is as though the competitors for shrinking space live in separate worlds and therefore have great difficulty understanding the perspective of their opponents. In some cases, they have two completely distinct worldviews. Each side sees itself as correct and rational, with its opponent clearly in the wrong. What is more, each is at times driven by the most intense of emotions: fear and love. For good or ill, these adversaries do not live in separate worlds. They live under one set of laws and therefore must somehow come to a mutually satisfactory solution to this intensely charged issue.

# Chapter III

## The Inevitable Turn to Politics

As leash laws have been more routinely enforced, dog walkers have had no choice but to turn to the political arena for help. That turn has sparked political conflicts in every region of the country and involved local, state, and national governments. While it is beyond the scope of this work to provide an exhaustive listing of these disputes, a brief review of selected conflicts demonstrates both their breadth and intensity. Clearly, these conflicts have become a national phenomenon and as such, present a challenge to public officials. In some cases, these officials have risen to the challenge and negotiated mutually acceptable compromises. Yet far too often, governments have responded inappropriately and have failed to uphold democratic ideals.

### THE LEASHING ISSUE ARRIVES ON THE POLITICAL SCENE

#### The Innovative West Coast

So often at the forefront of national trends, California was an early creator of dog parks. Indeed, one of the very first dog parks in the country opened in Berkeley in 1979.[1] Recognized as one of the best, Berkeley's Ohlone Park is still in existence and its steward, the Ohlone Dog Park Association, works to ensure its preservation and upkeep. Berkeley is home as well to *Bark Magazine*, which has become nothing short of an icon in "dog people's" culture. With beginnings as a newsletter for those seeking to create a dog park at the Berkeley Marina, *Bark* now has a national circulation in excess of 110,000 and has expanded its coverage to all things dog. The *New York Times* has labeled it the *New Yorker* of dog magazines.[2] In 2003, the editors published a best-selling book, *Dog is*

*My Co-Pilot*, which explores the depth of the canine-human relationship and unabashedly celebrates the connection. The rise of *Bark* in some ways portended the growth of local movements to advocate for off-leash recreation.

Across the Bay from Berkeley, San Francisco is the site of monumental struggles to retain off-leash areas, as we will see in detail later in the volume. Elsewhere in California, such as Santa Barbara, San Diego, and Los Angeles, citizens have banded together to convince cities and towns to establish off-leash areas. California's northern neighbors in Washington and Oregon have done so as well. The organizational efforts of those in Seattle, in fact, are often highlighted as a model for those seeking to create or retain off-leash areas in other parts of the country.

Seattle's animal control officers cracked down on off-leash walking in 1994, exponentially increasing the number of citations and operating in conjunction with the police department. Outraged at their sudden criminalization, dog walkers in February 1995 formed a non-profit group, Citizens for Off-Leash Areas (COLA), to obtain and maintain places to exercise their dogs in Seattle. With the aid of a sympathetic city council member, Jan Drago, several meetings and workshops were held that unequivocally demonstrated widespread interest in the creation of off-leash areas. Proposals for specific sites were generated at workshops, evaluated by several city departments and the city council. Finally, after extensive input from the public, Seattle approved an off-leash pilot program for seven sites on June 15, 1996.[3] The program was successful and became permanent in September 1997. Ultimately becoming an umbrella group through which any neighborhood groups seeking to establish a dog park could operate, COLA is the officially recognized steward group to the Department of Parks and Recreation . It not only advocates for off-leash areas, but ensures the maintenance of existing ones and educates the public about proper etiquette in those areas. By 2009, there were eleven off-leash areas in Seattle, with an additional three pending. One of the off-leash areas, Magnuson, even includes beach access.

Portland, Oregon is yet another example on the West Coast of a city where off-leash areas were created at the behest of organized citizens. Using an off-leash task force to make recommendations for specific sites, Portland established a pilot program for off-leash recreation in June 2003. The director of Portland Parks and Recreation then appointed a citywide Off-leash Advisory Committee to create "an off-leash program that balanced the needs of dog owners with those of other park users."[4] In December 2004, the city council approved its recommendations, and as a result Portland, in 2009, has thirty-two off-leash areas, five of which are fenced areas specifically for off-leash recreation and twenty-seven of which are multiuse with off-leash exercise allowed within a designated area for specific hours. Suffice it to say that the West Coast has been at the forefront of the movement to establish off-leash areas, with many cities and towns now proudly boasting about the existence of such areas.

### The Northeast— Give Me Your Tired, Your Four-legged?

With the highest population density of any city in the country, New York is home to approximately 1.4 million dogs. Describing its dog-friendly culture, Downey and Lau write, "We discovered that New York City has more dog runs than any other city in the country, more dedicated dog groups and owners actively working to make life in New York City a little bit better for both dogs and their human companions, and more spas, gyms, holistic healers, and stores all dedicated to making every pup as buff and beautiful as a New York dog should be."[5] Typically, dogs are most interested in open space and surprisingly, densely populated New York provides that as well. With its combined national, state, and city parkland, New York is the "'greenest' big city in the country, with fully 26.6 percent of its area blanketed by parks." However, not all of this area is available for recreational use.[6]

For over twenty years, New York has had a policy that allowed dogs off-leash in sections of various parks, including locations within Central Park, from 9 p.m. to 9 a.m. Additionally, New York City has fenced runs available throughout the day. In May 2006, the Juniper Park Civic Association, which opposed the off-leash hours, filed a lawsuit, arguing that the twenty-year-old policy violated the leash-law provision of the health code and was therefore illegal. Dog owners, who stood to lose their freedom to walk their dogs off-leash in the mornings or late evenings, organized and sought to defend their interests in the political arena.

On November 30, 2006, a New York State Supreme Court Judge ruled that the twenty-year-old policy, sometimes called timed-use, has been and continues to be legal. Following the decision, the New York City Board of Health unanimously approved amendments to the health code, proposed in September, that ceded specific authority to the New York Parks Commission to allow dogs off-leash hours. It was in defending those amendments that the New York State Department of Health cited the low incidence of dog bites in public parks. Acting on this newly assigned authority, the Parks Commission codified and formalized the timed-use policy. As part of the codification process, the Parks Commission held a hearing in February 2007. At this meeting, NYCDog, an advocacy group for dog owners and their dogs, presented over twenty thousand letters and petitions to codify this policy and over sixty people gave public commentary on the issue. Convinced of the policy's popularity and success, the New York Parks Commission has implemented it in at least eighty-eight locations. In this case, dog walkers were able to retain the status quo ante, but not without organization and a voice.

While New Englanders might joke that New York City is its own world, they share with that world a political agenda that now includes dogs and the issue of leashing. Far away from New York City, in every conceivable sense, is the small town of Manchester-by-the-Sea, Massachusetts. Located on Cape Ann, Manchester-by-the-Sea is a picturesque New England town with high property values and beautiful Singing Beach. It was once called plain-old "Manchester," but the town changed the name so that it would never be confused with Manchester, New Hampshire, which is a big city not at all like Manchester-by-the-Sea. During the summer months, no dogs are allowed on Singing Beach. Indeed, non-resident humans have to work to access the area. The small, adjacent parking lot is for residents only, with non-residents relegated to a lot about a half mile away that charges a hefty fee. The beach, though, is truly worth the effort. In the off season, from October 1 through April 30, dogs have historically been allowed sans leash on the beach, and their non-resident humans have an easier time parking as well. On those cold, winter days, few other than dog walkers venture to the beach for an oceanfront stroll. As *The Boston Globe* described, "It's been a tradition in Manchester-by-the-Sea for decades, heading to the beach for some off-season dog walking. . . . In the middle of winter, there they are: dogs and their owners, from Beverly to Boston, strolling up and down the beach. This is no dog park; this is a doggie destination."[7]

This popular tradition was threatened when a group of citizens, who were dissatisfied with the numbers of dogs at the beach, gathered the necessary ten signatures to introduce a dog ban at the Town Meeting. With approximately 5,200 residents, Manchester-by-the-Sea uses the Town Meeting as its form of government. At its Town Meeting on April 7, 2008, citizens voted overwhelmingly to continue the policy that allows dogs from October 1 to April 30. An amendment to lengthen the ban by two months was narrowly defeated as well. Proponents of the dog ban then sought a referendum on the matter, but that proposal was rejected too. The status quo ante thus prevailed, but dog walkers could no longer take it for granted.

The results have not always been so positive for dog walkers. In many cities and towns across the Northeast, there has been a crackdown on off-leash walking despite the political mobilization of dog owners. For example, in

Greenwich, Connecticut, an upscale town on the state's "Gold Coast" within commuting distance of New York City, authorities began enforcing a leash law in the 1990s on an area of beach that residents had long used to walk their dogs in the colder months. As we will later see, Avon, Connecticut, a picturesque New England town west of Hartford, completely eliminated off-leash walking in all of its parks despite much opposition in 1998. There are additional conflicts in towns on Long Island, such as Huntington, and in New Jersey. Dog politics, in other words, has arrived in the Northeast and has excited the residents in ways that few other issues do.

## Hot Dogs and the Gentile South

In cities and towns across the South, groups of citizens have banded together to ensure space for off-leash play as well. In densely populated Arlington County, Virginia, this issue came to a climax in the late 1990s. At that time, there were seven off-leash areas in the county, only one of which was fully enclosed. Dogs could swim or play in streams at selected areas, a veritable necessity for canines given the hot Virginia summers. In January 1997, the Arlington County Department of Parks, Recreation and Cultural Resources adopted guidelines, in the form of an "operating memorandum," with which all off-leash areas had to be in compliance by January 1999. Those that failed to comply by that deadline would be shut down. Since only two of the seven off-leash areas came even close to meeting these guidelines, dog walkers faced a massive loss of recreational space. The county's off-leash areas were already somewhat overcrowded given that seven areas were expected to accommodate approximately 18,000 dogs. Responding to this concern, citizens, led by Judy Green, organized Arlington Dogs to defend their interests and retain off-leash areas.

Their efforts were not in vain. According to the Arlington County Park Web site, there are still eight operative off-leash areas, two of which are not completely fenced. In August 1999, the county adopted new guidelines for off-leash areas that require private sponsorship. Dog owners quickly stepped up to form private groups and to raise funds to support these areas. The establishment of the first privately managed off-leash area at Utah Park in Fairlington was not without controversy. Opponents formed a group to advocate the area's closure and removal to a more "industrial" site, but so far the area remains open. As mentioned earlier, dog owners confronted officials regarding their unsubstantiated claim that dogs alone were responsible for environmental pollution in the Four Mile Run Watershed. In short, Arlington Dogs has been an effective voice in the face of official and private opposition. As Howard Hudgins, the Acting Division Chief of Parks and Natural Resources in 1998, noted, "The population of dog owners in Arlington is rivaling that of parents of school-aged children."[8] Given that Arlington County's leash laws have been strictly enforced since 1998, it became essential to this constituency that off-leash areas remain open.

Elsewhere in the South, citizens have prevailed upon officials to establish off-leash areas. In Bowie, Maryland, for example, dog owners organized a group and began advocating for an off-leash area in December 1996. After five years of persistent effort and the support of Bowie's City Council, Bowie opened a dog park on December 15, 2001. Greenbelt, Maryland could already claim the first dog park in that state. Disputes over off-leash areas have emerged in several other cities and towns, such as Decatur, Georgia and New Orleans. Florida is home to many dog parks (I refrained from asking for an exact count), including the first privately-owned one in the country located in Gainesville. Virtually all of these public parks, throughout the South and particularly in heavily populated areas, came about only with the persistent demands and work of grassroots groups.

## The Rocky Mountains, Southwest, and Midwest—Even with all that Land?

One would think that with so few people, relatively speaking, and the presence of so many rather more intimidating species, such as grizzly bears, that off-leash dogs would not be a concern in the Rockies. This is not the case. In this rapidly growing region, there are indeed conflicts over off-leash areas. Area natives, despite the mountains, might even be inclined to say, "land, what land?"

In Denver, Colorado, for example, dog owners had to take a trip out of the city to exercise their dogs in the mid-1990s. Even then, it was not easy. As the *Denver Post* reported, "as Denver's suburbs expand, it has become difficult to locate an open area where your dog can romp and you can enjoy nature's solitude."[9] One such area was Cherry Creek State Park, which is about a forty-five-minute drive from the city. In 1996, state authorities threatened to move this dog training and exercise area to a less favorable location within Cherry Creek State Park. Although the area had been designated for this use for forty years, authorities sought to protect wetlands and relocate the dog exercise area. Organized into a group, DenFidos, dog walkers fought this change and prevailed upon the city to establish off-leash areas. The first such area opened in January 2000, and the city now claims seven of these areas.

DenFidos is actually a chapter of a Boulder, Colorado organization. FIDOS is an acronym for Friends Interested in Dogs and Open Space, which was formed in 1994 when authorities considered banning dogs from certain areas of Boulder's Open Space and leashing them in all others. Prior to that time, Boulder had a leash law in all city areas, but dogs could be off-leash in the Open Space areas. Authorities cited increased use, more people in the area, and threats to wildlife in their case for leashing. This did not sit well with dog walkers, who found themselves with no place to exercise their dogs. By 1995, FIDOS had 1,500 members and had been able to prevail upon city authorities to create more off-leash areas in the city proper and ultimately, to evaluate the Open Space areas more discriminately. The group is active in local politics and fears that the Open Space planning process unfairly scapegoats dogs. For while FIDOS has had success in keeping some trail areas open to leash-free dogs, there has been a discernible shift from open, multiuse areas to dog parks, which are solely for the purpose of exercising dogs. In this case and in Denver, there has been vociferous opposition to dog walkers, whether in the form of the Sierra Club, Audubon Society, or reactionary individuals who monitor parks and report the "smallest infractions" of dog walkers.[10] Colorado is by no means the only state in the Rockies and great Southwest that is confronting this issue. At the urging of organized citizens, off-leash areas have been created in cities such as Bozeman, Montana; Cheyenne, Wyoming; Scottsdale, Arizona; Dallas, Texas; and many more.

The nation's agricultural heartland has experienced conflict over this issue as well. Similarly to other densely populated parts of the country, Midwestern dog walkers began to lobby for space to exercise their dogs when leash laws were enforced more regularly in the 1990s. Chicago, for example, started to open off-leash areas in 1995, with leashing required in all other places. In Minneapolis, citizens formed an off-leash advocacy group called Responsible Owners of Mannerly Pets (ROMP) and succeeded in establishing off-leash areas. Minneapolis listed five such areas in 2009. Its twin, St. Paul, has only one but efforts are underway to establish more given the popularity of that one area. Since St. Paul has approximately 41,000 dogs, it is not all that surprising that its *one* off-leash area is over burdened. A local group, Off-Leash Advocates, has been invited to assume a more formal role in the identification and maintenance of off-leash areas. Elsewhere in the Midwest, off-leash areas have been created in cities such as Indianapolis, Indiana; Akron and Cincinnati, Ohio; Omaha, Nebraska; St. Louis, Missouri; and many other cities and towns. According to a Web site that lists off-leash areas, Illinois and Ohio have over seventy-five and fifty, respectively, while Minnesota and Indiana have thirty-eight and twenty-two. Even Iowa lists twelve such areas.[11]

## Summary

Given the sheer volume of these disputes and their wide geographical spread, it is safe to say that they have become a national phenomenon. In the mid-1990s, the number of official dog parks or off-leash areas was marginal, approximately twenty-five or so. In 2010, that number now exceeds 1,600 and is growing. Even Anchorage, Alaska lists three, one of which warns dog walkers to "watch out for moose."[12] These areas, in many cases, have not been established without opposition. Indeed, it has only been through the efforts of large numbers of new advocacy groups that these off-leash areas have been created and preserved. In many cases, these groups have organized with formal structures and have expanded their missions to promote responsible dog ownership and stewardship of public areas. Despite such organized representation, dog walkers have nonetheless lost many battles to retain unofficial off-leash areas. What is clear is that across the country, these disputes have become commonplace.

## AWKWARD POLITICAL RESPONSES TO A NEW ISSUE

At the local level, this issue has burst onto the political scene. For as perhaps many local issues do, this one defies traditional alliances of politics. Knowledge of the partisan breakdown of a city council, for example, tells little about how this issue will be resolved. As the brief and incomplete sampling of conflicts indicates, the issue has struck both "blue" (Democratic) and "red" (Republican) states, though, for reasons we have already reviewed, it tends to manifest itself the most in densely populated areas. Such areas, even if in "red" states, tend to lean "blue," though there are, of course, exceptions. Indeed, the issue has not spared small towns, such as Avon, Connecticut, which are decidedly "red-leaning" despite their location in "blue" states. It is, in other words, a classic cross-cutting issue that honors no previous political alignments and, therefore, has the potential to strike terror into politicians' hearts. If the issue were to be introduced into a partisan election, it would very possibly shake up traditional patterns of voting. With that said, typically neither dog walkers nor their opponents comprise majority groups, but dog walkers are usually the much larger minority group. Logically, given its intensity and cross-cutting nature, legislators should prefer to contain this issue, as much as possible, in the realm of interest group politics where compromise carries the day.

Politics does not always work out according to the rules of logic, however. Some lawmakers get pulled into the fray in these battles and play important roles in either establishing or eradicating off-leash walking. Sucked into this emotional debate themselves, officials run the risk of losing perspective and worse still, treating the legitimate concerns of citizens with contempt. Most often, it is the interests of dog walkers that are dismissed as illegitimate. For example, officials might cast the issue as one pitting the well-being of dogs against that of humans and thereby treat the dog walkers as either invisible or second-class citizens. When government officials become partisans in this debate, particularly when aligned against dog walkers, they not only eliminate the possibility of achieving a fair outcome, but they fuel the fires of this already volatile controversy.

## THE IDEAL RESPONSE—DEMOCRACY

Ideally, government officials should stay neutral and work to achieve mutually acceptable solutions. To do that appropriately, governmental officials must resolve the leashing issue within a democratic framework. While there is considerable disagreement over the precise meaning of democracy, most theorists agree that popular sovereignty, equality, and civil liberties are essential ingredients in any definition. Popular sovereignty, or the placement of final decision-making authority in society with the people, is arguably the most important ingredient of democracy. However, it is also critical that the input of each and every citizen be treated equally and that citizens are free to speak and associate in their efforts to persuade others about the merit of their positions. In my case studies of the leashing disputes, of which we will soon learn, I ask a series of questions to assess whether these three ingredients of democracy are present and if so, in what degree.

### Democratic Ingredients

For popular sovereignty, I first examine the structure of the applicable units of government, whether it be a town, city, or federal agency. Are those in office elected? If so, are there competitive elections or does one party typically dominate? If elected or non-elected office-holders had the power to make decisions about the leash laws, I attempt to depict their degree of responsiveness to the public's interests. As Bruce Miroff has explained, there is an inherent tension between the concepts of leadership and democracy. However, as he also stipulates, certain forms of leadership are more reconcilable with democracy than others. Democratic leaders tend to be good listeners and to rely upon persuasive abilities and reason to convince the public about the merits of their actions, while non-democratic leaders adopt a position of superiority and are more inclined to manipulate the public.[13]

If public meetings and/or an election or referendum were held to address the leashing issues, I examine the level of participation. While the numbers alone can be important here, I go further to ask if diverse interests were represented and if any effort was made to accommodate the intensity of feelings on each side. Most difficult to assess is the degree of deliberation. To determine if a "healthy" level of deliberation was present, I examine the transcripts of the meetings when possible and rely upon coverage of the meetings and interviews of the participants when transcripts are not available. With this material, I assess whether participants listened to one another, treated one another with respect, and engaged in rational argument. Did any participants try to pull "trump cards" and thereby discredit the other side, or did they alternatively seek a common solution or one that called for mutual accommodation? Not surprisingly, I find examples of disrespect and irrational argument in all of my cases given the passions involved. There are those who refer to their opponents as "nuts" and "fascists," by definition unworthy of conversation. However, I attempt to glean the overall tone. Were "hotheads" in the majority or minority? Did cooler minds eventually prevail? Importantly, did the facilitators of meetings, mainly governmental officials, encourage or discourage a healthy form of deliberation?

Because of the growing size of localities, the mass media's role cannot be neglected either. Unfortunately, we depend on centralized media even for information about proceedings in our local areas. The media can tip the odds of these debates by influencing those without much of a stake in them. Because such persons are unlikely to have attended meetings, they tend to rely upon the media's depiction to form their own opinions. In some cases, those opinions might very well determine the outcome of the conflict. If the populace is "sovereign," but makes decisions on the basis of faulty or manipulated information that is supplied by an elite media, clearly that "sovereignty" is without meaning. Hence, it is important to pay some attention to the media, especially when a referendum is used to decide the issue. In those cases, it is worth asking how well and fairly the media portrayed the issue and the conflicting interests. Did the media show respect for each side, highlight rational arguments, and search for common ground, or did they dwell upon the conflict itself and publicize the most sensational aspects of the story?

Additionally, the impact of the populace must be weighed. Even if the meeting was deliberative, it would not be indicative of democracy if no one paid heed to its conclusions. We must therefore ask if the participants have the final say or indeed any say. What is done with the public input? Is it the modern-day equivalent of a petition to the King or does it carry power in and of itself?

To determine the degree of equality, I ask who was included and excluded from the debate. When the use of public space is in question, who should have input? Should taxpayers have the only say or should park users have some level of input as well? Given the scarcity of off-leash areas, dog walkers often go to parks outside of their town and tax-paying residents can sometimes object to the presence of these "out-of-towners." In other words, this abstract question has important consequences in this debate. Likewise, I inquire if the process was favorable to free speech and association. Did each side have a public voice? Did each side organize into associations? More broadly, was the policy outcome consistent with liberties? Did either a majority or minority tyrannize over others?

Finally, I consider the effects on the participants and community. In the end, did the decision-making process strengthen or weaken the ties of community? Did participants come away with a greater or lesser understanding of their fellow citizens? In what ways did participants grow, if any, from this process? Were participants more or less apt to get involved in other issues or forms of politics as a result of their experience?

**Table I.** Democratic checklist.

| | |
|---|---|
| **Popular Sovereignty** | -structure of government<br>-responsiveness of decision-makers<br>-levels of popular participation<br>-degree of deliberation<br>-impact of public input |
| **Equality** | -boundaries of electorate<br>-stakeholders vs. taxpayers<br>-treatment of interest groups |
| **Civil Liberties** | -formation and activities of organizations<br>-letters, petitions, rallies<br>-governmental restraint |

## Models of Democracy

Once we have the answers to these questions, we must interpret them and conclude as to whether or not the leashing disputes were handled democratically. With what standards can we judge this information? For example, how much equality is required to satisfy that particular democratic criterion? There are, it so happens, several opinions on this matter. In fact, political theorists have debated the goals and requirements of this form of government for centuries. While each participant in this conversation has contributed a unique version of democracy and added to the cumulative understanding of the concept, at least

**Table II.** Forms of democracy.

|  | Minimalist Democracy | Participatory Democracy |
|---|---|---|
| **Popular Sovereignty** | -competitive elections<br>-interest group politics | -competitive elections<br>-high level of participation<br>-deliberation<br>-impact of informed public opinion on policy |
| **Equality** | -political/universal suffrage<br>-legal/before the law | -political/universal suffrage<br>-legal/before the law<br>-minimize impact of economic or class differences<br>-inclusive |
| **Civil Liberties** | -no government obstruction of basic civil liberties (e.g., free speech)<br>-protection of property rights | -widespread use of basic civil liberties<br>-accommodation of minority concerns |
| **Goals** | -protection of freedoms or liberties | -community development<br>-education and development of citizens |

two schools of thought have emerged in modern times.[14] One of these schools is very demanding in its criteria for democracy, and the other has fairly basic requirements. Just as there are "easy" and "hard" graders among professors, there are easy and hard graders among theorists and observers of democracy. While these schools are labeled differently at times, I will refer to the easy graders as "minimalists" and the hard graders as "participatory democrats."

It is to these models that I will turn to interpret and thus to evaluate the actions of government in leashing disputes. Social scientists employ the use of models to avoid a purely subjective analysis, and that is my purpose here. I will provide a procedural analysis of the leashing disputes and conclude as to whether they were resolved in a manner consistent with these models. To be sure, the use of models does not eliminate the need for judgment given the qualitative nature of their criteria and evidence. When evaluating democracy, it is nonetheless especially important to invoke a well-defined model given the history of abuse of this term and the disagreements over its definition. After all, obviously undemocratic countries, such as North Korea, claim this word in their titles. An additional benefit of such a procedural analysis is its possible applicability to other issues upon which people passionately disagree.

For all of the democratic ingredients, minimalists would set lower standards than participatory democrats. If competitive elections are held and citizens have the opportunity to advance their goals via interest groups, a minimalist would conclude that popular sovereignty is present. Participatory democrats, in contrast, would additionally associate a healthy level of popular participation and public deliberation with popular sovereignty. Even further, they would expect public opinion, when informed, to matter and therefore, influence governmental decisions.[15]

Both minimalists and participatory theorists include political and legal equality in their definition of democracy. No adult should be denied the vote because of his or her identity, and the law should apply equally to all. However, participatory democrats go further to ask if people are effectively excluded from politics by their economic or social status. There is no agreement as to the degree of economic and social equality necessary for democratic governance, but participatory democrats at least seek to ensure processes that minimize the impact of class differences in the political realm and are as inclusive as possible.

Both groups additionally agree that a democracy must protect basic civil liberties, such as free speech, association, and press. For the minimalist, this criterion is satisfied as long as the government does not obstruct people from enjoying these freedoms. If there is no government censorship, for example, the press is free even if owned by just a few corporations. Participatory democrats are more likely to demand the realization of these freedoms even if that requires the government to take action, such as media regulation, to ensure it. For both groups, liberty might contrarily require the constraint of government at times. Democracy is not the same as majority rule, minority be damned. Instead, liberty implies some limits, albeit ill-defined ones, on governmental policies when they potentially impose severe deprivations on some people.[16] In this regard, minimalists emphasize the constraining influence of property rights, while participatory democrats are more inclined to express concern for all essential interests.

The participatory model values democracy as a goal in and of itself. Emphasizing the importance of the democratic process in educating the citizenry and developing healthy communities, this model offers the stronger theoretical justification for democracy. Minimalists, in contrast, value democracy for its proven ability to maximize liberties, such as speech and property rights. Other forms of government have utterly failed to secure these rights and in that comparative sense, democracy has done better. As Winston Churchill once put it, "democracy is the worst form of government, except all those other forms that have been tried from time to time."[17] The minimalists value democracy, then, for something external to itself, much as some students take a course solely to earn the grade or credits. Participatory democrats are more analogous to the student who loves the learning process itself and does not care about the external reward or grade.

Although the participatory model is more demanding, arguably it is a more appropriate standard for small-town or local politics. After all in American folklore, local towns are allegedly the most democratic. In reality, local towns and cities do not always live up to this ideal. In fact, they often are dominated by one party and therefore lack competitive elections, a basic requirement of even the minimalist model. As a result, I will invoke both models in my evaluation of leashing disputes.

## WHY THESE CASES?

My case studies by no means represent a sampling of leashing disputes. There are so many such disputes that I do not claim to provide an exhaustive listing of them. Instead, I have chosen to fully describe and analyze three case studies. Specifically, I have selected two separate but related cases in San Francisco, a bastion of progressive politics with a reputation for innovation, and one in Avon, Connecticut, a small and conservative town in New England. In all of these cases, off-leash advocates struggled to maintain their access to multiuse parks. At several locations in San Francisco and at one location in Avon, people were able to walk their dogs off-leash in parks used for other activities, such as fishing or hang gliding. Dog walkers became attached to these places and the people with whom they shared them. When authorities threatened to end off-leash walking, dog owners mobilized politically and attempted to thwart the unwanted change. The ensuing politics, in all cases, were intense and passionate.

I chose to focus on the fight to retain off-leash walking at multiuse areas because its very existence speaks volumes about our political culture. Just a generation ago, dogs often roamed neighborhoods unsupervised. It was almost as common to see someone walking a dog off-leash as it was to witness children at a playground. That is no longer the case. Now, dog walking is a much more regulated activity. The trend, as described partly above, is toward "dog parks," which often are not multiuse. They segregate dog walkers from other park users. Typically, again with important exceptions, they are areas for dogs to play and exercise with one another and for humans to socialize and rest. The multiuse areas more often allowed the humans to walk and therefore exercise themselves at the same time that their dogs played and exercised. In contemporary times, there is more likely to be specialization, a place to exercise the dogs and another to exercise the humans. Just as children are now more likely to play in regulated activities, such as soccer, than they are to explore neighborhoods and invent their own games with one another, adults are to exercise themselves and their dogs in areas created for those specific purposes. As we have noted, people are less likely to manage conflicting uses amongst themselves, and thus they demand single-use areas. The dog walkers' struggle to keep multiuse areas is, then, in some ways an effort to retain a storied part of the American past. While, as we already saw, they are having much success in establishing dog parks, this battle to keep multiuse areas is a more challenging one, as the three cases will unequivocally demonstrate.

After analyzing the three struggles in depth, I will attempt to draw some lessons for governmental authorities and off-leash advocates. I am concerned about drawing such lessons for the latter group because I am an advocate of off-leash areas. I consider recreational dog walking, off-leash, to be as legitimate an activity as golfing, skiing, biking, or any other common pastime. To be sure, the nature of this activity, like so many others, requires regulation as to time and place. In my view, the leashing conflicts should be about those issues, not whether or not such an activity can take place at all. The popularity of off-leash walking in and of itself attests to its legitimacy. When I evaluate cases, I will therefore treat this activity and its advocates as legitimate, and I will expect governmental authorities to do so as well. That does not necessarily mean that such authorities must always rule in favor of dog walkers, but their interests should be given fair consideration.

# Chapter IV

## The Land of Steady Habits? Avon, Connecticut

In the "Land of Steady Habits" otherwise known as Connecticut, there is no more quintessentially steadier town than Avon. It was there that a piece of property, for a time, came to be known as "dog heaven." Fisher Meadows won this designation because it was not only leash-free, but contained a body of water complete with small beachheads, a wooded trail that ran along the Farmington River, and lots of friendly people and dogs. Over time, it became *the* place to walk dogs for those who lived in Avon and its surrounding towns. For hundreds of people, a trip to Fisher Meadows became a treasured part of their daily or weekly routines. When the Avon Town Council recommended that a leash law be implemented at Fisher Meadows, there was, of course, an outcry from those that frequented the area. The ensuing politics cast Avon in the unwanted limelight.

The Town Council first threatened a leash law in 1995. Yet the Council, with prodding from dog walkers, struck a compromise at this time, and a large chunk of Fisher Meadows remained leash-free. Regulations were put in place to prevent off-leash walking in some areas and allow it in others. Although signs were posted, there was virtually no enforcement of these regulations. What is more, the popularity of Fisher Meadows continued to increase among off-leash dog walkers. Faced with a few complaints about loose dogs at this park, in 1998 the Town Council decided to forbid off-leash dog walking in all areas of the park once and for all. From the outset, the Town Council was convinced of the need to end off-leash dog walking and was not open to compromise. This attitude of the Town Council members, added to the already divisive nature of leash-law proposals, fueled the fires of this controversy to an explosive point. So it was that in the very "Land of Steady Habits," people on both sides of this conflict erupted in anger. As events unfolded, it also became clear that this conflict was about a great deal more than a leash law.

## COULD THIS REALLY HAPPEN IN AVON?

Described in the 1980s *The Official Preppy Handbook* as one of the "preppiest places in the United States," few would be surprised to learn that the wealthy town of Avon later went on to win a designation as one of the safest towns in the country.[1] Put simply, it is not the place where one would expect heated conflicts over anything, let alone dogs. Yet Avon, perhaps much to its citizens' dismay, is not an island unto itself, and therefore it is not insulated from the national trends that precipitated these conflicts.

Incorporated as its own town in 1830, Avon, which is divided into east and west sections by the Farmington River, most likely took its name from the Avon River in England. In fact, Avon had originally been a part of the neighboring town of Farmington before its own incorporation. At the time of its incorporation, the town had 1,025 residents. In 1950, its population had reached 3,171, a milestone that prompted Avon to formulate a development plan in 1954. The population continued to increase from 5,273 in 1960 to 14,000 in 1990 and then to 15,832 in 2000. Avon was still considered a "small town" in 1998, but it was a much more populated one, indeed with three times as many people as it had in 1960.

Additionally, the makeup of its population had changed in kind. In his analysis of this controversy, Joel Lang described "Avon's three-part power structure," which consisted of "descendants of Yankee farmers, descendants of Italian immigrants who settled in Avon before World War II, and corporate people who arrived after the war."[2] Before World War II, Avon was small enough for its citizens to know one another, at least casually. The more than threefold increase in population after the war was fueled by the newer "corporate" people, who, by some of their own accounts, never won acceptance or a sense of belonging in the town. While some members of this group stayed only a short time and moved, others had been in Avon for decades but still perceived themselves as outsiders.[3] From the perspective of those with generational ties to the town, these corporate, or more accurately, professional people were associated with wealth, as some of them lived in newly built tract mansions. To be sure, some of these newer professionals were not any wealthier than longstanding residents, with many of the newer group living in condominiums, and of course, there were more than a few wealthy individuals among the descendants of Yankee farmers and Italian immigrants. After all, the median Avon household income in 2000 was $90,934. In that year, 85.9 percent of its housing units were owner-occupied and only 14.1 percent were comprised of renters.[4]

In 2000, according to the US Census, the average travel time to work for residents of Avon was 23.3 minutes. The average household and family sizes, 2.53 and 3.03, respectively, were just slightly lower than the national averages. A household includes all who occupy a housing unit, whether a single person or multiple families, while a family is defined as a group of two or more people related by birth, marriage, or adoption residing together. Since household size was smaller than family size in Avon, it is possible that significant numbers of people lived alone. However, Avon had a much higher percentage of married males and females, 72 and 63.6 percent, respectively, than the national averages of 56.7 and 52.1 percent.[5] Avon is not an exception, then, to the trend toward smaller family sizes, a reality that elevates the attention lauded on pets and, of course, children.

Despite its high marriage rates and wealth, both the increase in population and a division between "newcomers" and old-timers arguably weakened community ties in Avon. More pointedly, Avon's "old-timers," defined not by age, but by generational longevity in the town and also cultural norms, seemed to have a strong sense of community, but its newcomers, even those there for more than a decade, were not a part of it. It was primarily these "newcomers" who populated and led the dog walkers. Given their lack of connection to the town's community, they perhaps treasured the sense of belonging found among the dog walkers at Fisher Meadows all the more. It is also probably not too much of a stretch to infer that, as professionals, they would be more likely than the "old-timers" to partake of the culture and demographics that have elevated the importance of a pet's companionship. For example, professionals would be more likely to have longer commutes, which result in declining attachments to geographical community and smaller families. For many of the newcomers, who lacked strong attachments to the community, Avon was basically a wealthy suburb that, despite its fairly small size, partook of the anonymity of suburbia. Some of these citizens, already alienated from the town, would be infuriated when what little sense of belonging they had in the town was threatened. Ironically, that very anger would cause the old-timers to condemn and stereotype the newcomers as rich, spoiled, and arrogant, traits that clearly marked them, from the old-timers' view, as outsiders to the real Avon. Those old-timers would thus coalesce around "their" Town Council, alienating the newcomers even more. The decline in community and the very definition of community, then, clearly fueled the fires of this debate.

Add to that painful tension the fact that Avon was not immune from the forces of development. In a nineteenth century history of the town, it is noted that "agriculture has been the leading pursuit of the inhabitants of this town, which is favored by the fertility of most of its soil and by its proximity to good markets."[6] This is no longer the case. In 1989, just 4 percent of the town's 22.6 square miles were used for agriculture, and that percentage shrank even further by the twenty-first century. By 2004, single- and multi-family residences comprised over half the land area of Avon.[7] The town lost 419 acres to development between 1985 and 1995, the year the first leash law was proposed for Fisher Meadows, alone. According to the April 2006 Town Newsletter, Avon has lost 2,000 acres of privately-owned, undeveloped land since 1989 as well.[8] Like so many suburban areas across the country, then, Avon has experienced a loss of undeveloped land and an increase in population. There are more users of less space. Because Avon is no longer a small farming community where most, if not all, of the residents know one another, many of these users compete for that space as strangers.

While such competition and the anonymity of suburbia might help to make public debates bitter, Avon's early history should remind us that local conflicts by their very nature can be the most intense, whether residents know and/ or like each other or not. Early residents of what later came to be Avon argued vociferously over the location of the parish's first meetinghouse. Since most of the residents lived east of the Farmington River, the meetinghouse was placed there despite a petition from twenty-two residents who lived west of the River and claimed "hardship at crossing the river to attend church." As Nora Howard, the town historian, explains, "Time and population growth—and a suspicious meetinghouse fire in 1817, resolved the one-meetinghouse problem."[9] Soon thereafter, there were meetinghouses on both sides of the Farmington River. It seems that when daily or weekly routines are in question, as they often are with local disputes, passions flare, whatever the century. Happily, there were no suspicious fires over the leash-law controversy, but new divisions, perhaps even deeper than the geographical one, reared their ugly heads.

## THE BONE OF CONTENTION: FISHER MEADOWS

Fisher Meadows is a park of approximately 233 acres, including a pond of about 42 acres. Stanley D. Fisher, Hinda N. Fisher, Lois F. Ruge, and Diane Fisher, all of the nearby town of West Hartford, donated the land to Avon in 1976. The Fisher family successfully incorporated several conditions on the gift. If Avon failed to comply with those conditions for the first twenty years, the land was to be given to the State of Connecticut. Specifically, the park was to "be dedicated to the uses of conservation, farming (to the extent recently so used), recreation, including fishing and swimming, open space and uses incidental to all the foregoing." The area was to "be open to the general public without regard to place of residence" and to "be maintained in as generally clean and orderly condition as existed immediately prior to the transfer."[10] Because the twenty-year period concluded in 1996, these specific conditions would be relevant in 1995, but not in 1998. Indeed, representatives of the Fisher family expressed support for the dog walkers in 1998, but their advice was not heeded. In a letter to the Town Manager, Diane Fisher Bell wrote, "As one of the grantors of the deed of the farmland which today is Fisher Meadows, I feel that the restrictive ordinance regarding dogs recently imposed by the Avon Town Council is misguided. Surely somewhere in Fisher Meadows' more than 200 acres there is an area which could be set aside for people to exercise their dogs off leads, as they have been able to do for more than 20 years."[11] In this letter, Fisher Bell also expressed dismay over the Avon Water Company's well sites at Fisher Meadows. In 1998, the town no longer faced even a remote threat that the property could be lost to the state, and thus it had to abide only by its own rules and certain federal regulations, given that it had obtained federal funds to develop the soccer fields and for work on the pond.

Fisher Meadows is quite clearly divided into areas, with one part set aside for soccer and other playing fields. Upon driving in the main entrance, the playing fields are on the left. Almost immediately in front of the entrance is the pond. One could drive straight on a dirt road and be between the soccer fields and the pond. To the right of the main entrance, a wide dirt path, which is closed to vehicular traffic, circles the lake and ultimately meets with the dirt road, which is open to traffic and between the soccer fields and pond. Most off-leash dog walkers stayed on the portion of the wide dirt path closed to vehicular traffic. The park also includes a wooded trail, which is accessed either from the far right side of the parking lot or more popularly, via an entrance on the wide dirt path just a short ways from the parking lot. Because this trail follows the banks of the Farmington River, it is also referred to as the River Trail. It is the farthest from the playing fields and woods separate it from the main dirt path that circles the lake. While off-leash dog walkers could be found on this trail as well, they were fewer in number here than the more popular wide dirt path.

Over time, Fisher Meadows attracted people from nearby towns, such as West Hartford, with strict leash laws. Even citizens from towns without such strict leash laws frequented Fisher Meadows because of its water access

*Entrance to Fisher Meadows.*

*Main walking path in Fisher Meadows.*

*"Dog beach," now abandoned.*

and its sense of community. Overwhelmingly, the largest group of users of the main dirt path, and probably the River Trail, were off-leash dog walkers. People also fished on the shores of the pond, but there were few or no problems between the fishermen and dog walkers. The dogs accessed the water from just a few open areas or "beaches." In particular, there was one beachhead, half-way around the pond, known popularly as "dog beach." There was no human swimming allowed on the lake, and that cut down on usage during the hot summer months. Children used the playing fields during the spring and fall especially, with soccer games and practices. Because Fisher Meadows is located very near Avon Old Farms School, its cross-country teams would sometimes run there as well during those seasons. Occasionally, perhaps a few times a year, the town granted a Boy Scout troop permission to camp there. Beyond that, there were some people who used the park for walking without dogs. It was primarily that group that took issue with off-leash dogs. However, there were also many complaints about dog waste on the playing fields.

By 1995, it is fair to say that Fisher Meadows was a vibrant place. Even in the dead of winter, one could find off-leash dog walkers there. In the spring and fall, especially on weekends, it was very popular, with games on the fields and many off-leash walkers around the lake. It was in fact the increasing usage and popularity that gave the Town Council concern. Its members feared that there were too many dogs and therefore too much potential for an accident of some kind. On the other hand, Fisher Meadows had become a haven for many people, a place to where they looked forward to going. Friendships had formed among people who regularly walked with one another as well. There was, in short, a strong attachment to the place and to the people there. Of course, there was also no denying the enjoyment of the dogs, who are not exactly the best at hiding their emotions! For those who loved their dogs, Fisher Meadows provided a spot not only to watch them have fun, but to enjoy nature and be among human friends.

## WAR AVERTED—1995

Citing concerns about the dangers of unleashed dogs and dog litter, Glenn Marston, the Director of Recreation and Parks, asked the Avon Town Council to pass a leash law for all town-owned properties at the April 6, 1995 meeting. He was especially concerned about litter on the playing fields and claimed that people had been knocked down by loose dogs. He went as far as to say that "dogs . . . have taken over Fisher Meadows."[12] Members of the Town Council were reluctant to embrace such a drastic change in policy and sought to find a compromise. Essentially, they asked for more signs indicating that animals are not allowed on the playing fields, better enforcement of that rule, and more public education. However, the Council indicated its willingness to revisit this issue shortly.

At the May 4, 1995 meeting of the Town Council, a couple of citizens strongly complained about loose dogs and described the situation at Fisher Meadows as dangerous. As a result, the Council agreed to revisit the issue at its June 1, 1995 meeting. While the Council members were leaning closer to a leash law at the subsequent meeting, they called for a public hearing on the matter, which was held on July 6, 1995. More than one hundred people attended that hearing, and the overwhelming majority opposed the leash law. In contrast, approximately five people attended the Town's budget meeting. As the *Hartford Courant* noted, the proposed leash law "caused a major flap in this usually unflappable community." Glenn Marston, who had proposed the law, could not recall a more contentious issue in his fourteen-year tenure as Director of Recreation and Parks.[13]

Given the strong desire for an area to walk dogs off-leash, the Council decided to strike a compromise. It did indeed pass a leash law for all Avon properties, but it exempted a section of Fisher Meadows. Prior to this time, Avon did not have a leash law on its books. The new ordinance (#49), which passed on August 3, 1995, allowed for an exception to the law in areas so designated.[14] At Fisher Meadows, dogs were forbidden from the playing fields, and they were to be leashed in the parking areas, the river trail, and the short space between the parking lot and the main entrance to the river trail. The compromise allowed people to walk dogs off-leash on most, but not all, of the dirt path surrounding the lake. The Council noted that it would revisit the issue if problems persisted. More ominously for dog walkers, the Council placed the burden of enforcement on the dog walkers themselves. Indeed, the *Hartford Courant* remarked that "Details of how officials will enforce the new ordinance must be worked out."[15]

## EVALUATING AVON DEMOCRACY—TAKE ONE

Critical to democracy is the notion of popular sovereignty or popular rule. Avon has a Council/Manager form of government, with the Town Manager the chief administrative officer and the Chairperson of the Town Council the chief elected official. Elections for the Town Council are held every other year in odd years. In 1995, there were five members of the Town Council: Chairman Richard Hines, S. Edward Jeter, Joseph Woodford, William Shea II, and Diane Hornaday. Four of the five Council members were Republican and one, Shea, was a Democrat. Hornaday and Shea were relatively new to the Council in 1995, while Hines, Jeter, and Woodford had all been on the Council since the early 1980s.[16] In 1998, these same individuals were still on the Town Council. Consistent with what one might expect from an "unflappable" community, Council members tended to be re-elected handily and serve lengthy tenures. Not surprisingly, this fairly wealthy and rather homogeneous suburb, with 94.9 percent of its residents white, leaned Republican in its local politics, with registered Republicans far outnumbering registered Democrats at this time.[17] Because the town's elections were not competitive, Council members had perhaps more discretion to handle controversial matters than they would in a more politically-competitive setting.

Notwithstanding that flexibility, Council members demonstrated a willingness to listen to constituents on this issue in 1995. Charged with passing legislation or ordinances for the town, they sought to find a compromise that would satisfy or at least appease the greatest number of their constituents. From the very outset, when the Director of Recreation and Parks asked for the leash law, the Council members were, for the most part, pragmatic. Their objective seemed to be to address the concerns with off-leash usage, while still permitting that activity. In fact, Chairman Hines explicitly stated that "we want to continue to do what is best for all of the people. The majority are [sic] being well behaved and that is the route we want to go."[18] In the course of the few meetings during which the issue was addressed, Council members offered several suggestions or compromises to continue some off-leash usage, such as fencing and a prohibition of off-leash walking on weekends only.[19] To be sure, the Council members took seriously the complaints of those in favor of a leash law. To address the concerns about dog litter, they called for better signage on the playing fields. In the view of at least one member, fencing would alleviate the concerns of those who do not want to be accosted by dogs. In other words, they intended their suggestions to provide some measure of satisfaction to both sides.

What is more, the Council *sought* public input on this matter in 1995. When just a few strong advocates of the leash law were present at the May 4, 1995 meeting, the Council heard their complaints but then called for a public hearing on the matter, ultimately scheduled for July 6. At that hearing, Chairman Hines explicitly indicated to the audience that the Council's mind was not already made up, as it was considering several options. At the outset, he explained the process and stipulated that a decision would not be rendered that evening. People, whether speaking for or against the ordinance, thus were assured that their input mattered in the decision-making process. When questioned specifically about the process, Chairman Hines responded, "We have had more and more complaints as time has gone on, and so it came before the Council and maybe we ought to consider a leash law. It does not necessarily mean that we are going to go ahead with it, you hold a public hearing and get input from the public and that becomes part of the input as to making our decision."[20] The Council then heard testimony from thirty-seven speakers, thirty-one of whom were opposed to the law and five of whom were in favor (for one, the position was not clear). Toward the end of the meeting, the Chair solicited "any ideas that are different than what we have already heard."[21] Additionally, the town received several letters, some with multiple signers. Twenty-four people voiced opposition to a ban on off-leash walking and eleven wrote in support of the law.[22]

In the aftermath of the public meeting, the Town Council, by a four to one vote, supported a compromise, as previously described, at its August 3, 1995 meeting. Council Member Hornaday, who noted her "initial feeling" about the need for a leash law, explicitly remarked that she was "trying to look for a compromise" and thereby supported the town-property leash law with an exception for part of Fisher Meadows. Interestingly, the only Democrat voted against the ordinance because he did not want to make an exception for Fisher Meadows.

Although this matter was resolved via a compromise, opponents of the leash law voiced some concerns about the process in 1995. Most significantly, they asked for documentation of complaints. There was a desire for an evidentiary basis to support the law. The Town Council was not forthcoming with the documentation and at one point, with prodding, became slightly defensive. At the July 6, 1995 meeting, Chairman Hines stated that "We have been getting increased complaints over a period of time, whether these are all documented in black or white or not I do not know. . . . So this has not been something that has just been pulled out of the air, we do not do things like that in Avon." To a response of laughter from an approximate crowd of one hundred in attendance, the questioner responded, "I have been here and I know you do."[23] Because the Town Council was open to compromise in 1995, such complaints about the process were few. In fact, just three people against the law expressed some frustration with the political process, mainly asking the Town Council for documentation or evidence of a problem.[24] However, this frustration and animosity on the part of one resident was a sign of things to come in 1998. The town made no effort to tabulate public comments on each side of the issue in 1995 or 1998, an omission that forced citizens to rely on their leaders' judgment. Without any records of citizens' input, there was also potential for Council Members to highlight only those comments supportive of their positions. Yet overall, in 1995, the Town Council listened to public input and crafted a policy in response to it.

If the Town Council received fairly good democratic grades in 1995, how well did the public perform? Over one hundred people attended the public hearing in July, with the vast majority of attendees opposed to the leash law.[25] From the public commentary and indeed, even from the attendance levels, it is clear that people cared passionately about this issue. In their statements, six people specifically cited their frequency of use and/or cited Fisher Meadows as a reason for their acquisition of property in Avon. Explicitly, one stated, "I moved to Old Farms Road because of Fisher Meadows, to be closer."[26] The proponents of a leash law, while much fewer in number, were as passionate in their advocacy of a leash law. One proponent described the situation as "very dangerous" and another threatened to sue Avon if he was knocked over by a loose dog, though he quickly backtracked to say, "That is not a threat."[27] Yet despite this intensity of feelings, six people, who were opposed to the leash law, specifically called for compromise to accommodate all users of the park. One of the five speaking in favor of the leash law called for compromise as well.

There were few expressions of disrespect at this meeting. In fact, just two, one pro- and one anti-leash law, made what were arguably disrespectful comments. A proponent of the law exhorted the crowd, "Oh shut up, I listened to all of you nuts." Understandably frustrated as a minority at the meeting, this speaker was reacting to noise from the crowd after making an implied threat to sue the town.[28] An opponent of the leash law asked the Council why it did not put a sign at the park instructing those who did not like dogs to stay away.[29] Arguably, this suggestion demonstrates no concern or respect for those who want to use the park and fear unleashed dogs. Another advocate of the law expressed concern that two people had confronted him after the last meeting to question his views, and he noted the importance of each side respecting the other's views.[30]

In their substantive arguments, the five advocates of the leash law cited safety concerns. Only one of the five cast the issue in a manner that belittled the interests of dog walkers. That person argued that the park was for "the human element . . . not the dogs" and therefore implied that the dog walkers' interests were not worthy of consideration.[31] Ironically, at least six of the opponents of the law contributed to this mind-set by emphasizing the benefits of off-leash exercise for dogs only. Cast as a conflict between human and canine interests, elected officials will undoubtedly opt for the former. Dogs do not vote. Indeed, Chairman Hines stipulated that "This is the property for all of our residents and . . . people come first."[32] One opponent of the law addressed this problematic casting of the issue in noting that "this room is full of people, what about people with a dog, what about their rights."[33] In their other substantive arguments, four opponents of the leash law cited their personal enjoyment of the area, while three others attested to the benefits of community there.[34] People, despite their intensity of feelings, were for the most part articulating their views in a reasonable manner, and there were even instances of respondents addressing points made by their opponents.

In the letters sent to the town, opponents of the leash law made similar arguments. Several stressed the unique nature of Fisher Meadows, the frequency of their use, personal enjoyment, and sense of community. At least three opponents asked for a compromise of some kind. Those writing in favor of the law were a bit more strident in tone. Some raised concerns about the dangers associated with so many loose dogs, as did the speakers at the meeting. A few, dog owners among them, noted that this situation prevented their use of the park. Two letters specifically complained about out-of-towners preempting their use. One suggested that dog owners simply "fence in their property" if they want their dogs to run free, which, of course, presents a problem for those without yards. A few complained about dog waste as well. On this matter, one opponent of the law asked if horses, which occasionally rode through there, were to be banned as well. Overall, most letters, but not all, did not denigrate the other side.

Media coverage of the 1995 controversy was less extensive than in 1998. Because the Town Council resolved the debate via a compromise, the media's role in educating non-stakeholders about it was less important. The *Hartford Courant*, the main newspaper in the area, ran at least six stories on the matter plus a few editorials. In the news stories, there was fair representation of the complaints and also of the importance of the area to dog owners. For example, one story described residents' complaints of being "knocked over, bitten and intimidated," while another explained that this was a "big issue" to dog walkers, who were described as "reasonable people who are open to compromise."[35] The *Hartford Courant* chose to highlight a proponent's worst moment, calling opponents "nuts," but otherwise did not lean excessively toward sensationalism. The numbers of speakers on each side of the issue at the public hearing were also depicted accurately. In its stories, the *Hartford Courant* was not guilty of exacerbating the conflict and indeed called for compromise in its editorial section.

Because the controversy ended with a compromise, it is fair to conclude that the Town Council not only listened to public input, but heeded it, to some degree. However, the Town Council placed the burden of the new policy's success on the amorphous group of dog walkers themselves. At least three opponents of the leash law condoned this type of collective thinking in calling for self-policing. Yet as one opponent indirectly cautioned, this approach could lead to penalizing "the 95% of us who take care of our dogs and care about other people's feelings" for the "5% who are rude, inconsiderate and ridiculous."[36] Indeed, this is exactly what would come to pass in 1998. At this time, though, the requirement of popular sovereignty appeared to be satisfied via participation, deliberation, and compromise.

Equality of input was an important concern in this controversy. Because several out-of-towners used the park to walk their dogs, the question of their role was an open one. Of those speaking against the law at the public hearing, sixteen were from Avon and fifteen were from other towns. Those from Avon were given preference in speaking first. Of the twenty-four signers of letters opposed to the law, eight were from Avon, four were from out of town, and twelve did not provide an address. All eleven of those writing in favor of the law were from Avon.[37] Prior to the public hearing, at the Town Council meetings, two advocates of the leash law emphasized the fact that several non-Avon residents used Fisher Meadows. Chairman Hines also noted "a feeling that a lot of out-of-towners come into Fisher Meadows . . . , which of course is allowed."[38] The Fisher family stipulated that the park was to be open to all, regardless of their place of residence. In the first twenty years of the park's history, then, it was not just allowed, but required, and because of federal grants, the park was required to be open to all as well. Because this controversy was resolved in a manner amenable to out-of-town dog walkers, this division did not become too much of an issue in 1995.

There were no organizations formed in 1995, as those with intense feelings expressed their views at the meetings. Given that the opponents of the law outnumbered the advocates by such a wide margin, advocates might have been a little more defensive or confrontational, but there seemed to be no inhibition in stating their views.

## FROM POLITICS TO WAR: THE END OF COMPROMISE IN 1998

Between 1995 and 1998, dog walkers continued to use Fisher Meadows, and the town did not enforce the compromise (or did so very infrequently). While perhaps the majority of dog walkers stayed in the off-leash area, there were a good number who did not. There was also confusion about the boundaries; in particular, the River Trail which was an on-leash area, was not marked with appropriate signs. In its proposal for a workable plan at Fisher Meadows, the dog walkers' group noted that the vast majority of dog walkers thought this trail was off-leash. The group claimed, "There is no sign at the beginning of this trail marking it (nothing as the trail enters the woods) as a leashed area; and in fact, many of us used it to be courteous to people around the pond who might not want to be bothered with dogs."[39] Instead of calling for stricter enforcement of the 1995 compromise, the Town Council decided in 1998 to hold all dog walkers collectively responsible for failing to adhere to the compromise. At its May 7, 1998 Town Meeting, the Council voted to pass a leash law for Fisher Meadows. The matter had not been on the meeting's agenda, but an individual raised the issue in complaining about loose dogs at Fisher Meadows. If two-thirds of the Council agrees to add an issue to the agenda, as they did in this case, then legally the Council can do so. Politically, however, this was astonishing. Even Town Manager, Philip Schenck, Jr., according to the *Hartford Courant*, "appeared surprised."[40] Prior to the May 1998 meeting, the town had received only two written complaints after the resolution in 1995.[41] Unlike in 1995, when the Council called for a public hearing in response to the Director of Recreation and Parks' recommendation of a leash law, the Council in 1998 simply passed the ordinance with no warning to the hundreds of dog walkers who enjoyed the park. Also unlike in 1995, the Town Council promised to enforce this policy and in fact, did so.

Dog walkers, of course, were livid. In May, they organized a group called Trails for Tails, with co-presidents C. J. Hauss and Heidi Lewis. In response to public anger and demand, Chairman Hines placed the issue on the Council's June agenda. More than four hundred people attended that meeting, most of whom were against the leash law. The Council heard testimony, but decided to retain the ordinance. Unlike in 1995, the Town Council had made up its mind and was adamantly opposed to all forms of compromise. To demonstrate some concern for the interests of dog walkers, the Council sent letters to them instructing them to go instead to a state-owned wildlife management area to exercise their dogs off-leash. This area, which is on the Avon-Simsbury line, allows hunting and is closed most weekends from May through October for dog field trials. What is more, the field trial groups also use it for training during the week in those months and in some cases, discharge live ammunition even then.[42] Needless to say, dog walkers did not consider this to be a compromise in good faith.

Faced with a Town Council that was unwilling to negotiate a compromise, the dog walkers sought to use Avon's rules to their advantage. They obtained the required one thousand signatures from registered Avon voters to call for a Special Town Meeting at which citizens could vote on the ordinance. Instead of responding to this outpouring of concern from registered voters in Avon with an offer to compromise, the Town Council dug into its position. Some Council members, in fact, became almost openly hostile to dog walkers, with Councilman Shea referring to them as a "special interest group" and a small "element."[43] The very same ideas, such as fencing, that Council members had themselves suggested in 1995 were now not given any consideration.

Because the Town Council knew that its ordinance would be rescinded at the Special Town Meeting, it exercised its legal prerogative to bring the matter to a referendum. As a result, the town noticed the Special Town Meeting, held on July 27, 1998, and the referendum on September 14, 1998 at the same time. A map was distributed with the notice, but leaders from Trails for Tails deemed it inaccurate. Because of problems with the noticing, which had been the Council's responsibility, and the Council's exercise of the option to send the matter to a referendum, the Council itself questioned the legality of the vote at the Special Town Meeting.

Given the clearly hostile attitude of the Council and the confrontational nature of the politics that provoked, the Special Town Meeting on July 27 was the most intense of all. The few proponents of the law and the many opponents were equally furious, but dog walkers had the numbers. They prevailed in the vote by a very large margin, but questions immediately arose about its legality and implementation. Scott Lewis, a member of Trails for Tails, said that the ordinance or leash law would be rescinded in ten days or on August 6. The town, armed with an opinion from its attorney, disputed that statement, and one advocate of a leash law promised to patrol the park on that day, with cell phone in hand, reporting loose dogs.[44]

The media coverage of that meeting focused on the anger of dog walkers and was very negative. In the aftermath of the meeting, the dog walkers refrained from using the park in August and waited until the September referendum. During that time, advocates of the leash law formed their own group, Save Our Park, led by William Cooper. The group could boast of a very influential membership role. As Lang writes, "Among [its members] . . . were Buck Tilson, who has served on town boards for decades . . . ; Tony Rice, who led the Fisher Meadows Building Committee; Penny Woodford, the vice chairwoman of the Republican Town Committee and wife of Councilman Joseph Woodford; and William Shea, the father of the Councilman."[45] This was an organization that would likely be sympathetic toward official viewpoints, as expressed by the Town Council. Cooper himself claimed that his motivation for political activism had little to do with dogs and much to do with control over Avon politics.[46]

The contest was set between the grassroots upstarts, ironically comprised of wealthy professionals who are not the usual demographic for revolutionaries, and the establishment. With the sides drawn, the matter went to a referendum on September 14 and 2,243 citizens voted for a leash law, while 1,192 voted against it. At 36 percent, the turnout was significantly higher than it had been for municipal elections. After the vote, the matter was settled. Neither the Town Council nor the advocates of the law made any offer of compromise. In their view, they had "won the war" and so there was to be unconditional surrender. Almost one year later, "feelings [had] not yet healed," according to the *Hartford Courant.* Between October 1, 1998 and June 30, 1999, twenty-two tickets and eighteen warnings had been issued for off-leash dog walking at Fisher Meadows. Both sides agreed that there had been a dramatic decrease in the use of Fisher Meadows. It is now a very quiet place, reserved for "passive recreation," which is what the Town Council intended.[47]

## WAS THIS DEMOCRACY? AN EVALUATION

### The Town Council

The exact same Avon government was in place in 1998, with no turnover on the Council and the same Town Manager, Philip Schenck, Jr. These same Council members, however, handled the leash-law controversy in the opposite manner from their actions in 1995. Obviously, the final outcome was different, but the *process* was also dissimilar to that in 1995. While the Council rebuffed its own Director of Recreation and Parks' recommendation for a leash law in 1995 and claimed the need for public input on the matter, it voted a leash law into effect in 1998 when a citizen raised the issue. No representatives of dog walkers were present, and their input was not sought. Further, Council Member Jeter now called for "stern, serious enforcement of the leash law," despite admitting that "we probably should have been more firm during this trial period," since 1995.[48]

Contrary to the process in 1995, the one in 1998 *started* with a *final* decision. The Council had made up its collective mind *before* hearing from those opposed to a leash law. As a result, it would spend a summer defending its decision without ever showing any inclination to revisit the issue. Dog walkers were shut out and thus had to take the offensive or risk total loss of their ability to engage in their recreational activity at Fisher Meadows. What is more, they had something very valuable taken from them, without any sense that the Council recognized the depth of their loss. In effect, dog walkers experienced relative deprivation or the phenomenon of losing something of value to which one is accustomed. Some political scientists consider this to be a recipe for revolution, explaining that people are more likely to revolt when their status is reduced than they are with a constantly low status or chronically poor conditions. Theoretically, the most revolutionary situation is when people's conditions improve, but then begin to deteriorate again. Consider that Americans without health care complain very little, while citizens with health care threaten strikes when benefits are reduced. If you have never had something, you are less likely to revolt than you are if someone takes something from you. The dog walkers were losing something of great value to them, while those who might go to Fisher Meadows if there were no loose dogs were potentially gaining something. Trips to Fisher Meadows, for most in this latter group, were not a part of their daily routines yet, but might become so. Unlike a loss of something valuable, that dynamic does not provoke conflict. The dog walkers, in contrast, were likely to respond intensely to such a profound loss.

In passing the leash law, the Town Council cited complaints, repeated violations of the 1995 compromise, and safety concerns. Chairman Hines articulated the rationales for the change at the Town Council Meeting on June 4, as the issue was placed on the agenda in response to citizens' requests. He alluded to "three years of concerns and complaints by Avon residents" and liability worries. While admitting that more could have been done to enforce the compromise, he cited the changing landscape of Avon from rural to suburban as a need for change as well. Finally, he noted that the Nod Brook Wildlife Management Area, state-owned but on the Avon-Simsbury line, could serve the interests of dog walkers. Specifically, Hines claimed, "This could be a win-win situation—the dog owners return Fisher Meadows to the residents and reduce the Town [sic] potential liability."[49] Of course, many of the dog walkers were residents and would, as a result, lose Fisher Meadows, but the humanity of the dog walkers seemed to be a point lost on the Town Council. What is more striking is the difference in Hines's approach from 1995 to 1998. In 1995, he explained the *process* to those attending the public hearing and assured them that their input mattered in the Town Council's decision-making. In 1998, Hines *defended* the *substance* of a decision already made. It was a fait accompli, and residents were left to conclude that their input had no relevance. To be sure, he said that all of the information presented would be taken "under advisement," but no compromises were forthcoming from the Council in 1998.

Because two members were not present at the June meeting, the issue was placed on the July 2 agenda. At the outset of this meeting, the Council members once again took the opportunity to explain their initial decision, but this time, they were defensive. Councilman Shea, who was probably the strongest advocate of the leash law and indeed the only one to vote against an unleashed area in 1995, opened with a decidedly biased lecture to the dog walkers, which, of course, is his right. Stipulating that some "good" had come from this process with public involvement, he then noted that "bad . . . has come" too, with "some members of this special interest group" attempting "to bully and intimidate the Town Council" and manipulate the media to boot. He proceeded to complain about an "element of people who were a bit hostile" without stating the fact that such hotheads were found on each side of this issue. In his view, only the dog walkers behaved poorly, and he condescendingly explained that "you do not have to succumb to people who appear to yell the loudest." The new policy would "give the park back to the people," in his opinion.[50] Obviously, it would also take it away from the group of people in front of him. In using the negative term "special interest group" repeatedly, Councilman Shea, intentionally or not, denigrated this collection of human beings. Were other walkers a special interest group? Were soccer players? Were fishermen? No, apparently in Councilman Shea's view, those other interests were legitimate, while dog walkers were not.

The condescending lecture angered dog walkers even more. In response to such anger, Councilman Shea opted for a siege mentality. He criticized the media for not reporting the many positive things that happen in Avon. Then the lone Democrat said that he "has never been more proud to serve with a group of people than he is with the Town Council."[51] If the Council was not at outright war with the dog walkers, it was clearly engaged in highly confrontational politics.

To be sure, the other Council members were not as openly hostile to the dog walkers as Shea. Councilwoman Hornaday, for example, specifically noted that all callers were "courteous to her" and that after an extensive review of the matter, she was convinced that a majority of Avon citizens, while not as emotionally involved, supported a leash law. Chairman Hines maintained that calls were three-to-one in favor of a leash law. At the end of the meeting, he stated that the leash law would remain.[52]

With the issue closed, dog walkers, led by the group Trails for Tails, gathered more than enough signatures to call for a Special Town Meeting. To plan for that large meeting, another small Special Town Meeting was held on July 10 with a representative from Trails for Tails, Scott Lewis. Although faced with one thousand signatures, the Town Council did not relent. No offers of compromise were entertained. Pointedly, Chairman Hines remarked, "We will return the property back to the residents." In his view, a compromise would not work.[53]

In an unprecedented move, which had the blessing of the Town Attorney, the Council opted to adjourn the Special Town Meeting, which was held on July 27, to a referendum vote in September. Given the fervor of dog walkers on this issue and the lack of zeal of most proponents of the law, the dog walkers were more than likely to control the meeting and in fact, did so. A referendum would allow the silent majority to register its opinion. Officially, Councilman Jeter defended the call for a referendum by noting a lack of a facility large enough to accommodate all attendees, the problematic presence of out-of-towners and the need to separate them, and the fear of intimidation in voting.[54] A referendum, of course, would also cast the issue in black and white, with no opportunity for compromise. What is more, the Council itself was clearly aligned with and invested in one side. Insisting that it wanted to return the park to its residents and depicting the dog walkers as an intimidating special interest, the Council framed the referendum as a vote for or against Avon itself.

In its absolute refusal to compromise, the Town Council did not serve democracy well in 1998. A minimalist democrat might forgive the Council given that a referendum decided the matter. In the end, the citizens of Avon set policy and did so by a wide margin. Yet even a minimalist would lament the lack of party competition in Avon and would have much preferred the Council to have brokered a compromise among these competing interests.

A participatory democrat would assuredly condemn the Council for inviting such a confrontational form of politics in the first place, casting the issue in stark, non-negotiable terms, and ignoring and denigrating the passions and interests of a substantial minority. A leash law need not be cast in such winner-take-all terms. More disturbingly, a participatory democrat would criticize the condescending attitude of some Council members. The Council, in its view, knew best and seemed to resent any criticism of its decision. There was not deliberation here, but defensiveness; not conversation, but lecture. Citizens were effectively told that their participation was meaningless because the final decision had been reached before they had any opportunity to give input.

## The Citizenry

If the Council did not live up to the standards of participatory democracy, how well did the citizens perform? Keep in mind that the Council's behavior influenced citizens negatively. In other words, the Council did not work to create a forum in which the best traits of people would emerge, but rather one that would invite the worst behavior from both sides. Since the Council considered the matter closed, there was no committee with representatives from both sides charged with finding a consensus or compromise. Instead, opponents, equally passionate but with far greater numbers on the anti-leash side, confronted one another in open meetings where they would state their views with no real need to engage the other side.

There were three such meetings—June 4, July 2, and July 27—at which citizens gave commentary on the issue. At the first Town Council Meeting following the passage of the leash law, the *Hartford Courant* estimated that approximately four hundred dog owners, who were "polite" but "unhappy," and a "smattering" of equally adamant proponents of the law attended the meeting.[55] At this meeting, eight individuals, all from Avon, spoke on behalf of the law, and one alluded to a letter sent to the town with twenty-five signatures in support of the leash law. Eighteen Avon residents spoke against the law, and the co-president of Trails for Tails, C. J. Hauss, presented a petition with the signatures of 277 Avon residents in opposition to the law. Seven out-of-towners spoke against the law, and a petition from out-of-towners was also given to the Council.[56] There were four additional speakers who were either neutral or whose position could not be determined from their words.

This was the meeting at which pro- and anti-leash advocates made their substantive arguments to the Council. At the July 2 meeting, the Council limited comments on this issue to six speakers. In June, fourteen of the twenty-five speakers opposed to the leash law called for a compromise that would accommodate all users of the park. Scott Lewis, speaking on behalf of Trails for Tails, asked that a committee of representatives from both sides, administrators, and neutral people be established to resolve the matter. Others seconded that idea and otherwise called for peaceful coexistence. One speaker claimed a desire to be a "part of the solution," and another acknowledged that there were "strong views on both sides" and exhorted the Council to "find a solution so that everybody can enjoy this park."[57] No advocates of the law called for compromise. Given the dynamic established by the Town Council, that is not surprising. In making its decision *before* the public meeting, the Council gave the victorious side absolutely no reason to compromise and placed the onus on the dog walkers to beg for some sort of a compromise (a bone, if you will). Proponents viewed compromise as equivalent to a loss in this context. There was little disrespect at this June meeting on either side, though two leash advocates were somewhat confrontational. In particular, one assigned collective blame to the dog walkers and told them that they should be "ashamed," while another personally insulted Scott Lewis, telling him to apologize for "trying to be a comedian which he was not."[58]

Among the dog walkers, there was frustration with the political process, with six anti-leash advocates specifically speaking to this issue at the June meeting. Dog walkers were upset with the lack of enforcement of the 1995 compromise, the lack of objective evidence in support of the policy change, and the lack of a public hearing on the matter. As one Avon resident explained the latter, "I felt as though I did not have an opportunity to stand at this mike and tell you what my perceptions were. To me that was what was troubling."[59] The pro-leash advocates had no such complaints in June.

In their substantive arguments, both opponents and advocates of the law demonstrated passion for their respective causes. Three advocates of the leash law explained that they were effectively denied access to the park before it was passed. For example, one mother described how her daughter was afraid to walk there. She complained that her daughter had "been lunged at by young dogs, and she actually latched onto me in sheer terror."[60] On the other side, at least five dog walkers testified to the importance of Fisher Meadows in their lives. Two explained that they moved to Avon partly because of Fisher Meadows, and three others noted their frequency of use. One person specifically claimed that Fisher Meadows was "a significant part of my life in the Town of Avon. . . . This is personal." Another noted that he had been at Fisher Meadows with his dog "every day during blizzards and everything else, for 14 years."[61]

Otherwise, both advocates and opponents made similar arguments to those in 1995. Opponents of the leash law cited the unique aspects of Fisher

Meadows, their personal enjoyment, their sense of security in the company of others, and repeatedly, their sense of community with other dog walkers. This law would destroy that community, they explained. As one non-dog owning opponent of the law stated, "I can tell you that I loved the place the way it used to be, now the life that was there is missing. There was a community of people there that was friendly. . . . And without the dogs and their people, it is completely changed."[62] A dog owner reiterated this sentiment in claiming, "We humans are losing a very important place, a community not a place, a community of people. Unless you belonged to that community . . . , you could not know what that community meant."[63]

Advocates of the law excoriated dog walkers for their irresponsible behavior, with dogs out of control and litter everywhere. Given the uncontrolled dogs, they noted the danger of lawsuits. They applauded the Town Council for giving the park back to the people and the residents of Avon. As Diane Carney, the Treasurer of Save Our Park, phrased it, "We are all tired of being told that this is a park for dogs and if we don't like it find someplace else to walk. The park is for everyone to enjoy."[64] Proponents found it particularly galling when out-of-towners communicated this message.

At the Special Town Meeting on July 27, dog walkers, as expected, comprised an overwhelming majority and were able to rescind the law. The legality of the vote, though, was questioned even before it took place. As previously mentioned, the Town Council had exercised its authority to send this matter to a referendum, which was to be held in September. Scott Lewis, an attorney working on behalf of Trails for Tails, disagreed with this interpretation of the Town Charter. He argued that a Special Town Meeting, per that Charter, is not the same as a regular town meeting and as a result, the Council did not have the authority to refer this matter to a referendum. Despite the disagreement, Trails for Tails did not challenge the legality of the referendum in court. There was a dispute as to whether the leash law was, in fact, rescinded in the period between the Special Town Meeting and the referendum.[65] However, even there, Trails for Tails deferred to the Town Attorney's interpretation of the law and instructed their members not to walk unleashed dogs at Fisher Meadows before the referendum vote.

The Special Town Meeting itself almost certainly worked against the interests of dog walkers. Hundreds had come to the meeting with the expectation that they could vote on the law itself. By this point, they were furious with the Council for refusing to compromise and now, for opting to go to a September referendum. Prior to the second call for a vote, which was acted upon, sixteen people, excluding officials, spoke at this meeting. Of the twelve speaking against the leash law, nine emphasized their frustration with the political process and/or disgust with the Council. One citizen, who had no position or stake on this issue, attended the meeting simply to deliver a verbal complaint to the Council for its handling of this matter. Noting that the Town Attorney's reading of the Charter was "unprecedented," this individual asked why this issue had been so sharply drawn when "there is so much middle ground and room for compromise."[66] Heidi Lewis, co-president of Trails for Tails, directly asked the Council if there was "something other than ego here" and questioned the truthfulness of Councilman Shea's claim that compromises were explored. Explaining the cause of their anger, another said, "We come to you in numbers, we have tried to be polite, we have tried to be respectful, but when we get faces that have no expressions and you turn a deaf ear to us, we get upset."[67] Indeed, the crowd of dog walkers was boisterous at this meeting, with the minutes noting "extremely noisy chatter," "hissing," "much noise," "boos," "whooping," and "noisy clammer," among other descriptions.

From the perspective of the very few advocates of the leash law at this meeting, the dog walkers appeared as a mob. The crowd booed and hissed Diane Carney, the Treasurer of Save Our Park, when she challenged the three-minute time limit for speakers. In her view, the dog walkers had cut into her time via their noisy interruptions, and she wanted the opportunity to complete her rebuttal. When the moderator refused her additional time, she attempted to finish her statement but was then loudly interrupted. Symbolically, an out-of-towner, Dorothy Mader, who was charged with giving the microphone to speakers, sought to take it from Diane Carney, who concluded simply, "This is wrong."[68] Years later, she explained that the denial of her right to speak infuriated her all the more. The dog walkers' behavior, in her view, was inappropriate and denoted a lack of respect for others. She also received a few pieces of hate mail as a result of the incident. Ironically, it was that very same sense of wrong, of not being heard, that drove the anger of the dog walkers.

It was this raw display of anger that the undecided Avon voters saw. Devoid of the context and knowledge of the passion surrounding this issue, onlookers concluded that the dog walkers were behaving outrageously. They saw a mob bully a minority. To the casual observer, the dog walkers were insisting on getting their own way, other interests be damned. A picture is worth a thousand words in the minds of most, but the context is absent. Ironically, the actual words of the dog walkers, while they expressed great anger at the Council, were not aimed at other users of the park and in fact, six speaking against the law still sought compromise. On the other side, a proponent of the law exhorted, "It is not the dogs that we should be afraid of it is you people."[69] What onlookers caught, though, were not the words, but the emotion and anger. C. J. Hauss, the co-president of Trails for Tails, explained that it was the Council that "pushed me over the edge and you have pushed a lot of people over the edge here tonight," but the Council's *appearance* was passive.[70]

## Media Coverage

Appearances were critical, as voters, with little stake in the matter, were now called upon to vote for one side or the other. There was no option to vote for a compromise. Media coverage thus became important, as that was how most people learned of the situation. After the July 27 Special Town Meeting, the *Hartford Courant* turned decidedly against the dog walkers and used extremely negative language to describe them. In an article describing the meeting, Elizabeth Hamilton wrote, "[D]og owners . . . staged a rebellion to free their pets.

"Four Town Council members sat through a two-hour tirade at the town meeting as dog owners chewed them out, shouted them down and then proceeded to override the Council's decision."[71] There is no mention in the article of the substantive complaints about the political process that fueled their anger. Instead, the article depicts the dog owners as out-of-control rebels upset only because of the law itself. Further, the *Hartford Courant* endorsed the Council's view, labeling the dog walkers "obnoxious."[72] Just two weeks before the vote, Denis Horgan, a columnist, described the dog walkers as a "stubborn, noisy minority." While he also questioned why this issue had not been resolved via a compromise, voters were note afforded that option.[73] They had to side with the "stubborn, noisy minority" or the Town Council. Repelled by the inexplicable conduct of dog walkers, many Avon voters sided with the Council. Given this coverage, it was fairly easy for the Council and advocates of the leash law to cast the dog walkers as antithetical to Avon's mores, or as outsiders.

## The Impact—Citizens' Input and Community

Turnout was high for a local vote, at 36 percent, and voters, by a margin of almost two-to-one, opted for the leash law. In this sense, the input of citizens mattered, as they literally decided the issue. Intensity, however, counted for nothing. If gun control laws, to take one rather contentious example, were decided this way, there would be much stricter controls and probably fewer places to hunt. Most people support gun control, but it is not the issue of greatest importance to them. For the minority of gun owners, though, they feel passionately about the issue, and the legislature typically accommodates that. Snowmobiling, too, would most likely be limited, as would riding a motorcycle without a helmet and any other activities enjoyed by a minority, but with some potentially negative effects. Even issues of citizens' rights do not fare well in this forum, as the recent bans on same-sex marriage attest. Referendums do not allow for compromise, and minority interests are therefore almost certain to lose completely in this venue. All votes count equally, and thus there is no emphasis given to intensity of feeling. A vote of someone who never has and never will go to Fisher Meadows counts equally with someone, pro- or anti-leash, who visits every day. For all those citizens who testified to the importance of Fisher Meadows in their daily lives, this form of resolution rendered those efforts futile. The Town Council seemingly had washed its hands of the matter. The media did not explain the significance of this issue to people's lives in the weeks before the referendum, but focused instead on the dog walkers' anger and rebellious behavior. As a result, those voters with little stake in this issue chose between an angry mob at war with its Town Council and a law-abiding minority supportive of the Town Council.

What effect did this resolution have on the community? There is no question that this casting of the issue was divisive. Yet for the leash advocates, there was vindication and perhaps a strengthening sense of community. Diane Carney, Treasurer of Save Our Park, noted that she was "proud of her town" and considered the vote a condemnation of the dog walkers' inappropriate behavior. A relative newcomer to Avon herself, she bonded with others over this issue and continues to be involved in local politics. She clearly retains positive feelings about Avon, its government, and the majority of its citizens.[74] For those who lost the referendum, however, the effect seemed to be precisely the opposite. After this battle, the leaders of Trails for Tails retreated from any involvement in local politics. C. J. Hauss considered herself an "outsider" despite long years of residence in Avon. Frustrated with the town's handling of this issue, Hauss deemed it a "lost opportunity" to bring Avon together.[75] To paraphrase President George W. Bush, you were either with the Town Council or against it, and your treatment and sense of belonging seemed to depend on that status. Outsiders, defined much more by lifestyle than longevity in the town, experienced total rejection, and their status as "other" was therefore solidified.

Arguably, Avon held onto its old identity in this battle, one that excluded the professional types and their style of politics. There was much made of the rebelliousness of dog walkers. Yet it was a legal rebellion, a nice oxymoron if there ever was one. Their rebellion involved collecting signatures and exercising free speech rights to question and harshly criticize the Town Council. Dog walkers reminded Town Council members that they were elected and could be voted out of office, and one asked if there was a recall or impeachment procedure. There was legitimate disagreement over the legality of the vote at the Special Town Meeting, but the worst case scenario seemed to involve a court's resolution, and even that did not come to pass. It was, then, the style, the challenge, the display of anger, and the whole spectacle that were so upsetting to traditional Avon. The dog walkers were "those people," outsiders, other, and to vote against "them" was to vote for Avon itself. The dog walkers, whose brand of democracy was as deeply offended by the arrogant, father-knows-best style of the Council, considered it entirely appropriate to make elected officials answer for their behavior. What exactly is wrong with reminding elected officials that they can be voted out of office? The Council's absolute refusal to negotiate was as maddening and alienating to the dog walkers as their behavior was to traditional Avon. The resolution, then, left a deeply divided community in its wake or more accurately, two separate communities.

Given this negative impact on community, a participatory democrat would condemn this process. To be sure, participatory democrats would applaud citizens for attending meetings, collecting signatures to call for a Special Town Meeting, and voting. However, it was all for naught, as the Town Council was not open to any reconsideration of its original decision. There was no deliberation, as that requires two sides to engage in good faith. What is more, there was no positive reinforcement for any forms of participation besides voting. No other input was given serious consideration, and that was apparent to dog walkers. Indeed, one person who supported off-leash walking but did not own a dog wrote letters to each Town Council member and asked each one to reconsider his/her decision. In his letter, he specifically stated that he did not own a dog. As he recounts, the Town Council clearly paid no attention to his letters. In response to my questions, he wrote, "I did not receive a personal response from any of them. Instead I received a letter advising me to take my dog to a hunting training park in a neighboring town (in spite of the fact that I began my letter by stating that I did not have a dog)."[76] No one seemed to have read his letter. That message—that one's input is not worthy of attention—is utterly irreconcilable with participatory democracy.

## Equality and Out-of-Towners

A referendum counts all votes equally, and so that basic requirement of democracy is satisfied, superficially at least. The Town Council has the legal authority to refer a matter to the voters for their resolution. Yet all of those out-of-towners who so enjoyed the park were shut out of this process. To be sure, they could speak at the town meetings, but the Council had already seemingly decided the issue. If a committee had been formed, all stakeholders could have been represented. Instead, these out-of-town stakeholders had no input in the final decision. That is a function of our governmental boundaries, but there were other options in this case. Interestingly, proponents of the leash law cast the vote as one for Avon, with the self-described outsiders of Avon aligned with the real outsiders or those from out-of-town. Despite the Fisher family's wish for the park to be open to all, out-of-towners were politically toxic in the framing of this issue. A participatory democrat would consider this exclusion and casting problematic. A minimalist, on the other hand, would not, as the basic legal requirement of equality was satisfied.

## Liberty

Liberty seemed alive and well in this dispute, with both groups forming associations. The dog walkers formed Trails for Tails almost immediately after the Council's passage of the leash law. This grassroots group had effective leaders, hundreds of members, and a system of communication. The advocates of a leash law formed their own group, Save Our Park, in the aftermath of the July Special Town Meeting to ensure victory in the September referendum. This group, while decidedly more establishmentarian, too had leaders, held meetings, and consisted of contributing members. Both participatory and minimalist democrats would applaud the formation of these groups.

Dog walkers clearly exercised their speech rights. Given their intensity and the resultant numbers who attended town meetings, there were legitimate concerns about intimidation for those opposed to them. A handful of people spoke in favor of the leash law, but surely there were some not willing to express a minority view in that forum. More should have been done to allow leash advocates to speak without interruption. No citizen should be booed at a public meeting for expressing unpopular views. While not a perfect substitute, citizens could also express their views to Council members via letters and calls. According to Lang, the Council received many letters on both sides of this issue, and Council members alluded to phone calls as well.[77] It is thus fair to conclude that each side had an opportunity to state its case.

## CONCLUSION

The resolution in this case produced clear winners and losers. For those who won, there was a psychological victory of sorts. The *Hartford Courant* described the members of Save Our Park as "practically howling with jubilation."[78] Voters rejected the confrontational politics associated with the dog walkers and rallied behind the Town Council. In contrast, the dog walkers were devastated. They lost their community at Fisher Meadows and their use of the park. Because this large group of users could no longer partake of their recreational activity at Fisher Meadows, there was a dramatic reduction in activity at the park. Both sides emerged with a sense of bitterness, or at least distaste, for their adversaries. Dog walkers repeatedly recount that the town mobilized and bused elderly residents from nursing homes to vote against them. They consider such votes to be particularly mean-spirited, as the voters had no intention of using the park but were ending the dog walkers' use of the area. Likewise, one proponent of the law claimed that the whole episode, especially the behavior of dog walkers, left such a "bad taste" that the individual rarely visits Fisher Meadows anymore.[79] Not surprisingly, this brutally confrontational style of politics left no one, even the "winners," fully satisfied in the end.

The Town Council had the legal prerogative to handle the matter as it did, confrontationally. Elected by the voters, the Council can pass ordinances that it deems in the best interests of the town. Faced with so much opposition to this leash law, the Council sought its attorney's advice and acted consistently with that advice, choosing to bring the matter to a referendum. While Trails for Tails disputed the town's interpretation of the Charter, the group did not bring suit, and if it had, both sides could have made credible cases for their interpretations. Such is law. Because no suit was brought, the town's actions must be acknowledged as legally legitimate.

Politically, however, the Town Council handled this matter poorly in 1998. A large number of people, including Avon citizens, felt shut out of this process. Never validating their concerns, the Council instead depicted these citizens as problematic. For many, their first experience with political involvement was thus negative and as a result, would provide an inducement to stay out of local politics. Perhaps because the Council made its decision before soliciting any public input, it clearly developed a stake in the outcome. Its very legitimacy, as a decision-making body, somehow became associated with the particulars of this policy decision. That was misfortunate. As an advocate of one side of this issue, the Council not only lost sight of the very real desires of a minority of its constituents, but it became consumed in the confrontation itself. People expect governmental bodies to balance the interests of competing groups, not to fight on one side against the other. To be sure, the Council seemingly did not consider recreational dog walking to be a legitimate interest, as it did fishing, sports, and other activities. That rejection was stinging, especially when aimed at people who pay taxes and play by the rules. The Council effectively criminalized the recreational activity of many professional people, attacked their status as upstanding citizens, and "put them in their place," if you will. Leash disputes are divisive enough on their own accord, with plenty of hotheads on each side, without a governmental body's involvement. Arguably, the Council's total immersion in the politics of this issue is what catapulted this controversy to such a fiery level. Ironically, the Council, despite its passive appearance, put the town in the limelight more so than the interest groups themselves.

The outcome was as problematic as the process. Instead of finding space for recreational dog walkers somewhere in Avon, the Council attempted to direct people to state-owned land. The solution was to let another governmental body deal with the dog walkers, despite the protestations of the state. While Avon has experienced a loss of undeveloped space and population growth, it is not quite yet Arlington County, Virginia or San Francisco. There are parks in Avon that get fairly light use. Fisher Meadows itself, which now also gets light use especially in the winter, has 233 acres. Somewhere, a space could have been found *if there was political will*. Even the enforcement of the law was galling to dog walkers. Unable to devote significant resources to this matter between 1995 and 1998, the Town Council found the means to enforce the total ban diligently, not just at prime time, but at all hours, as though it were a public water supply.

The Town Council can rest assured that it satisfied the majority of its constituents, even if many in that majority rarely, if ever, walk at Fisher Meadows. All Council members have been re-elected, and one continues to serve on the Council in 2010. Three members retired, but of their own volition. Another lost his seat in 2007 after serving for twenty-four years. Such is majoritarian democracy, conflict-style. For the minority, the loss was real. It changed people's lives. A non-dog owner, who supported off-leash walking, said, "I still do go to Fisher Meadow. It was initially very sad to go there and see the trail virtually empty, where I used to encounter so many people who were there enjoying themselves with their dogs. The 'vast number' of people, who supposedly had not been able to walk there because of the dogs, apparently had lost interest in the place as soon as it had been ruined for the dog walkers."[80]

# Chapter V

## San Francisco: The Patron Saint of Animals

Named for the patron saint of animals, Frances of Assisi, San Francisco is indeed home to animal lovers of all kinds. Even the leashing controversies in this city often pit one form of animal lover against another. There is no question, though, that dog lovers abound in this area. As one reporter explained, "Nobody beats San Francisco when it comes to doting on dogs. It's a city with luxury dog hotels, rooftop dog cocktail parties, . . ." and more dogs than children![1] It is no wonder, then, that at one time, San Francisco was rated the best city in the United States for dogs.[2] Although hotels and cocktail parties are fine as far as they go, most canines are concerned with parks, and San Francisco does not disappoint on that score either. Surrounded by the natural beauty of water on three sides, the city boasts several gorgeous parks where dogs historically have been allowed off-leash. One of those parks, Fort Funston, is nationally renowned as a "dog heaven." Given this culture, it should come as no surprise that when authorities began to curtail and in some cases, end off-leash walking in the 1990s and 2000s, "dog politics" exploded onto the local political scene.

While other leashing conflicts take the form of battles, this one is more akin to a war. Since the 1990s, dog walkers in San Francisco have, in fact, been fighting a two-front war. On the "eastern front," they face Washington, DC in the form of the National Park Service (NPS). Almost all of San Francisco's coastline and over half of its park space are a part of the Golden Gate National Recreation Area (GGNRA), which is managed by the NPS. Encompassed in the 75,000 acre park, which goes well beyond county limits, are Fort Funston (or "dog heaven"); Crissy Field, Baker Beach, Land's End, and Ocean Beach, four other very popular off-leash, dog-walking places; and many others. In 2001, the NPS announced a ban on off-leash dog walking in all areas of the GGNRA. Both the politics that led up to that decision and the ensuing politics have been confrontational, passionate, and complex. A federal court reversed the ban in 2005, but the NPS is now engaged in the process of rewriting its dog policy for the GGNRA. The final outcome of this process is expected to restrict off-leash dog walking significantly.

On the "western front," dog walkers confront City Hall. Prior to the 1990s, the city had very lax enforcement of its leash laws. When the NPS limited off-leash dog walking in the GGNRA, city parks experienced an increase in this activity. Even well before the 2001 ban, the city, managing multiuse neighborhood parks, began to reconsider its leashing policies. Indeed, the city established a new, official dog policy in 2002 with promises of enforcement after a lengthy process that began in the 1990s. As you might imagine, the development and announcement of this policy were highly contentious political events. To be sure, there are off-leash areas at many of the city's parks, but their number and size do not begin to accommodate the demand. What is more, the city has charged a commission with studying its open space, which could have profound impacts on the availability of recreational dog walking as well.

When all is said and done, what was once a mundane, daily enjoyment—walking the dog—is becoming a highly regulated activity in San Francisco. As a result, dog walkers are as embattled on the western, city front as they are on the eastern one. The outcome, at this writing, remains uncertain. Whatever that outcome, though, this war is sure to continue given the dynamics in place, the history, and the reality of an urban landscape with approximately 120,000 dogs whose guardians, not just owners per the San Francisco Board of Supervisors, for the most part have no land.[3]

## SAN FRANCISCO AND DOGS: A LOVE STORY

In the American imagination, San Francisco is home to liberal activism and all that includes, such as protests that often take the form of spectacle, cutting-edge policies, and most importantly, championship of minority rights, youth, and underrepresented groups. Perhaps its tolerant reputation stems from its Barbary Coast days when literally all types of unsavory activities, such as warfare and prostitution, were accepted and practiced. Recent history, though, cements a decidedly more progressive milieu of causes. San Francisco, after all, was home to the beat generation, whose members challenged the materialism and conformity of 1950s America, and later to the hippies, who famously flocked to the city's summer of love in 1967.[4] In that turbulent period, San

Francisco was in the forefront of the movements against the Vietnam War and for the rights of youth. It later became the center of the gay rights movement in the 1970s and continues to have an honored place in that struggle.

Long a tolerant and welcoming culture, the city was profoundly impacted by the rise of the computer industry and the subsequent dot-com boom of the 1990s. Entrepreneurs and computer programmers descended upon the city and transformed its economy. As a result, at that time, San Francisco claimed the highest household income and property values of any city in the United States and a very well educated populace. Surely, such gentrification has challenged the city's character. Instead of students sleeping out to protest national policies, now the underprivileged sleep in its streets and parks for want of housing. A youthful counterculture, which made San Francisco famous at one time, would be hard pressed to pay today's rents. As Frommer's put it, in the 1990s, "San Francisco no longer opened its Golden Gate to everyone looking for the legendary alternative lifestyle—unless they could afford a $1000 studio apartment and $20-per-day fees to park their cars."[5] The bursting of the dot-com bubble in spring 2000, the impact of 9/11 on tourism, and a general economic downturn cooled the excesses of the 1990s, but the city has generally rebounded from those woes and remains decidedly upscale when compared to its pre-boom days.

Despite such changes, a social conscience persists in this city. Perhaps reflecting its demographics, its focus tends to be social and environmental more so than economic. This is not to say that San Francisco has not shown compassion for its economically distressed, but it is to say that social and environmental issues are more salient. The restoration of natural areas is an example of one such environmental issue, as is the city's efforts to curb the use of plastic water bottles among public employees. Generosity and care for animals of all kinds, wild and domestic, abound in San Francisco as well. The Golden Gate Audubon Society has a strong presence in the city and is vociferous in its defense of wild birds. Of course, San Franciscans also treasure their sea lions, who are themselves a tourist attraction. It is not surprising, then, that pets would be treated particularly well in this city. Home to a $7 million shelter with comfortable accommodations for abandoned pets, San Francisco has the lowest canine euthanasia rate of any city in the country. One in ten people, per estimates, contribute to the Society for the Prevention of Cruelty to Animals (SPCA), and they do so generously, as the $10 per person contribution to animals for all citizens compares to a national average of only $1.70. Additionally, the SPCA has over 1,200 volunteers, a number that is three times higher than any other city.[6]

*Tribute to Bummer and Lazarus, Transamerica Building.*

Clearly, man's best friend holds a special place in this city's heart. Even well before the Spanish settled in the area, its native tribes, unlike ones to the south, were said to have named dogs, kept them inside, and buried them with a care given to humans. Tribes such as the Northern Yokut believed that dogs possessed immortal souls.[7] When the Europeans arrived in large numbers during the 1848 Gold Rush, they kept this tradition somewhat alive. Inundated with rats and stray dogs in the 1860s during its growth period, city dwellers managed to fall in love with two strays, Bummer and Lazarus. They were impressed with their rat-hunting skills, but arguably most captivated by the bond between these two dogs. According to newspaper accounts at the time, Bummer, a Newfoundland-type dog, came to the rescue of Lazarus when the latter found himself on the losing side of a fight. Bummer chased off his canine attacker and then escorted the wounded Lazarus to a doorway. Every night until Lazarus's severely wounded leg was healed, Bummer slept with him. He also brought him food. As his name might imply, Lazarus came back from near death to become Bummer's partner. Henceforward, the newspapers regularly reported evidence of their friendship, their antics, and rat catching. Indeed, they were nicknamed Damon and Pythias for the two Pythagorean philosophers of ancient times "whose steadfast friendship for each other had become proverbial."[8]

Because of the large number of strays at this time, the city began round-
ing up, impounding, and killing them. When Lazarus was caught in that
frenzy, people paid the fee for his release and prevailed upon the city's Supervisors to exempt both Bummer and Lazarus from an ordinance that banned
unleashed dogs downtown. Upon the deaths of each of the dogs, tributes were
written in the newspaper, and ultimately their bodies were stuffed and put on
display in the saloon they frequented. In recognition of the special place that
Bummer and Lazarus had in the city's heart, a plaque stands in their memory
at the base of the Transamerica Building, located in the very neighborhood
that they once roamed. Bummer and Lazarus were not the only dogs to find a
place in the city's heart in those ruthless days, as other dogs, too, according to
Barker, merited funerals and obituaries in the press. Yet no others had quite
the status as Bummer and Lazarus.[9]

Added to this historical friendship with dogs is an exaggerated impact of
modern trends that have otherwise increased the emotional ties between humans and canines. San Francisco has the lowest percentage of children of any
major American city, a statistic that increases the likelihood that dogs will assume very important roles in the family. Indeed, compared to a national average
of 25 percent, only 14.5 percent of San Franciscans are under eighteen. While
the average household size of 2.3 is only slightly below the national average
of 2.6, 39 percent of San Franciscans, a very substantial minority, live alone.[10]
What is more, San Francisco is a large city where people are anonymous, unless they find small communities within. Indeed, San Francisco, noted for its
high percentage of foreign-born, attracts newcomers from all over and is thus
a city constantly in flux. Only a minority of San Franciscans, approximately
35 percent, were born in the city. In such a world, dogs and the relationships
established with other dog walkers are likely to assume great importance. These
communities not only offer a third entrance to social life, along with family
and work, but can compensate for distant or non-existent families as well.

While the citizens of San Francisco demonstrate an ethic of care for
animals and dogs in general, they naturally express great love for their own
dogs in particular. This love manifests itself ubiquitously in the culture. There
are dog nights at popular restaurants, off nights when dogs are welcome; dog
days at Giants games, when the first five hundred patrons can bring their dogs
in the bleachers; and dog fairs, most famously, the Pet Street Fair or Animal
Wingding that features dogs dressed in drag, among other things. San Francisco invented doggie day care and pet résumés to convince reluctant landlords, in a city with 65 percent renters, to accept their dogs.[11] *Dog Fancy* rightly
deemed this the most dog-friendly city in the country. Even the climate suits

the canine aversion to heat, with temperatures averaging between sixty and seventy degrees. Of course, such weather is great for hiking and swimming year-round, for canines at least, and until the great leash wars, San Francisco boasted some of the best parks in the country for precisely these activities.

## DOG HEAVEN AND OTHER GREAT PARKS

Prior to the mid-1990s, dog walkers had only to choose which great park to visit. San Francisco has a "green index" (or park space) of 25.4 percent, second only to New York City. There are approximately 7,594 acres of parkland in the city itself, with over half of that space, or 4,106 acres, under the control of the national government or NPS.[12] That land is the GGNRA, and it includes such popular dog-walking spots as Fort Funston, Ocean Beach, Land's End, Baker Beach, and Crissy Field. The GGNRA is spread across three counties, Marin to the north, where it is vast, and even to San Mateo in the south. Inclusive of such hot tourist spots as Muir Woods and Alcatraz and approximately twenty-eight miles of shoreline, it is the largest urban park in the world.[13] In San Francisco County, with which we are concerned, its holdings also include Fort Mason and the Presidio. Consisting of 1,491 acres of coastal scrub, dunes, prairie grassland, a planted forest, historical buildings, and residential sections, the Presidio sits in the northwest corner of San Francisco and includes bay and ocean fronts. Once an army base, it became part of the GGNRA in October 1994. Crissy Field and Baker Beach are in this area, but it also includes other fields once used to walk dogs as well. Fort Mason, with some fields and historic buildings, is on the Bay and connected with the Presidio.

With dunes, trails, ocean, and wide-open space, Fort Funston is the dog walkers' hands-down favorite despite all of these great choices. It is dog heaven, after all, and therefore considered the best place to walk dogs not only in the area, but in California, and maybe even the country. In fact, dogs themselves are a draw for children and others to watch. Approximately 230 acres in size, the park occupies a rugged stretch of coastal headlands with dunes reaching heights of 200 feet or more and trails leading down to the coast. The views are stunning and include ocean surf, cliffs, a lake, and cityscape. What is more, it is user-friendly with plenty of paved pathways.[14] Dog walkers can remain on high ground in a large open area, or they can walk down the dunes and head to the beach area. The park thus accommodates both those people with limited mobility and those who want a walk themselves. Indeed, there are benches for the humans who need to sit and community water bowls for thirsty dogs. While its geographical assets are phenomenal, they are not the only or even

*Community water bowls, Fort Funston.*

*Walking path, Fort Funston.*

the main reason why this park is so special. Repeatedly, dog walkers applaud the social nature of this park—its great people. It is a place where friendships have formed, a social center. In an interview, Linda McKay, who has been a leader in the Fort Funston Dog Walkers group, noted how this park was a community for many people and as a result, filled an important role in their lives.[15] That *living* component of Funston, the social component, greatly enhances its allure, as, of course, do the dogs.

I visited Funston on a rainy Saturday morning and nonetheless sensed its friendly and peaceful ambience immediately. The rain did not keep people away. Tourists, however, were missing, as the park is located on the extreme southwestern edge of the city. Indeed, one has to be creative in the use of public transportation to access this park. (My hotel concierge suggested renting a bicycle, albeit problematically from a place that rented only surfboards, a definite no-no for a New Englander more accustomed to snow shoes.) While adjacent to a main road, the park is completely removed from traffic and provides a safe place to walk dogs. All of the dogs I encountered were well behaved and clearly having an equally enjoyable time as their human companions.

Fort Funston connects to what was another great dog-walking place, Ocean Beach. Stretching approximately 3.5 miles from Fort Funston to the Cliff House near the mouth of San Francisco Bay, Ocean Beach is the city's largest beach and defines its western edge. This, too, is part of the GGNRA. It is a long, flat area and is therefore perfect for a great many activities, including dog-walking. Ocean Beach "has always been a destination for pleasure-loving San Franciscans. . . . It is arguably the best big city seaside walk in the world."[16] Crissy Field was yet another popular dog walking spot. Originally an airfield, this area, which has recently been rejuvenated, includes open space and beachfront. Its restored marshlands, which are fenced off, serve as a buffer between a busy street and the beauty of the shoreline. A well-maintained walkway receives heavy use from runners, bikers, and dog walkers. Baker Beach is on the northwestern, ocean shore and as a result, has spectacular waves. The beach is known for its "laid-back vibe," which Fodor's advises could include nude sunbathers.[17] Also on the west coast, Land's End offers great hiking trails atop cliffs. That area also encompasses former Fort Miley, which offers "a grassy picnic area" amid "turn-of-century gun emplacements."[18] All of these areas, then, were multiuse, with Funston, for example, attracting hang gliders as well as dog walkers.

San Francisco additionally has 3,317 acres of parkland within city limits and under its own control. Before the mid-1990s, San Francisco had leash laws for all of its parks with the exception of eighteen designated off-leash areas, though the laws were not seriously enforced. As a result, people could exercise their dogs at many city parks without a realistic fear of a ticket. City and federal authorities cracked down on off-leash dog walking around the same time, and their actions were related to one another's. In the 1990s, as will be noted later, the NPS began closing off significant sections of Fort Funston to dogs and people, which, of course, put more pressure on city parks to accommodate dogs. City parks, then, began to reconsider both their dog policy and its enforcement, which, in turn, put increasing pressure on the NPS to provide space for this activity. Dog walkers, caught in a vicious circle, were being pushed out from both sides, and this combined assault on their favorite pastime created a political firestorm.

## WHY THEN?

On one level of analysis, San Francisco has all the ingredients for a leash war; it is home to many dogs and dog lovers. Yet while the city might claim to have more dogs than children, approximately 15 percent of its 2000 population of 776,733 are under 18. That is about 116,510 children. There is bound to be competition among a percentage of these children for playground space. Coleman Advocates for Children and Youth specifically works for the interests of children. While some argue that children like to play with dogs off-leash, this organization fights for fewer off-leash areas and for these areas to be fenced. In other words, there are children and parents who want park space without dogs present. Besides children, there are many other competitors for park use in San Francisco. The now upscale city boasts a healthy lifestyle, with its citizens among the fittest in the nation. Surely, such people must go to parks to do whatever it is that keeps them fit. According to the 2000 census, San Francisco has the second highest population density in the US. There are, in fact, 16,526 persons per square mile, a number exceeded by only New York City. There are, then, *lots* of competitors. In such a populated city, most of these competitors are unlikely to know each other.

But why was there an explosion at the turn of the century? Surely, all of the above factors had been in place for some time. In fact, San Francisco's 2000 population was only slightly above its 1950 peak population of 775,000.[19] Outdoor exercise has had popularity since at least the 1970s, and tourism has been a staple of San Francisco's economy for some time as well. In other words, there should not have been a dramatic change in park use at this time. Yet there were two significant changes in the 1990s. First, the gentrification of the city brought wealthier people to its neighborhoods. It is possible that this increasingly sized demographic group was likely to include both those less prone to tolerate the eccentricities of others, inclusive of a love for dogs, and those more likely to have strong attachments to dogs. This demographic group is also more likely to partake in outdoor recreation. Second, and arguably more importantly, there was a change in park philosophy. Both the NPS and the city, the two managers of parkland, began to adopt an environmental approach that favored the protection and restoration of natural areas, including animal and plant life indigenous to the Bay Area.

Defining itself as a "movement," natural-areas supporters seek to restore native habitats. Unlike other forms of environmentalism, the goal is not necessarily conservation in all cases. Instead, the restoration of native habitat might require the removal of trees and plants that Europeans introduced to the area. In San Francisco, for example, natural-areas supporters recommend the removal of Monterey cypress and pine trees, eucalyptus trees, ice plants, and other non-native weeds and plants.[20] More controversially, certain animal species non-native to the area, such as species of deer, have been hunted and killed pursuant to restoration plans.[21] The goal is to reclaim the original biodiversity of the area. According to this school of thought, a healthy ecosystem, which "requires a balance of plants, insects, herbivores, and carnivores which have evolved together . . . ," is most likely if native animals and plants are restored and non-native species, such as those introduced by Europeans, are removed.[22] Obviously, the application of this theory to San Francisco must be limited or Golden Gate Park, for example, would exist no more. That largest of city parks was built entirely on sand dunes, and the construction required the introduction of non-native trees and plants. Indeed, per Manning and Dickson, at one time, "The whole western edge of San Francisco was a series of sand dunes with no trees in evidence. The flora was primarily coastal brush and dune scrub."[23] However, supporters of this view cite the need to save endangered plant species and retain San Francisco's standing as one of the world's top twenty-five biodiversity hot spots.[24]

There are powerful and active supporters of this form of environmentalism. The Center for Biological Diversity, for example, actively pushes for the restoration of natural areas and does so via a combination of "conservation biology with litigation policy advocacy, and an innovative strategic vision."[25] As one might expect, the Yerba Buena Chapter of the California Native Plant Society (CNPS) also promotes these policies. Significantly, the local chapters of the Sierra Club and Audubon Society advocate the restoration of natural areas as well. They have successfully equated this approach with San Francisco's popular mantra of environmentalism. As a result, there is significant support for this movement.

The National Park Service is clearly an advocate, with much information about natural areas and biodiversity provided on its Web site. This is not surprising. The mission of the NPS is to preserve "unimpaired the natural and cultural resources and values of the national park system for the enjoyment, education, and inspiration of this and future generations."[26] One reading of this mission could focus on preserving unimpaired natural resources, which can be defined fairly as those indigenous to the area. Those attracted to jobs at the NPS are most likely committed to this mission and to ensuring the survival of threatened plant and animal species. What is more, this organization is accustomed to overseeing parks in the wilderness with very different recreational uses than would be found in a city. More problematically, the NPS has undoubtedly developed relations with the Audubon Society, Sierra Club, and the Center for Biological Diversity in fulfillment of its national mission. These organizations are *its own natural-areas* supporters, and a cursory study of bureaucratic operations confirms the likelihood of friendly relationships with such organizations.[27] The pleas, then, of such organizations are most likely to fall on receptive ears at the NPS, both because of a longstanding relationship and shared beliefs among NPS staff. San Francisco, too, has been fairly supportive of this movement. Given that city officials are elected, they might be responding to both the popularity of the movement and the political power of its supporting organizations.

The natural-areas framework, accepted wholeheartedly by the NPS and increasingly by the city, is highly prejudicial to recreational dog walkers. As a domesticated species, dogs are of no use to natural-areas environmentalists. In this framework, they are, by definition, a problem. Given the numbers of recreational dog walkers in San Francisco, dogs have, in fact, been targeted as enemies in this perspective. Almost every environmental problem is attributed to their presence. This attribution goads the dog walkers, who cite, for example, the NPS's use of bulldozers to remove non-native ice plants, as more threatening to sand dunes and migrating birds than human or canine walkers. Additionally, dog walkers argue that birds are just as likely to have been displaced by the *removal* of non-native plants, helicopters, hang gliders, and myriad other reasons. From this perspective, the natural-areas supporters and the NPS have turned dogs into scapegoats, concluding that they are the source of problems without sufficient evidence. The various dog-walking groups, such as Ocean Beach Dog, Fort Funston Dog Walkers, and SFDog, have cited studies that challenge the negative assumptions about dogs made in the natural-areas framework.[28] To be sure, there are indeed natural-areas supporters who love dogs and some seek forms of sustainable dog walking.

More often, however, dog walkers and natural-areas supporters find themselves in competition.

For the most part, dog walkers claim the label of environmentalism also. However, their environmentalism seeks to retain trees and includes dogs as an animal species whose exercise needs should be accommodated. Dog walkers repeatedly *celebrate* the human and canine use of parks, emphasizing that they are often the primary users of the land. From their perspective, it is healthy that people go for walks daily. Those people enjoy partaking in nature. Dog walkers would deem it a shame to ban this activity and have these beautiful lands go unused, while natural-areas advocates would applaud the reduced use for its benefits in protecting endangered plant and animal species. They are wholly distinct land-use philosophies. To be sure, there are others, not necessarily dog people, who challenge other aspects of natural-areas restoration, such as the removal of trees. As Rodriguez explained, it is at times a battle between "tree huggers and sand huggers." He writes, "On one side are self-proclaimed environmentalists who want to preserve and restore 'natural areas' to look as San Francisco did more than a century ago, when most of the land was covered with sand dunes and wild shrubs.

"On the other side are self-proclaimed environmentalists who prefer their open space as 'cultural areas'—places where dogs run free, families picnic on vast lawns, softball players circle the bases and children seesaw and swing."[29]

Perhaps because the NPS is aligned with the natural-areas movement, there are some who might have been turned off from environmentalism entirely. They fault the NPS for not differentiating an urban recreational area from other parks and consider its actions extremist. Additionally, they can cite the flexibility inherent in the mission of the NPS, which includes both cultural and natural preservation. Concerned about the city's Natural Areas Program, one professor worried that "regulatory styles perceived as arbitrary and authoritarian can and have pushed groups of people normally friendly to environmentalism and conservation . . . into anti-government positions."[30] To some extent, this is already happening among dog walkers in San Francisco, long a bastion of liberalism and environmentalism. In response to written interview questions, one respondent emphasized his/her perception that "the NPS was ***not*** neutral!!!! They favored those groups who opposed people walking with their dogs on NPS lands. Same with San Francisco City Government. . . ." It seems to be, from the dog walkers' perspective, a fact that this agency is not neutral, but an opponent of their interests. This particular respondent then commented that s/he has already moved from the Bay Area: "I now live in an area with lots of open space where off-leash recreation is allowed and secured. This is why I moved. If I still lived in San Francisco, I would become an outlaw." In phone conversations, two others claimed new sympathy for libertarians, with one pessimistic about the future of dog walking in San Francisco.[31]

One journalist, Ilene Lelchuk, observed that leash battles in San Francisco "always boil down to dogs versus native plants, off-leash advocates versus protective parents, [and] pedestrians versus dog poop."[32] Perhaps they do, but her first-listed antagonism, dogs versus native plants, shorthand for these two very different land-use philosophies of natural and cultural areas, is what catapulted this war on San Francisco. As recreational areas became restricted for restoration, dog walkers began to frequent new areas and to have greater numbers in those remaining areas still off-leash, which then set off tension with children's advocates. Given the changing economic demographics in San Francisco, it is also likely that more people wanted to engage in this activity. With greater numbers of park users, San Francisco has experienced a loss of *recreational* space, but not a loss of *open* space. Dog walkers have fought natural-areas advocates to keep open spaces recreational. As they have lost those battles, they have then experienced the ugly political dynamic of more anonymous users competing for fewer acres of recreational space. Although San Francisco is not a suburb with shrinking areas of open space, this new environmental philosophy of public management has ironically foisted upon it the same dynamic that has fueled these debates elsewhere. In short, the dog walkers are in a war to stop the loss of recreational space and to have their rights to the usable areas remain in place.

## ATTACK ON THE EASTERN FRONT

### The Birth of the GGNRA

Citing the "pressing" need "for open space and recreational opportunities" in "our great metropolitan centers," President Nixon signed the enabling legislation for the GGNRA in October of 1972. Both the GGNRA and the Gateway National Recreational Center in the New York City area were consistent with the Nixon Administration's philosophy of bringing "parks to the people."[33] Originally, the GGNRA covered a much smaller land area, approximately 34,000 acres, than it does today. However, the plan was to convert military bases to parkland over time. At the outset, the GGNRA was divided into three distinct units: San Francisco County, Marin County, and the islands of Alcatraz and Angel. In Marin County, much of the 27,000 acres was in private hands and therefore was to be purchased. The law allotted over $60 million for such land acquisitions. The San Francisco County Unit, with which we are concerned, consisted of approximately 2,200 acres, almost all in public hands at the time of the new park's creation. However, there were three sets of "public hands." According to the US House Report, the army and other federal agencies administered much of this acreage, but a considerable 632 acres were under state or county control, and 12.5 acres were privately owned.[34] The non-federal, public lands, which consisted of four state and nine county/city parks at the time of acquisition, were to be donated to the federal government. The private acreage, which included the famous Cliff House, was to be purchased after the public lands were donated.

In San Francisco County, then, the GGNRA was formed from a patchwork of public lands. Fort Funston, the place of such value to dog walkers, is a good illustration of the complexities of GGNRA's beginnings. As a "fort," it originally belonged to the national government, but that government sold 116.4 acres of it to San Francisco County in 1961 for $1.1 million. At the creation of the GGNRA, the county returned this portion to the national government, which itself converted 71 acres there from military control to parkland. Because the county donated some of the GGNRA lands to the national government and retained a right to rescind those donations if the national government did not administer those lands for recreational and park purposes, the precise acreage at point of origin is potentially significant. During the debates over leash laws and other matters, such as closures to human access, many called for rescission of the county-donated lands. There was frustration with the NPS not only for its substantive policies, but also its procedures, which were said to violate a memorandum of understanding between the city and the federal government. Understandably reluctant to part with its control over beachfront parkland, the city expected to consult with the national government about significant administrative decisions for the GGNRA.[35] It is important to note that any reclamation would apply only to the donated lands.

The original act establishing the GGNRA is also critical to the leashing dispute and indeed, potentially to the broader arguments over land usage. There are at least two very different readings of this enabling legislation. Dog walkers highlight the unique nature of the GGNRA, while the NPS is prone to emphasize its similarity with other national parks, in law at least. In its own words, the law states, "In order to preserve for public use and enjoyment certain areas of Marin and San Francisco Counties, California, possessing outstanding natural, historic, scenic, and recreational values, and in order to provide for the maintenance of needed recreational open space necessary to [an] urban environment and planning, the [GGNRA] . . . is hereby established."[36]

Dog walkers can cite the repeated emphasis on recreational use throughout the Congressional Record and hearings and indeed, the *celebration* of that use. On both the House and Senate Floors, the need for recreational space in densely populated San Francisco was noted. In one fairly representative comment, Joe Skubitz explained, "We need more parks and recreational areas across the country so they can be enjoyed on a daily—or at least weekly—basis."[37] Lest there be any doubt about the scope or type of recreational activities, members of Congress cited the "variety of recreational uses," including swimming, boating, hiking, camping, and nature study.[38] In fact, the Senate Report of the Committee on Interior and Insular Affairs specifically stated that the lands in San Francisco County would "satisfy the interests of those who choose to fly kites, sunbathe, walk their dogs, or just idly watch the action along the bay."[39] While the legislative record noted that foreign visitors and American tourists, from other parts of the country, would visit the GGNRA, it also clearly identified San Franciscans and those in the Bay Area as the primary users. In fact, the population increase in the greater Bay Area and the expansion of leisure time were cited as reasons for the creation of the GGNRA. Explicitly recognizing that there will be extensive use of the GGNRA, the House Report stated, "Great numbers of people can reasonably be expected to use the area—particularly those portions located in San Francisco County."[40] Interestingly, the Committee Reports distinguished Marin and San Francisco Counties of the Recreation Area, not only geographically but by *function*. The House Report noted three important differences in these two areas, including the fragility of lands in Marin County. About Marin County, the House Report stated that, unlike San Francisco County, "it comprises relatively delicate natural areas which will not lend themselves to such extensive visitor use."[41] In that more extensive area, the House Report noted that "water areas are used by vast numbers of water fowl and shore birds as important nesting, feeding and resting places."[42]

Based on a review of the Committee Reports and the Congressional Record, it seems clear that the GGNRA was to serve the recreational interests of San Franciscans and also to protect open space and nature. The holdings in San Francisco County, dog walkers can argue, were to lean more heavily on the recreational side, while the more extensive Marin County holdings were more amenable to ensuring the preservation of nature itself. The *use* of San Francisco County holdings was expected, celebrated, and the motivating factor behind the legislation. Because dog walkers celebrate the use of the San Francisco parks, they can claim consistency with the spirit of this enabling legislation. While walking dogs off-leash is not specifically addressed in the legislation itself, the record certainly indicates a hope to accommodate as many activities as possible.[43] If large numbers of San Franciscans enjoy this activity and it brings them to the GGNRA, a strong case can be made that accommodation of this public demand is consistent with, indeed mandated by, the spirit of this law.

In contrast, opponents of off-leash walking can cite the silence in the record about this *particular* activity. Walking dogs, which is stated in the record, can be done on- or off-leash. Additionally, they can cite the myriad references to the importance of this natural area. One of the House co-sponsors of the bill, Representative Robert Kastenmeier, asserted that the GGNRA "will not only preserve and enhance the ecology of the bay area, it also will provide a program of open space preservation which will be woven into the whole fabric of urban development."[44] Natural-areas supporters can emphasize the value of bringing nature to urban residents for purposes of observation, study, and appreciation. That goal is not hindered via the regulation and curtailment of certain human activities. What is more, the law itself gives the Secretary of the Interior ample discretion to administer the land. It states, "The Secretary shall administer the lands, waters and interests therein acquired for the recreation area in accordance with the provisions of the Act of August 25, 1916," which established the first national park at Yellowstone, "as amended and supplemented, and the Secretary may utilize such statutory authority available to him for the conservation and management of wildlife and natural resources as he deems appropriate to carry out the purposes of this Act."[45] Such wording provides legal cover for the Secretary and the NPS to regulate areas so as to protect natural areas and species. In this sense, the NPS, in attempting to ban or sharply curtail off-leash dog walking in San Francisco County, can claim consistency with the letter of the law. However, in treating San Francisco County similarly to Marin County and other national parks, the NPS arguably is breaking from the spirit of this law. The legislative intention was undoubtedly maximum recreational use in San Francisco County. If one of the main recreational uses is forbidden or made unpleasant, that original goal is thwarted.

The enabling legislation established an Advisory Commission, composed of fifteen unpaid members, who would meet with the Secretary or his designee at least annually for purposes of consulting on general policies and specific matters related to the administration of the GGNRA. It was this Commission that created the 1979 Pet Policy. According to the Policy, dogs could be under voice control at Fort Funston, Ocean Beach—with some areas possibly restricted on crowded days—Lands End, Fort Miley, the north area of Baker

Beach, Crissy Field, and additional areas in Marin County. Several other areas, such as Fort Mason and Sutro Heights, required leashes and still others, such as Fort Point, prohibited dogs entirely. All told, dogs could be leash-free on a very small percentage of GGNRA land. These guidelines were issued on letterhead from the Department of the Interior, and the NPS implemented them for more than twenty years.

There is nonetheless a dispute over their legality. The dog-walking groups contend that the policy was in accordance with the unique enabling legislation for the GGNRA, as that legislation recognized the needs of an urban area and sought to retain the longstanding uses of the land. Further, they highlight the NPS's involvement in the development of this policy, as well as its promulgation and enforcement. A special regulation, which would have codified the policy, was submitted to the Western Regional Director of the Park Service and ultimately to officials in Washington, DC, but it was never finalized. Because that final authorization was never given, the NPS maintains that the policy was never legal and therefore never in effect. Much like the Supreme Court can declare a law null and void via its power of judicial review, the NPS claims that the policy's lack of legality has the effect of erasing its existence. In its advance notice of rulemaking, the NPS states that the park, "in error, implemented the 'voice control' policy, in contradiction to service-wide regulations."[46] In other words, absent a special regulation or exemption, the leash policy for national parks must be in effect. The legal requirements in the NPS's view trump the de facto policy of over twenty years. Dog walkers, of course, disagree.

## Downsizing Heaven

From 1979 to the early 1990s, the NPS adhered to the pet policy, inclusive of its voice-control or off-leash areas. President Bill Clinton's Secretary of the Interior, Bruce Babbitt, presided over a substantive change of managerial philosophy at the GGNRA. That change, which had begun tepidly under the previous Bush administration, treated the San Francisco County Unit of the GGNRA more akin to the other national parks and as a result, spelled trouble for the dog walkers. In the early 1990s, the NPS implemented policies to restore native habitat, destroy "exotic" plants and trees, and aggressively protect native plants and animals. Delighted with this approach, the Sierra Club, Audubon Society, California Native Plant Society, and the Center for Biological Diversity supported the NPS fully and lobbied for even greater application of this philosophy. From the perspective of the NPS itself, this philosophy, which would limit human and canine use of parts of the GGNRA, was consistent with its own mission as stated in the legislation creating Yellowstone National

Park in 1916. That Organic Act empowered the NPS to regulate the use of parks "by such means and measures as conform to the fundamental purpose of said parks, . . . , which purpose is to conserve the scenery and the natural and historic objects and the wild life therein and to provide for the enjoyment of the same in such manner and by such means as will leave them unimpaired for the enjoyment of future generations."[47] With the Clinton Administration now sympathetic to this charge, the protection of native plants and animals would trump recreational use at the GGNRA.

Before the early 1990s, the NPS treaded lightly and slowly. Rangers began to fence off limited sections of Fort Funston (or "dog heaven") along the top of bluffs, thereby closing it to all human and canine traffic. With a change in presidential administration, the closures accelerated. In the closed areas, bulldozers ripped up exotic ice plants and exotic trees fell to chainsaws. In 1995, the closures became extensive, with twenty-five acres closed in that year alone. At this time, the NPS threatened a leash law for the open areas of Fort Funston as well, but that was rebuffed. Such a dire threat to the interests of dog walkers, though, prompted their organization into the Fort Funston Dog Walkers (FFDW). While this new organization lacked paid employees and a national organization, as the Audubon Society and Sierra Club have, it none-theless allowed the dog walkers to resist the NPS's assault on their interests.

After closing coastal bluffs in 1998, the NPS again sought to close ten more acres in 2000. These closures were disruptive for dog walkers because they prevented them, in some cases, from taking a popular walk down to the beach area. Frustrated with the NPS's closures, its destruction of trees and ice plants, and its lack of consultation with the city on these matters, the FFDW brought suit in response to the 2000 closures. The legal challenge was proce-dural, not substantive. Because the NPS did not hold public hearings on the closures, a federal judge granted an injunction to stop the closure. However, the NPS remedied the procedural error and then received the green light to go ahead with its closure, which it then increased from ten acres to twelve.[48]

Why was the NPS closing off more and more sections of dog heaven? First and foremost, the NPS sought to protect nesting shorebirds called bank swallows and to increase the biodiversity of the area by restoring coastal dune scrub habitat. It also cited public safety concerns, as the closures kept visitors away from the cliffs. Most frustrating of all to dog walkers, the NPS addi-tionally claimed the need to protect the dunes from accelerated erosion. Dog walkers contended that the very removal of exotic ice plants *contributed* to erosion and was harmful to the bank swallows' nesting patterns. While dog walkers also contested the negative impact of dogs on the bank swallows, the

NPS and the Audubon Society successfully defined this as a dog-versus-bird issue. This framing infuriated the dog walkers, as they argued that the NPS itself was the main source of harm to the swallows. This was not an unfounded, self-serving claim. According to the San Francisco chapter of the Society for the Prevention of the Cruelty to Animals (SPCA), studies verify that "bank swallows often purposely locate themselves in populated areas, possibly because recreational activity scares away predators. In fact, the bank swallows moved *away* from an area *closed off* by the GGNRA in 1998 *to* an area where ice plant and recreational activity is [sic] more prevalent" [emphasis is mine]."[49] In interviews with dog walkers, they repeatedly cite frustration with the NPS for its unwillingness to consider these studies with an open mind.

The lawsuit over the Funston closures, to put it mildly, did not help the antagonistic relationship between the NPS and dog walkers. While the NPS ultimately prevailed in the lawsuit, one reporter noted that the NPS got its "nose whacked" over its secretive procedures. That reporter, and many dog walkers, suspected that the ban on off-leash dog walking the following year was a "retaliatory move" over the lawsuit.[50] Of course, the NPS denies that charge and maintains that the original policy was illegal.

Troubles in the 1990s were by no means limited to Funston, as limitations were put in effect in other places that had been leash-free. For example, the NPS instituted a ban on off-leash dog walking at the popular Ocean Beach, effective January 1, 1997. At issue in this restriction was the rare western snowy plover, a six-inch bird with dark markings across its forehead. According to the NPS, free-running dogs disturb the plovers, of which there were approximately seventy at Ocean Beach. Once again, dog walkers contested that claim and highlighted that the NPS had failed to document a single instance of a dog harming a plover.[51] Bird lovers and dog lovers were once again cast at odds, to the great dismay of the latter who disputed the conflict. One group, Rovers and Plovers, tried to seek a compromise but was disregarded. As with the Funston closures, the unwillingness of the NPS to discuss evidence and to prove its claims against dogs goaded the dog walkers. To understate the matter, relations were poor between the NPS and dog walkers at the turn of the century.

### Prelude to War—The Arrest and Trial of a Dog Walker

With its new, more restrictive policies in place, rangers stopped hundreds of people for having their dogs off-leash at Ocean Beach in the late 1990s. No citation or arrest received more attention, though, than that of Michelle Parris at the Presidio on April 8, 1997. As the reader might recall, Parris, who rescued dogs with special needs, was arrested for allowing her dogs off-leash after she declined to show her license to a ranger and left the scene. That arrest took place at Hicks Field, which is an "unused, weed-covered baseball diamond" in the Presidio.[52] When this portion of the Presidio was under the jurisdiction of the US military, it was acceptable to walk dogs off-leash. However, it was now part of the GGNRA. As Christine Powell of the NPS explained to a reporter, "It wasn't the purview of the Department of Defense to pay as much attention to the resources as the National Park Service. . . . Now that we've come in, it is our mission to document and list endangered plants and to conserve cultural and natural resources."[53] As a result, leashing restrictions were now in place at Hicks Field and Parris was in violation of them.

Prosecutors decided to try Parris on the charge of preventing a park ranger from doing her job. The trial, which was packed with dog walkers, bordered on farce at times. In the cross-examination of the NPS ranger, Angelina Gregorio, the public defender established that the leash law applies to all pets, not just dogs, and that the ranger herself had violated the law by allowing her cat out sans leash in the Presidio. Overwhelmingly sympathetic to Parris, the audience responded with laughter.[54] This exchange was not without a touch of irony, however, as bird enthusiasts, who were advocating leashing restrictions, ordinarily would be expected to have more concerns with cats than dogs. Typically, cats are better than dogs at hunting song birds. After this attempt to embarrass Gregorio, the public defender more seriously argued that there was "no probable cause to cite Parris because she had ceased breaking the law when she loaded her dogs into her truck and left the scene." The public defender, Heidi Hudson, also claimed that the leash law was applied arbitrarily.[55] In response, the US Attorney's Office argued that Parris "interfered with the officer by refusing to hand over her license, leaving the scene without permission, refusing to stop her car, and essentially, making a federal case out of a minor incident."[56] That last claim, of course, is precisely the dog walkers' accusation about the NPS's behavior in this case. A federal magistrate decided the case in favor of the prosecution, but suspended any punishment of Parris. Magistrate Larson could have imposed a $5,000 fine and six months in jail, but said the "deterrent purpose has already been served."[57]

While the Magistrate opted not to punish Parris, dog walkers were horrified at the message of this arrest and trial. Their recreational activity was effectively criminalized, with their own government redefining them as criminals. Not surprisingly, this case provided the proverbial wake-up call to dog walkers, with membership in SFDog soaring. That group, originally founded in 1976, organized formally in 1997 in reaction to the ban on off-leash walking at Ocean Beach. Given the salience of Parris's story and its importance in motivating people to join SFDog, the case was a hot topic of discussion on the organization's e-mail list. Members can post to the e-mail list and comments are not supposed to be forwarded without the permission of the sender. To the shock of Parris's supporters, approximately 61 e-mails from this online discussion were provided to the prosecuting attorneys, who alluded to them and used them against Parris in the course of the trial. Apparently, a GGNRA employee joined the list and turned the e-mails over to prosecutors. There was a spy in the midst of the dog walkers! While confirming the fact that an employee had forwarded SFDog e-mails to them, NPS authorities vehemently denied that there was an orchestrated campaign on their part to obtain this information.[58] Given the now overtly hostile relations between the dog walkers and the NPS, at least some dog walkers concluded otherwise.

## The NPS Declares War

Because of the litigation about the 2000 Fort Funston closures, the Advisory Commission for the GGNRA held public meetings on that matter to satisfy the procedural requirements of the court. Dog walkers generated over 1,100 comments against the closures in a short time, and they also made their strong support for off-leash walking known to the Advisory Commission. Acknowledging receipt of the dog walkers' sentiments on January 23, 2001, Commission Chair Bartke stated, "During the past 12 months, this Commission has heard from the dog walkers on four separate occasions. In each case, we've heard from dog owners, how important their dogs are to them. We've heard that the City has not provided space for off-leash dogs, that the state and county parks have also not provided space for off-leash dogs. We've heard, at great length, and we're convinced."[59] Ironically, though, he made this statement at the start of a public meeting convened for the purpose of rescinding the 1979 Pet Policy and thereby requiring all pets to be leashed in the GGNRA. Whether the Commission and the NPS were motivated to rescind the policy to retaliate against dog walkers for the Funston suit, as the dog walkers claimed, or the US Attorney gave the Commission no choice but to rescind the policy, as the NPS claimed, dog walkers faced the imminent reality of an end to off-leash walking at the GGNRA on the night of January 23, 2001. Dog heaven was about to be shut down.

The response to this threat was extraordinary. Well over two thousand people came to the Presidio for the meeting. The building could not accommodate this number of people, who then had to stand outside in the rain. So many people wanted to speak against the change in policy that time constraints prevented that opportunity as well. Eight members of the San Francisco Board of Supervisors, the legislative branch for San Francisco, and two other San Francisco officials spoke against the change, as did spokespersons for two members of the California State Assembly. In their statements, the city officials not only cited concerns about the impact on city/county parks, but they emphasized the depth and breadth of public opposition to this change. For example, Supervisor McGoldrick pleaded with the Commissioners to "please abide by what is an overwhelming sentiment in this city," while Supervisor Leno explained that "this is a very important issue. A very, very important issue to my constituents."[60] Similarly, Richard Schulke, the Chair of the San Francisco Animal Control and Welfare Commission, exclaimed, "I'm here to speak to you about the incredibly outraged community of San Francisco constituents. . . . I have never, in 8 years, heard so many absolutely both livid and extremely concerned folks, seniors, children, people who have AIDS and other chronic diseases, and just regular folks, who have literally begged me to try and convince you to hold off on the decision to rescind the '79 Pet Policy. . . . Not to mention the devastating and crushing effect this will have on our city parks..."[61] No public official spoke on behalf of the change.

The Commissioners responded to the city and state appeals by asking what accommodations these governmental levels had made for off-leash dogs. Of course, the state and city had donated some of the GGNRA parkland, a fact that left the state, at least, with very little parkland in the city. While the San Francisco Supervisors nonetheless expressed a willingness to make more room for this activity at city parks, Supervisor McGoldrick responded that the "first place for them to be allowed to run their dogs is on the lands where they've been running the dogs for nearly four decades."[62] Clearly, there was a tension in the relationship between city officials and the Commissioners, undoubtedly fueled by the city's threat to consider reclaiming donated lands.

Thirty citizens, some representing organizations such as the San Francisco SPCA and dog-walking groups, additionally had opportunity to speak against the change. Hundreds of others yielded their time, as the meeting adjourned after eleven at night. The Chair of the Commission asked speakers to offer suggestions about how to proceed in light of the 1979 Pet Policy's illegality and not to rehash their arguments for off-leash areas. Some dog walkers made suggestions, including one to challenge the US Attorney's interpretation of the enabling statute. Perhaps because of the Commission's unwillingness to defend the 1979 Pet Policy, others nonetheless felt compelled to emphasize the importance of the issue to them. Speaking on behalf of the San Francisco SPCA, its president commented that off-leash recreation for dogs is an "experience that is deeply cherished . . . that resonates to the quality of life in the

Bay Area."[63] Another noted that this was "a major quality-of-life issue for us."[64] Claiming that this was the "first time" that she had "spoken or really being [sic] involved in any public issue," another dog walker stressed, "That's how important it is to me."[65] A senior citizen literally begged the Commission not to change the policy, exhorting "please, please, please reject this resolution."[66] Dog walkers additionally expressed frustration with the lack of fairness in the process. There was a sense that the Commission had not listened to their arguments and what is worse, was aligned against them. At least two noted concerns about the latter, with one commenting, "I'm bothered by the feeling that you're the enemy."[67] Only three people spoke unequivocally in favor of leashing restrictions, with one of those speakers representing the Audubon Society. All three expressed concern for other, wild animals.

Although most conducted themselves with decorum, this was unquestionably a raucous meeting. The minutes stipulated, "Throughout the meeting, and because the building did not accommodate all the participants, there were loud comments, boisterous conduct, and many interruptions."[68] Dog walkers were overwhelmingly in the majority, as it was they who stood to lose a valuable piece of their daily or weekly routines. That is a revolutionary dynamic, which not surprisingly prompted displays of anger. The Commission and the NPS, whom the dog walkers perceived as aligned against them, fueled this anger all the more. Unfortunately, in this environment, the few proponents of the leash law were booed. The Superintendent of the GGNRA, Brian O'Neill, could thus note with legitimacy that the NPS heard from "a lot of people who felt intimidated about coming tonight."[69] While disrespectful behavior is unacceptable, the NPS shares fault here in not arranging for the meeting to take place at a larger facility and for creating this very hostile dynamic. Similarly to the leash battle in Avon, Connecticut, the NPS, in rescinding the 1979 Pet Policy, placed dog walkers at a distinct disadvantage. Once this policy was rescinded, they would be left to beg for some off-leash areas, while leash advocates would be happy with the status quo and would therefore lack any incentive to compromise. It is a bit disingenuous, then, for the NPS to criticize the dog walkers for their outrage at the prospect of this monumental shift in power.

In light of the torrent of requests to delay rescinding the 1979 Pet Policy, the Commission did not act that night. Instead, they voted to ask the park staff to continue to meet with other land-owning agencies for purposes of finding other off-leash areas, to ask the Superintendent to meet with all stakeholders within 120 days, to consider the possibility in these discussions of an application for a special rule for this park, and to ask the park staff to have no changes in enforcement during the next 120 days.[70] Despite that promise, the Commission quietly voided the 1979 Pet Policy on February 1. Signs and enforcement followed on April 1. As promised, though, the NPS launched an Advance Notice to Proposed Rulemaking, albeit almost one year later, on January 11, 2002. Potentially, this process could result in a special rule for the GGNRA and thereby allow some off-leash areas. However, the advantage had decidedly shifted to the pro-leash advocates, as the burden of change was now on the dog walkers. As Supervisor Peskin explained at the January 2001 meeting, "it's a bad way to start a conversation."[71] That tactic and the resultant shift in power were not lost on dog walkers.

## Tragedy Follows Protest

A tragedy followed the January 23 meeting and undoubtedly served to mute public criticism of the Commission's decision to rescind the 1979 Pet Policy. Three days after thousands gathered in support of off-leash walking at the Presidio, on January 26, two Presa Canario dogs fatally mauled Diane Whipple in her own apartment building in an upscale section of San Francisco. Just thirty-three years old, Whipple was an exceptional athlete who coached lacrosse at St. Mary's College of California. The killing was shockingly brutal, with Whipple sustaining seventy-seven bite wounds. She died five hours after the attack from massive blood loss and asphyxiation. Residents of San Francisco were stunned at this horror, and Whipple's partner, family, and friends were, of course, devastated. Because of the brutality of the attack and the unremorseful behavior of the dogs' keepers, the media provided extensive coverage of the case not only in San Francisco, but nationally.

California convicted the two owners, Robert Noel and Marjorie Knoller, of manslaughter and owning a dangerous animal that killed someone. Knoller, who was present during the attack, was additionally convicted of second-degree murder.[72] Prior to the trial, which was held in Los Angeles, the defendants appeared on television interviews and made outrageous statements, even going so far as to blame the victim. The case became exceptionally bizarre when investigators learned how the couple had come to acquire the dogs. As attorneys who had represented prison guards, the couple had come into contact with Paul "Cornfed" Schneider, an inmate serving a life sentence. Immediately prior to the mauling, Noel and Knoller had *adopted* this thirty-eight-year-old prisoner. Schneider apparently had plans to breed and sell aggressive Presa Canario dogs to drug dealers, who could use them to guard methamphetamine labs. Using the Web and outside helpers, Schneider could run this "business" and make money for his white supremacist prison gang. Upset with the efforts of one of those perhaps unwitting helpers, Schneider prevailed upon Noel and Knoller to take the two dogs, Bane and Hera, a mere five months before the mauling.[73]

While there was not evidence to suggest that Noel and Knoller were training the dogs for Schneider's original purpose, it was clear that the couple did not know how to handle them. At trial, the prosecutor presented several witnesses who recounted aggressive encounters with these dogs and inappropriate responses from the owners, which all took place in the short span of a few months. What is more, the briefest of perusals about dog breeds should give warning to any keepers of these dogs. According to one reputable Web site, "The Canary Dog [Presa Canarios] requires a very dominant owner who understand[s] the alpha nature in canines. No member of the family can be uncomfortable around the dog. Canaries make outstanding guard dogs. Just their appearance is a deterrent not to mention their ability to confront any intruder. In the wrong hands this dog can be dangerous."[74] Obviously, these dogs were in the wrong hands. At best, Noel and Knoller were criminally irresponsible and at worst, they contributed to making these dogs dangerous. Diane Whipple paid for their crimes with her life.

In such a high-profile case, it is perfectly natural and healthy to consider possible changes in public policy so as to prevent another tragedy. Already, this case was groundbreaking for two reasons. Whipple's partner, Sharon Smith, became the first person granted the right to file a lawsuit for the wrongful death of a same-sex partner. She contributed the monies from that suit to St. Mary's lacrosse team. The state's successful prosecution of second-degree murder in a dog mauling case was also a first. In setting these precedents, the case changed future policy, but in both instances, these were remedies in the aftermath of a tragedy. Could any lessons be drawn about the prevention of another such tragedy? Surely, the case raises questions about the keeping of dangerous dogs in apartments or multi-family dwellings and the responsibilities of landlords and tenants to prevent the presence of such dogs. The specifics of accomplishing that goal are subject to debate. Public officials should also anticipate that many people, especially those unfamiliar with dogs, would be made wary of all dogs in the aftermath of such a case. A public discussion about breeds, the signs of aggressive behavior, and the responsibilities of dog owners might be in order as well. Such public education has the potential to help prevent dog bites or attacks.

Arguably, though, the application of this horrific tragedy to the NPS's effort to create natural areas devoid of free-running dogs is out of place. Worse, the issues are so distinct that the use of this tragedy appears politically motivated. It so happens that the loudest voices in opposition to the NPS's change in policy are the very same organizations that promote responsible dog ownership. For example, the San Francisco SPCA and SFDog both attempt to educate people about the responsibilities of dog ownership, and the former makes every attempt to place abandoned pets in appropriate homes with responsible owners. What is more, those who regularly walk their dogs off-leash have strong incentive to ensure that their dogs are well socialized. Indeed, many trainers applaud off-leash exercise for its positive impact on a dog's proper socialization.

Recall that two of the three most popular breeds in 2001 were Labrador and golden retrievers. These dogs are so popular because of their temperaments. Described as "good-natured, loyal . . . stable, [and] calm," the Labrador retriever is said to be "a good companion for children" and "never aggressive."[75] The golden retriever is similarly characterized as "a gentle, loving dog with a tender intelligent facial expression." It too is recommended as great with children.[76] Fostered from generations of dogs working closely with humans in hunting, the temperaments of these breeds and several other sporting breeds could not be any more distinct from Canary dogs. Several non-sporting breeds boast of extremely gentle temperaments as well. In many cases, those too have developed from a close working relationship with humans. However, the very trait that makes these dogs so popular has been cultivated via a physically demanding relationship. The breeding has not only made the dogs gentle, but in the case of Labrador retrievers, golden retrievers, and others, it has also made them the jocks of the canine world. These friendly, family dogs need a substantial amount of exercise when they are young. It is in fact cruel to deny exercise to such dogs. The owners or guardians of these types of dogs advocate for off-leash areas to keep the dogs well socialized, adequately exercised, and on their best behavior. There are also many people who know how to handle the behavioral needs and challenges of other breeds and train those dogs for off-leash activity. To equate such responsible owners, who specifically chose friendly breeds or who have properly socialized others, with the likes of Noel and Knoller, is grossly unfair. In citing the Whipple case in its Advanced Notice of Rulemaking, the NPS, whether intentionally or not, insults responsible dog owners and contributes to their perception of an agency biased against them.

## Legal Victory for Dog Walkers, but is it Pyrrhic?

With the 1979 Pet Policy rescinded, the NPS ticketed walkers with dogs off-leash. A few of those walkers, who were ticketed at Crissy Field in 2002, challenged the legality of the old policy's rescission. They argued that the NPS changed governmental policy without soliciting public notice and comment.

According to NPS's regulations, notice-and-comment procedures are required before any "highly controversial closure or opening of NPS land or before any such action would have a major impact on visitor-use patterns."[77] Surely, the dog walkers argued, the institution of a leash law in areas where off-leash recreation was allowed for over twenty years qualified as highly controversial and would have a major impact on visitor-use patterns. In December 2004, US Federal Magistrate Elizabeth LaPorte agreed with them and dismissed their tickets.

Since the NPS considered "its off-leash ban still in effect" after this ruling, it is not surprising that it appealed the case to a federal judge.[78] In 2005, US District Judge William Alsup not only upheld Magistrate LaPorte's ruling, but rejected in no uncertain terms the NPS's argument that the off-leash areas were illegal. In his ruling, he cited ample evidence that the NPS had been aware of off-leash areas for years. On the basis of that evidence, he wrote, "for more than twenty years, the GGNRA officially designated at least seven sites for off-leash use. This was not accidental. It was a carefully articulated, often studied, promulgation. The responsible GGNRA officials in 1978 and thereafter presumably believed they were acting lawfully."[79] Indeed, Judge Alsup highlighted that the NPS's rules in 1978 were not inconsistent with allowing superintendents the authority to make "activity designations on a park-by-park basis contradicting the national regulations. That restriction came later in 1983."[80] As a result, the NPS now cannot change this policy on the basis of a fine distinction in law without first adhering to its procedural rules, which require an opportunity for the public to have input before any such change. As did the Magistrate, Judge Alsup concluded that "the GGNRA clearly engaged in an 'activity restriction' when it suddenly reversed field, closed all areas for off-leash use, and started citing off-leash dog walkers. Not only did this activity restriction work a 'significant alteration in the public use pattern of the park area, but it was of a highly controversial nature.'"[81] The rescission of the 1979 Pet Policy, in other words, was procedurally flawed and therefore, the rescission, not the Policy itself, was illegal.

Importantly, Judge Alsup cited no substantive problem with the elimination of off-leash areas. Like in the suit over the Funston closures, the dog walkers prevailed because of NPS's procedural errors. The NPS, which had already initiated its rulemaking process in 2002, now advanced it to the next stage. Given the problems with its early decisions and the public scrutiny surrounding this issue, the NPS was now adhering closely to its procedural guidelines. If dog walkers were to salvage off-leash areas, they arguably had to prevail in this process. Their only choice was to participate, but some nonetheless resisted and most undoubtedly feared the outcome.

Judge Alsup's decision, in effect, reminded dog walkers of the NPS's biases on this issue. He wrote, "it was and remains curious that it was the agency itself, not a member of the public (for whose benefit that notice and comment was intended), that invoked the procedural omission to revise the designations." In other words, the NPS highlighted the "illegality" of its own original policy. Further, he commented that the "new" interpretation of the law, which requires leashing, was "conceived by the United States Attorney's office in the *Fort Funston* litigation," the very claim that dog walkers made.[82] Recall that dog walkers considered the rescission of the 1979 Pet Policy retaliation for their lawsuit over the Funston closures. Their procedural victory in that case was not only temporary, but Pyrrhic, as the closures came later anyway and all off-leash areas were eliminated. It is understandable, then, that dog walkers are wary about the outcome of the rulemaking process. There is absolutely no guarantee that they will prevail in the process, structured by the NPS, simply because they won in the procedural suit over the rescission. What is worse, from their perspective, this victory too could be Pyrrhic, as the NPS holds the cards at the substantive level and might yet again be angry over this lawsuit. However, there is little choice but to participate. To continue the war analogy, the dog walkers have been occupied and need to work within the rules of the occupying force. They face this rather unpleasant reality despite their procedural victories. We turn now to this internal rulemaking process and then, finally, to an evaluation of the democratic nature of both that process and the preceding politics.

# Chapter VI

## San Francisco's Eastern Front: Dog Walkers versus Bureaucracy

Since dog walkers must succeed in the NPS's rulemaking process to retain off-leash areas in the GGNRA, that process has taken center stage in their fight. As we will see, though, there are dog walkers who lament this fact and they do so with good reason. Since we are following dog walkers in their war, even if they are headed toward an ambush, it is to this rulemaking process that we now turn. As a part of the Department of the Interior, the NPS is a component of the executive branch (the federal bureaucracy). Agencies of the executive branch are primarily charged with implementation and enforcement of the law. Yet as we have noticed already, they also have quite a bit of latitude to make rules that are of extraordinary importance to people.[1] This leashing rule is a case in point. Rulemaking is not the same as legislating, which is done by elected representatives, but it can be equally complex and challenging.

Rules must be in service to laws, or at least, not in contradiction of them. Just as Congress must work within the constraints of the Constitution, executive agencies must work within the allegedly tighter confines of both the Constitution and statutory law. Any evaluation of the rulemaking process must keep this distinction in mind. What exactly does democratic theory require, then, of an executive agency when it is making rules of such importance to people? The very fact that an executive agency, not a legislative body, is making this policy decision might, in and of itself, be problematic. That notwithstanding, how well did the NPS perform procedurally? Clearly, it was off to a rough start in its relations with dog walkers, as a federal judge chastised the agency two times for its failure to comply with its own procedures. In both of those cases, the noncompliance was to the detriment of dog walkers' interests. Such behavior creates a perception of bias, whether one exists or not. With adherence to its rulemaking procedure, can and does the NPS ever overcome that perception? Can it salvage a decent democratic grade?

## ORGANIZATIONAL STRUCTURE OF THE NPS

As in other executive departments, the president appoints the top-level officials at the Department of the Interior, of which the NPS is a component. Those officials are transient and typically reflect the ideology and priorities of the current president. For example, Bruce Babbitt, President Bill Clinton's secretary, was committed to using governmental power to protect the environment, while Gale Norton, President George W. Bush's secretary, was more concerned with balancing the needs of the environment with business and recreational uses. Below these "political appointees" are the civil servants, or those permanent employees of these agencies who are supposed to be "insulated" from politics. Typically, but not always, these employees are dedicated to the mission of their agency. There can be tension between the civil servants and political appointees, especially when the latter order the former to balance the mission of their agency with other values and interests. With changing leadership dependent upon national elections, the executive departments are supposed to reflect the priorities of the American people. Yet they are additionally *executive* agencies and charged with enforcement of law. The presence of the civil service theoretically ensures that function is not corrupted via partisanship. When there is discretion in interpreting the law and thus a need to formulate rules, the goals and ideals of political appointees and the civil service matter and can, at times, clash.

A director, who is politically appointed, heads the NPS, which consists of headquarters in Washington, DC, seven regional offices, and multiple park and support units. The director establishes "overall policy and strategic direction" for the NPS, determines "legislative goals and strategies," and guides implementation of national goals and objectives. "Each regional director serves as the principal authority and spokesperson for the area as a whole and ensures consistency with national policies and priorities."[2] Below these directors are the superintendents, who manage the park units. These superintendents, who are civil servants, report to their regional director and manage all park operations. Brian O'Neill was the superintendent of the GGNRA throughout the leashing controversies and reported to the Pacific West Regional Office. O'Neill held the post of superintendent, in fact, from 1986 until his death in 2009.

After earning a degree in geography from the University of Maryland,

O'Neill soon thereafter joined the federal Bureau of Outdoor Recreation in 1965. That marked the beginning of a long and prestigious career in the stewardship of national parks and open spaces. In fact, he was part of the team that persuaded President Nixon to establish Golden Gate and Gateway as urban national recreation areas. While he worked elsewhere after his involvement with that team, he returned to the GGNRA in a senior managerial role in the early 1980s. As superintendent, O'Neill developed a "stewardship investment strategy" that depends upon partnership with community groups, such as the Golden Gate National Park Conservancy, to raise the requisite money for the needs of an urban park.[3] Given that O'Neill's entire career was dedicated to the service of national parks, it is not at all surprising that he would be very responsive to concerns about endangered wildlife. His initial relationship with dog walkers, also as one might expect, was a bit rocky. He was the one upon whose shoulders rested the final decision to replace the 1979 Pet Policy with a leash law. In alluding indirectly to the wrath that decision would unleash, one reporter noted, "The final decision rests with GGNRA Superintendent Brian O'Neill, an intelligent man who appears headed down an unwise path."[4] For O'Neill, the decision had to be grueling. Wholly invested in the GGNRA, inclusive of a part of its "birth," O'Neill now faced angry city supervisors threatening to take portions of the land back. What is more, he confronted large numbers of people whom his decision alienated from the land when he had spent a large chunk of his career giving people reasons to identify with the land and partner in stewardship of it. Despite this inauspicious introduction to the leashing issue, O'Neill approved the negotiated rulemaking process and involved himself in its effort to reach compromise.

## THE ROAD TO NEGOTIATED RULEMAKING—DOES IT LEAD TO OZ?

### Advance Notice to Proposed Rulemaking

An Advance Notice to Proposed Rulemaking (ANPR) is a "preliminary step in the rulemaking process, published in the *Federal Register* to present options, questions, and ideas for a rule. During a specified period, the public is asked to comment on these options or to present ones of their own. An ANPR does not include a preferred approach upon which comments are being solicited."[5] On January 11, 2002, the NPS published an ANPR for pet management in the GGNRA. Initially, comments were invited for sixty days, but that deadline was extended until April 12, 2002.[6]

In its ANPR, the NPS provides background information about pet management in the GGNRA and cites its rationales for rulemaking on the matter. Because the ANPR was published years before a federal judge ruled the 2001 cancellation of the 1979 Pet Policy illegal, the NPS asserts in the ANPR that the 1979 Policy was "in error" and has been replaced with the 2001 prohibition on off-leash recreation. It promises to enforce leashing requirements, per the 2001 policy, until such time as off-leash areas are established via this rulemaking process, if indeed they ever are. Additionally, it treats the GGNRA no differently than other national parks, another claim that dog walkers contest. Per the NPS, if "there is a conflict between conserving resources and values and providing for the enjoyment of them, conservation is to be predominant."[7] That is the case at all national parks, inclusive of the GGNRA. This section, then, does not acknowledge the controversial nature of either the 1979 Pet Policy's cancellation or the GGNRA's enabling legislation.

Citing "increased visitation to GGNRA, litigation concerning the Fort Funston area of the park, public concern about visitor and pet safety, park resource management issues involving wildlife and vegetation protection and the review of dog-walking issues by the Golden Gate National Recreation Area Advisory Commission," the ANPR asserts a need both to consider dog management at the GGNRA and to solicit public comment. All of these reasons seem to invite skepticism about off-leash recreation. Indeed, the ANPR, while presenting arguments on both sides of off-leash exercise, devotes more space to its possible harms. The numbers of rare or special-status wildlife and vegetation are stated along with citation of "scientific studies" that attribute "disturbance, harassment, displacement, injury and direct mortality of wildlife to domestic dogs that accompany recreationists."[8] In counterpoint to this "scientific" claim, the ANPR cites two observations from dog walkers and not other "scientific" studies that are available and would dispute the claim of harm.[9] This presentation makes the dog walkers' case seem weaker. Also troubling is a quotation from the Funston litigation, as the ANPR neglected to mention the earlier procedural problems with the closures and noted only the approval of a judge upon completion of his ordered procedures. It thereby depicts the suit as frivolous when, in fact, the judge initially found the NPS in violation of its own rules. Thus, while the ANPR is technically accurate in its background information, there is legitimate reason for dog walkers to worry about the impartiality of the NPS on this matter.

That notwithstanding, the ANPR seeks broad public comment on several alternatives. Specifically, it asks if the leash law should remain intact, if additional areas should be closed or open to dogs, if there should be time restrictions, fencing, liability waivers, and/or other requirements. To the NPS's credit, one question solicits comment on whether "analysis of any alternatives be measured from the current baseline of no off-leash dog walking, or the long-standing former policy that allowed off-leash dog walking in certain areas." While these open-ended comments are invited, the ANPR posits two main options. Option A would enforce the 2001 policy that requires leashing in all areas of the GGNRA where dogs are allowed at all. Option B would identify specific locations and ways to address off-leash use in the park. Under this option, off-leash dog walking would be allowed in specific locations, "with the remainder of the park subject to enforcement of the existing regulation requiring pets to be leashed where permitted."[10]

## The Public's Response

In the ninety-one-day period, the NPS received thousands of comments. The NPS paid the Social Research Laboratory at Northern Arizona University to analyze the commentary, a task that it completed in August 2002 with the issuance of a report. After purging the data of duplicates, this report identifies 8,580 documents or comments. However, fourteen of those documents are in the form of petitions, all of which support Option B, and the number of signatories of those petitions is not stated. Notwithstanding that fact, the comments overwhelmingly favored Option B, allowing off-leash recreation in the GGNRA. Indeed, 71 percent supported Option B, while only 28 percent advocated Option A.[11] What is more, the Report noted that 86 percent of Bay Area residents, who accounted for 6,042 comments, supported off-leash recreation, while the bulk of leashing supporters were from outside the Bay Area. Of the 1,628 comments received from outside the Bay Area, 88 percent supported Option A. Those who lived outside of California were even more lopsided in their support for leashing, with a full 96 percent behind Option A. Those who supported Option A were also much more likely to have sent a form letter, as such letters accounted for 67 percent of these comments. It seems probable that the well-organized Audubon Society and Sierra Club were able to mobilize their members to send form letters, while the dog walkers lacked a national organization capable of producing such support. Despite that organizational disadvantage, the dog walkers and their supporters accounted for more than two-thirds of the commentary. It seems reasonable to conclude, then, that the commentary supported a special rule or exception for the GGNRA.

The rationales and suggestions shed light on the debate about this issue as well. The Report identifies eighteen rationales cited by the supporters of Option A. By far, the two most common rationales were that off-leash dogs harmed wildlife and had a negative impact on the environment. The third most common rationale, concerns about the precedent of changing an NPS policy, was cited in 49 percent of supporting comments for Option A, while the top two, wildlife and the environment, were cited in 84 and 83 percent, respectively, of those comments. Almost half of Option A advocates noted concerns about dangers or threats from unleashed dogs and fears that the park would be unsafe for visitors. Other rationales, which were mentioned by a substantial portion of Option A supporters, include concerns that off-leash dogs would discourage minorities, the elderly, children, and those with special needs from using the park (39 percent of A comments), there would be increased need for rescue and interventions (38 percent of A comments), and the policy would violate the NPS's mandate (13 percent of A comments). Six percent complained about dog excrement as well.

Problematic rationales, or those that display a lack of respect for dog walkers, are made, but they comprise a smaller percentage of the pro-leash commentary. For example, just 6 percent (155 comments) alleged that dog owners were selfish and inconsiderate, while 3 percent or (67 comments) argued that the land was for humans. In that latter argument, the enjoyment of the dog-walking humans, of course, registers for nothing. Less than five percent of Option A supporters alluded to their right to enjoy the park, with 2 percent claiming they had a right to do so without dogs. Such reference to "rights" frames the issue in confrontational terms, as rights cannot be compromised. Indeed, one said, "I see no reason whatever that dog owners should trample on the enjoyment of the parks by hikers, bikers, walkers and horse riders."[12] They are the one group, in other words, not entitled to enjoyment. Confrontational or antagonistic comments, though, represented only a small portion of the total. Given the geographic breakdown of the commentary, this makes sense. The bulk of Option A supporters were not from the area and therefore probably lacked the passion and anger usually common in these fights. For those who do not reside in the Bay Area of California, for that matter, this issue is an abstract one with little to no effect on their daily routines. It would be surprising for such a demographic group to express anger in their comments. The overwhelming thrust in this commentary, namely concerns for wildlife and the environment, are consistent with the theory that a change in managerial philosophy from recreational use to natural-areas preservation sparked this fight. Additionally, these rationales are what would be expected from those mobilized by the Sierra Club and Audubon Society.

In contrast, those supporting Option B, off-leash recreation, are much more likely to be from the Bay Area. For these commentators, this is not an abstract issue, but one with profound effects on their quality of life. There are fewer "form" letters as well, which might account for a greater diversity in supporting rationales. Perhaps indicative of this group's lack of political savvy, or more charitably, their honesty, two of their three most common rationales cited benefits for dogs, exercise (27 percent of B supporters), and sociability (16 percent). Recall that dogs do not vote. It is for that reason that rationales emphasizing their gains are less likely to persuade policymakers. They also play into the hands of leashing advocates who argue that human interests trump canine ones. Importantly, though, Option B supporters cited general benefits (15 percent) and sociability benefits (14 percent) for *people* as well. As in disputes elsewhere, dog walkers attested to the importance of the community of dog walkers in their comments. For example, one stated, "The community of people we have encountered while walking dogs is an extremely warm and supportive one. . . . We have had long conversations with other older people who thrive on the social outlet that dog walking provides."[13] Second in ranking (17 percent) among Option B supporters was the rationale that cited the origins of the GGNRA, specifically claiming that the land was given with the assumption that existing uses would continue. Others (14 percent) argued that dog walkers were responsible and self-regulating, another somewhat politically naïve rationale because it can be disproven by the actions of very few.

Similarly to Option A supporters, only a small percentage made comments that could be construed as disrespectful of the other side. In fact, no rationale for Option B insulted those advocating a leash law, but 8 percent framed the issue in confrontational rights language and 6 percent claimed that dogs were friendly and enjoyable. One could, with a decidedly uncharitable reading, infer that such an assertion does not pay heed to the concerns of those who do not want to encounter dogs. For example, one of these commentators said, "Rarely have the [off-leash] dogs ever bothered me," a statement that does not acknowledge alternative experiences.[14] However, this is a harsh reading because Option B is to set aside only a limited portion of the park for off-leash recreation, and those who dislike dogs would retain large on-leash and no-dog areas.

Other rationales respond to the arguments of leashing advocates. For example, off-leash recreation is said to make the park safer, not more dangerous; to encourage, not discourage, use by minorities, the elderly, children, and those with special needs; to pose no harm to wildlife; and to have no negative impact on the environment. Option B supporters note as well that exceptions to NPS regulations exist elsewhere and that the GGNRA is an urban park, not a wilderness. Given the passion among dog walkers, the stated rationales are incredibly responsive to the concerns of leashing advocates. By definition, dog walkers are seeking a compromise, as only a small percentage of GGNRA land might be made off-leash. In conclusion, there is little evidence of disrespect on either side, at least in the formal report.

Commentators made helpful suggestions as well, almost all of which were premised on retaining off-leash recreation. Of the four most popular suggestions, three implied support for off-leash recreation. Five percent suggested that off-leash walking should be in designated but not fenced areas; four percent recommended citations only for irresponsible dog owners; and two percent proposed specific time periods for off-leash dog walking. Five percent suggested fenced or clearly separate areas for this activity, a recommendation that was against the previous multiuse areas and therefore more pro-leash in orientation. The other suggestions were individually cited by one percent or less than one percent of commentators. All of these suggestions were premised on the continuation of off-leash recreation and all were aimed at improving the situation. For example, some proposed limiting the number of dogs per person, increasing educational efforts, licensing off-leash dogs, encouraging stewardship of off-leash areas, and scientifically studying the impact of off-leash dogs. Based on these suggestions and commentary, it is fair to conclude that off-leash advocates were supportive of compromise. Those supporting a ban on off-leash recreation, by definition, were not. It is also obvious that, per the public commentary, off-leash recreation had substantially more support than the ban.

## Survey Results

The NPS requested that the University of Northern Arizona conduct a phone survey and provide analysis of those findings in addition to its analysis of public commentary. Those with little or no concern about the leashing issue can be included in a phone survey. In fact, surveys are even worse than referendums on this score, as the latter require, at least, some act on the part of the citizen. Seeking a more representative sample than provided from those commenting, the NPS commissioned the survey to learn what Bay Area residents thought about leashing restrictions. Such a survey theoretically can detect overwhelming hostility or support for a law, if such a sentiment exists. However, results can be problematic as well in that questions might be biased and respondents might know or care very little about the issue.

Researchers surveyed four hundred adult residents in four counties: Alameda, Marin, San Francisco, and San Mateo. Both county and regional results were tabulated, with validity rates of plus or minus 5 and 2.5, respectively. As would be expected in a telephone survey, respondents had less of a direct stake in this decision than commentators. While 96 percent had visited a GGNRA site in their lifetimes, 26 percent had not visited a GGNRA site within the last year. Of the most popular sites—the Cliff House, Alcatraz, Muir Woods, Stinson Beach, and Baker Beach—only portions of two allow dogs at all, leashed or not. The Cliff House, Alcatraz, and Muir Woods forbid dogs. Along with these sites, Ocean Beach, the Presidio, and Crissy Field— all areas that had previously allowed some off-leash recreation—were named as most popular within the last twelve months only. Recall that 74 percent of respondents had visited a GGNRA site within that period. If respondents had visited areas that had previously forbidden dogs or required leashing, their perception could be that new regulations would change that policy when, in fact, none of those areas would be impacted. It is also worth noting that "dog heaven," known otherwise as Fort Funston, did not make either list of "most popular sites." It is fair to conclude, then, that many respondents had probably not visited that site or certainly did not do so regularly.

Dog owners accounted for 29 percent of all respondents. Of that group, half had taken their dogs for a walk at a GGNRA site. However, only 39 percent *of that smaller subset* walked their dogs at the GGNRA regularly, at least once a week. As intended, then, this survey does not give weight to the passion or intensity of regular users. It is instead a snapshot of public opinion.

Researchers asked respondents if they had seen dogs off-leash in the GGNRA. Almost half had not, but in San Francisco County, that percentage was much smaller, 25 percent. In the four-county region, 76 percent reported that off-leash dogs either did not affect or added to their visit. In San Francisco County, that number was 79 percent, with 34 percent claiming that off-leash dogs *added* to their visit. Those who said that off-leash dogs detracted from their visit comprised approximately one quarter of the total, although only 20 percent in San Francisco County. These survey results would support the existence of off-leash areas in portions of the park.

However, researchers proceeded to ask a "loaded" question. Specifically, respondents were told: "Current NPS regulations allow for walking dogs on-leash at most GGNRA sites; AND, prohibit any off-leash dog walking." Then the respondents were asked, "Do you support or oppose this current regulation?" Given the fact that this NPS regulation was brand new and later determined illegal, its inclusion would be confusing to respondents. Seventy-five percent of San Francisco County and 52 percent of all respondents reported seeing off-leash dogs on visits. Basically, this statement conveyed to respondents that these dog walkers were acting illegally or that off-leash recreation was possible despite the regulation. In other words, the statement contradicted their experiences. It is difficult to conclude, then, that their support of this "policy" is indicative of their satisfaction with the status quo, which until very recently allowed some off-leash dog walking, or their desire for a prohibition on off-leash dog walking. The policy read to them, that is, was a *new* one and therefore represented a *change*, despite NPS denials. Yet it was presented to respondents as though it had been the status quo. That was misleading.

When presented this way, a full 71 percent either strongly or somewhat supported the leashing regulations. That percentage dropped to 63 percent among San Francisco County respondents. When a more open-ended question about respondents' positions on off-leash dog walking was asked of San Francisco respondents, only 47 percent somewhat or strongly opposed it, and 46 percent supported it somewhat or strongly. That was a statistical dead heat. In the four-county region, 53 percent opposed off-leash dog walking, while 40 percent supported it. While that latter result indicated support for leashing restrictions, it did not square with questions about respondents' experiences. For example, 49 percent in the four-county region who stated that dogs did not affect their visit to a GGNRA site might very well attribute that happy fact to the new NPS policy, which had been read to them, and thereby expressed support for it. In reality, the old policy, which included off-leash areas, might have forbidden dogs or required their leashing in the area they visited. Neither that fact nor the change in policy was clear to respondents.

Survey results highlight support for leashing, but with low intensity and a problematic presentation of the policy. To be sure, about 25 percent of respondents claimed that off-leash dogs detracted from their visit, and thus clearly they would be supporters of the new policy. On the other hand, about the same number claimed that such dogs added to their visit. The middle group, for whom dogs did not impact their visit, is harder to read and was likely influenced by the presentation of NPS policy. While the public commentary and survey results were cited as reasons to proceed with the rulemaking process and "create" some off-leash areas, they arguably demonstrate support for the *old* policy before the NPS prohibition, with perhaps some adjustments to accommodate the justifiable concerns of a minority who wanted to avoid off-leash dogs.[15]

## A Long Start

On November 19, 2002, Superintendent Brian O'Neill recommended to the director of the NPS that negotiated rulemaking be invoked for purposes of pet management in the GGNRA. This recommendation was consistent with that of a federal panel of five senior NPS administrators who convened in August 2002. Based on six findings, that panel concluded "that off-leash dog walking in GGNRA may be appropriate in selected locations where park resources will not be impaired if the standards for appropriate use can be met and if public safety incidents and public use conflicts can be appropriately managed."[16] Specifically, the panel found that the GGNRA parkland is immediately adjacent to San Francisco, one of the most densely populated urban centers in the country, and manages a significant portion of recreational open space in the city. As a result, most residents do not own private space to exercise their pets and rely on the GGNRA. Secondly, the GGNRA manages the majority of recreational waterfront in San Francisco and Marin Counties, a fact that leaves few non-GGNRA alternatives for beach access. Thirdly, the panel found that there was a significant expression of demand for off-leash dog walking within the GGNRA. That finding was based on a review of the public commentary and survey. The panel additionally concluded that there was longstanding off-leash dog use with the NPS's tacit acceptance, that locations exist within the GGNRA that appear suitable for off-leash dog use, and finally, that public safety and user conflicts with off-leash walking may be mitigated via appropriate measures.[17]

There would be an almost three-year delay between Superintendent O'Neill's recommendation to the national office and the "Notice of Intent to Establish a Negotiated Rulemaking Advisory Committee," which was published in the *Federal Register* on June 28, 2005. This delay can be attributed, at least in part, to the requirements and novelty of the process. The park unit's administration had to write a justification, which had to undergo full legal review, and then be approved by the national office. There were few precedents upon which to model this justification and that need for originality lengthened the process. Indeed, the GGNRA would be just the third national park to create regulations via a negotiated rulemaking process.[18] Approximately one-half to three-quarters of a million dollars had to be secured in the budget as well. Prior to publication, several steps in the rulemaking process additionally had to be completed.

To assist in the determination of the consistency between the legal framework of the Rulemaking Act and the formation of a Negotiated Rulemaking Committee for this particular issue, CDR Associates and the Center for Collaborative Policy at California State University, Sacramento, under contract with the US Institute for Environmental Conflict Resolution, studied the matter and issued a report to the GGNRA on September 14, 2004. The GGNRA needed this situation assessment report before proceeding with the formation of the Committee. Indeed, the goals of this study were 1) to identify the key interests concerned about dog management in the GGNRA that would be significantly affected and therefore require representation on the Negotiated Rulemaking Committee per the Rulemaking Act, 2) to evaluate the potential for reaching consensus on a rule, and 3) to identify prospective candidates who were able and willing to serve on the Committee. Such individuals had to be identified prior to publication of intent in the *Federal Register*. To achieve these goals, the assessment team conducted interviews of approximately 45 people, individually or in groups, from May to August 2004. Ultimately, the Report recommended that the GGNRA proceed with the negotiated rulemaking process.[19]

In reaching its conclusion, the Report noted, among other things, the need for a rule, a limited number of identifiable interests significantly affected, a reasonable likelihood that a committee with balanced representation and participants willing to negotiate in good faith could be formed, and a reasonable likelihood that such a committee could reach a consensus within a fixed period of time. This optimism was based on findings of a broadly shared expectation that some off-leash dog walking would be allowed as well as substantial agreement over the importance of participation. However, the Report noted the "challenging" nature of this context and specifically found that this issue was a "highly emotional" one that "implicates core values for many people and is often closely linked to personal and group identity."[20] It also cited several areas both of disagreement among stakeholders and unknown variables. In that latter category, the Report alluded to the lingering consequences of past conflicts on this issue, the impact of the City's process and environmental analysis as well as other factors. The optimism, in other words, was cautious and for good reason. Approximately nine months after receiving this Report, the Notice was published in the *Federal Register*. The timing was somewhat unfortunate given dog walkers' perceptions about the NPS, as the publication was within one month of the *U.S. v. Barley* decision, which overturned the NPS's prohibition on off-leash dog walking. Given the extensive legal requirements, it is understandable that the approval process, in the federal bureaucracy, would take some time. Critics could note the possibility that the court's decision brought the issue to the NPS's front burner, so to speak, but it is clear that the NPS was pursuing this process well before that decision.

# NEGOTIATED RULEMAKING—THE PROCESS— THERE IS NO WIZARD

No one has ever charged the federal bureaucracy with the crime of simplicity in procedures, an omission this process, really process*es*, might help to explain. Changes in rules require *both* a planning process, which in this case must incorporate an environmental review, *and* a rulemaking process, however these processes can occur concurrently (much like prison sentences can be served). They can also be conducted sequentially, but that is a more lengthy process. Mercifully, in this case, the rulemaking and planning processes took place concurrently.

## Negotiated Rulemaking—Steps in the Process

Federal agencies need not invoke negotiated rulemaking, but when they do, they supplement traditional rulemaking with a negotiation process. Ideally, all stakeholders participate in the negotiation and reach a consensus on a new rule. The Negotiated Rulemaking Committee for Dog Management in the GGNRA first met on March 6, 2006. According to the Notice of Intent to establish this committee, advocates of off-leash recreation were represented by the Crissy Field Dog Group, Fort Funston Dog Walkers, Ocean Beach Dog Owners, Pacifica Dog Walkers, Presidio Dog Walkers, and the San Francisco Dog Owners Group. Additionally, ProDog represented the interests of commercial dog walkers. Environmental organizations, which were opposed to off-leash recreation, were represented by the California Native Plant Society, the Center for Biological Diversity, the Golden Gate Audubon Society, the Marine Mammal Center, the Sierra Club, and the San Francisco League of Conservation Voters. Visitor interests were represented by Coleman Advocates for Children and Youth, equestrian groups, Senior Action Network, the Marin Humane Society, and the San Francisco Society for the Prevention of Cruelty to Animals. Finally, local governments, such as the city/county of San Francisco, the defunct GGNRA Citizens Advisory Committee, and the Presidio Trust had representatives as well. Of course, the NPS had its own representative, Christine Powell. Notice that no fewer than eighteen individuals, including representatives from six dog walking and six environmental groups, all of whom represent a membership with strong feelings on this issue, must reach a consensus. To be sure, such an inclusive approach may well be mandated in this case given the numerous separate areas, such as Crissy Field and Funston, to which different groups of dog walkers are attached. If those areas must be separately represented to ensure fairness, then, of course, multiple environmental groups must be at the table to provide balance. The end result, though, is a large group and that makes consensus less likely.

As envisioned in the Assessment Report, this Committee was to hold six meetings, with potentially four subcommittees meeting during the Committee's tenure as well. By the second meeting, the full Committee was to identify potential locations for off-leash dog walking and seek agreement on criteria for decisions. The final three meetings were dedicated to crafting a proposed rule. All of the Committee's meetings were to be open to the public, with some time limited for commentary. It could continue its work until it reached consensus or its authorization, which could not exceed two years, expired. If this group of individuals reached a consensus, that would be used as a basis for a new rule. As with any rule, it would be published in the *Federal Register* for public commentary. After the NPS reviewed that commentary and made any necessary changes to the rule, the final rule would be published provided that the requirements of the National Environmental Policy Act (NEPA) were satisfied.

## Reality

In actuality, the Committee's meetings did not quite adhere to this ambitious plan. The full Committee held meetings on March 6, 2006; April 18, 2006; May 15, 2006; July 31, 2006; September 21, 2006; April 15, 2007; and October 27, 2007. While its first full meeting was largely an organizational one as planned, the second meeting did not begin to identify areas for off-leash dog walking. At that meeting, per the summary, the Committee spent much time discussing and amending the protocols for the behavior of participants, a sure sign that relations were tense among some Committee members. To make matters worse, the deputy superintendent of the GGNRA explained that the agency would be seeking accelerated resource protection rules for Crissy Field and a portion of Ocean Beach. Such rules would prohibit off-leash dogs. Even into the third meeting, these two contentious issues, protocols and accelerated rulemaking, were still discussed. There was no discussion of specific areas *for* off-leash activity, as intended, but areas were identified as off the table if accelerated rulemaking was successful. The process itself, which now included the NEPA portion, seemed to occupy much of the third meeting's agenda. By the fourth meeting in July, at least a Technical Subcommittee had been formed and had started to meet. However, that full Committee meeting itself included reporting and complaints antithetical to the building of trust. For example, per the "Meeting Summary," "The representative of the Center for Biological Diversity expressed his concerns about . . . Ms. Kennedy-Routhier's ability to constructively participate as a Committee member."[21] Additionally, the representative of birding interests noted that members of the Golden Gate Audubon Society had observed dogs harassing wildlife at Ocean Beach.[22] In other words, the Committee had obviously not yet turned its attention from points of disagreement to building a consensus. Yet at this meeting, site visits were scheduled.

At the fifth meeting on September 21, the Technical Subcommittee reported that it was engaged in the discussion of substantive issues, such as the definition of "voice control," and enforcement situations and actions of NPS rangers. Importantly, the full Committee "supported going forward with the recommendation that the Technical Subcommittee develop proposals and recommendations for Committee discussion and decisions, with the understanding that Committee members not on the Subcommittee are welcome to attend the meetings."[23] Public observers, who could attend but not comment at these meetings, could not record discussions. Meeting summaries, in fact, would only be provided to subcommittee members. The Technical Subcommittee would therefore conduct the substantive discussions without a written public record. Given the lack of progress in the full Committee, it seems reasonable to charge a smaller body with this task and to give its members some room—or distance from their interest groups—to work out a compromise. The full Committee would not meet again until April 2007.

At the September 2006 full Committee meeting, the ongoing NEPA process was additionally discussed. Recall that this mandatory process was taking place concurrently with negotiated rulemaking. Ultimately, this process had to yield an environmental impact statement (EIS) for dog management in the GGNRA. By law, this statement must analyze the impact of a range of reasonable alternatives. As a result, any recommendations from the Negotiated Rulemaking Committee would be alternatives in competition with others. That is to say, even if a consensus was reached, there is no guarantee that consensus would form the basis of a final rule. In explaining the relationship of these processes, the NPS writes, "The park intends to integrate the recommendations of the committee's efforts into one or more alternatives for analysis in the EIS. This approach brings affected groups into the process at an early stage so they can share in the decision-making and also share responsibility for the outcome."[24] It seems that the hope is to generate support for a final rule, but with the clear stipulation that such a rule might not meet with the approval of the full Negotiated Rulemaking Committee or a portion thereof. Indeed, a brochure about this process notes, "The park will evaluate alternatives for managing dog walking in the dog management plan/EIS and identify a preferred alternative. . . . The final plan/EIS will become the basis of a formal 'rulemaking' process that will establish regulations for dog walking in GGNRA."[25] In other words, the NEPA process trumps, and the NPS has control over that.

To be sure, the NEPA process requires a "public scoping of issues." In accordance with that requirement, the NPS published a notice of intent to prepare an environmental impact statement in the *Federal Register* on February 22, 2006. That notice "invited comments regarding the scope of the Plan/EIS, relevant environmental information, or issues or concerns."[26] The comment period ran until April 24, 2006. Interestingly, the notice stated the NPS's displeasure with the 1979 Pet Policy, which by this time had been re-instituted by court order. In the background section, the NPS writes, "A history of dog management policy that has been inconsistent with NPS regulations has resulted in controversy and litigation, compromised visitor and employee safety, affected visitor experience and resulted in resource degradation."[27] That notwithstanding, the NPS held two workshops about the process and invited input, a large amount of which was received. Over five hundred pieces of correspondence were entered into the record. The NPS published a Public Scoping Comment Analysis Report in August 2006. There were at least 197 suggestions for new alternatives, running the gamut from no dogs to off-leash areas. Unfortunately, the format of this Report, dictated by its purpose, prevents conclusions about the number of pro- and anti-leash comments. For example, a "concern statement" about an alternative could include pro- and anti-leash suggestions. In some cases, concern statements are associated with one side or the other, such as a call to continue the 1979 policy. However, it would be misleading to highlight only some portions of the commentary. Further, the purpose of the Report is qualitative, as it seeks to cover all impacts, on humans, dogs, wildlife, and vegetation. The information gained during the public scoping is to inform the work of the Negotiated Rulemaking Committee and, of course, the draft NEPA document. Once such a draft is prepared, the public has additional time to comment.

The Negotiated Rulemaking Committee met twice more in April and October 2007. Given that there was still discussion about the protocols of members' behavior at the April meeting, it seems reasonable to infer that relations among members were still tense. Deputy Superintendent Mai-Liis Bartling of the GGNRA expressed the NPS's concern that external activities, such as interactions with the media, were disrupting the negotiating process. Because protocols require consensus adoption and the final version did not contain media prohibitions, members expressed reluctance to surrender their use of other forums to protect their interests.[28] Left unsaid was the underlying assumption of distrust in the negotiation process itself to accommodate members' interests.

Despite that distrust, the Committee achieved perhaps its most significant accomplishment at this meeting, an agreement on nine guiding principles or starting points for determining where off-leash recreation can and cannot take place (see Table I). In the discussion, recreational use (Principle 6) and historic and social use (Principle 9) were said to include dog walking. The summary noted that the Technical Subcommittee had met on four occasions and that smaller groups would continue to work so as to make site-specific recommendations to the full Committee.

**Table I.** Guiding principles for design and evaluation of dog management options.

*Preamble: The following principles are intended to assist the Committee in evaluating "starting points" and related proposals for dog management within GGNRA, consistent with National Park Service statutes and policies, including the Organic Act, GGNRA enabling legislation, and current management plans.*

| | |
|---|---|
| 1 | Minimize conflicts with other visitors and park staff |
| 2 | Protect sensitive species and their habitat. Sensitive species means federal-listed, state-listed, unique or rare species |
| 3 | Protect native wildlife and their habitat |
| 4 | Minimize soil/water resources degradation |
| 5 | Ensure consistency with National Park Service visitor experience definition |
| 6 | Continue recreational use including special events |
| 7 | Avoid obstruction/barriers to wildlife, except where the purpose of barriers would be protective of wildlife |
| 8 | Ensure public safety/visitor protection |
| 9 | Consider historic and social use values |

Source: April 5, 2007 Meeting Summary, Negotiated Rulemaking Advisory Committee for Dog Management at Golden Gate National Recreation Area

The facilitation team indeed submitted a draft progress report from Work Group Meetings to the full Committee at its final meeting on October 27, 2007. Even the Work Groups themselves were able to agree upon very few areas by the requisite consensus. The Report recommended off-leash areas in Oakwood Valley, Pedro Point, and Upper Fort Mason and had reached partial agreement for a few other areas. Because the full Committee reached consensus on only one site, Oakwood Valley, that was the only one forwarded for inclusion in the NEPA analysis. Oakwood Valley is not even in San Francisco, but is in Marin County. Two variations for that area, one with continuous fencing and the other without, were forwarded. No consensus was reached for the most popular dog walking areas, such as Fort Funston, known previously as "dog heaven"; Crissy Field; Ocean Beach; or Land's End. The progress report from the work groups ominously remarks, "Time did not allow discussion of the remaining six sites, which include all the beaches under consideration."[29]

The full Committee could not even reach consensus on seventeen guidelines intended to operationalize the nine starting points (see Table II). The work groups agreed to almost all of these, with the exception of Guideline 9, which asserted the need for clearly delineated boundaries between off-leash and other areas. Those boundaries could include fencing or other barriers. The facilitation team asked the full Committee to forward this list, excluding Guidelines 9 and 16, which required dog guardians to participate in a tag program confirming their understanding of the rules, to NPS and NEPA, but the Committee declined to do so. Off-leash proponents had advocated for the tag program to ensure that those with dogs at the GGNRA abided by the rules. Under this program, which was modeled on a similar one in Boulder, Colorado, only dogs wearing these special tags would be allowed off-leash privileges. The full Committee did forward the Work Group's proposal for commercial dog walking to NPS for the NEPA process, but with several caveats and amendments. One of those required that the NEPA analysis address the question of whether to allow commercial dog walking in the GGNRA at all.[30]

The Committee reached no consensus on off-leash walking at the most popular sites, its main task. Superintendent O'Neill not only presided over the final meeting, but had personally met with off-leash and environmental caucuses, the Technical Subcommittee, and Work Groups prior to this meeting. Such an active role undoubtedly denoted an appreciation of the significance of this issue. Concluding that "everyone is now better informed and educated about the issues due to this process," Superintendent O'Neill thanked all of the participants for their efforts. Because virtually no consensus was reached, it was up to the NPS to craft a rule that identified specific sites for off-leash dog walking. Michael Edward, of the NPS Environmental Quality Division, indicated at the final meeting that the draft EIS and rule could be expected in fall 2008. Once released, the public would have sixty days to comment upon them, and the EIS and/or rule could be modified as a result of the commentary. A final EIS and rule were originally anticipated in summer 2009.[31] As of this writing in 2010, a draft rule is still pending.

Preliminary indications are not promising for dog walkers. The NPS has proposed three planning frameworks for the GGNRA's San Francisco holdings, "Connecting People with Parks," "Preserving and Enjoying Coastal Ecosystems," and "Focusing on National Treasures." If one of the latter two ap-

**Table II.** Proposed dog management guidelines.

1  All GGNRA visitors should have clear notice about the potential for interactions with a dog at all GGNRA locations where dogs are permitted.
2  Dog management policies should support the reasonable expectation of personal safety for all GGNRA visitors.
3  Dog guardians have a responsibility to prevent unwelcome (non-consensual) interactions between their dog(s) and people, other dogs, horses and wildlife at all areas within GGNRA.
4  Dog guardians have a responsibility to ensure their dog(s) does not create negative impacts (such as digging, harassing wildlife or sensitive habitat) on GGNRA resources (such as plants, soils, wildlife and water bodies).
5  All GGNRA dog use areas shall have well-maintained signage that clearly describes conditions of use by dogs and guardians, located to maximize visitor education and awareness.
6  GGNRA dog rules and regulations shall be followed by dog guardians; dog guardians should be made aware that otherwise they shall be subject to enforcement actions.
7  An area designated for off-leash dog activity within GGNRA will be called a Regulated Off-Leash Area (ROLA).
8  ROLAs are the only areas within GGNRA where off-leash dogs are allowed, and dog guardians are responsible for ensuring that their off-leash dogs remain within ROLA boundaries.
9  ROLA boundaries should be clearly and effectively delineated to achieve visitor safety, provide notice regarding appropriate uses, protect natural resources, and provide a range of visitor experiences. A variety of delineation measures shall be considered, including fencing, vegetation, other natural or man-made barriers (e.g., bluffs, sea walls), buffers or some combination of the above.
10 Dog guardians must have a current license to visit GGNRA dog use areas, and each dog must wear a collar exhibiting their registration/vaccination tag.
11 Dog guardians must have a leash for each dog in their care, complying with NPS regulations that currently stipulate a maximum length of six feet.
12 Dogs must be leashed at all times in parking lots and designated picnic areas.
13 Dog guardians must at all times be in possession of bags to clean up dog waste and ensure that their dog's waste is picked-up and disposed of at designated locations.
14 Dogs in ROLAs are to be kept under control at all times. Dogs are considered under control when they are within direct eyesight of the owner/handler and when they immediately respond to their owner/handler.
15 Visitors must have reasonable notice of the boundaries of a ROLA and what they should expect within those boundaries. Notice shall include signs at ROLA access points, in transition zones, and in conjunction with fencing or other physical barriers.
16 Dog guardians wishing to utilize ROLAs must participate in a Tag Program confirming their understanding of the locations and conditions under which dogs may be allowed off-leash, the natural resources of GGNRA and other relevant information.
17 In the event of a live stranded marine mammal's presence in a ROLA, e.g., on a beach, all dogs must be immediately leashed (if not already on leash) within 100 yards of the marine mammal. This will stay in effect until the marine mammal is no longer present on the beach. (The presence of a dead marine mammal on a ROLA does not require that dogs be leashed.) Additional signage to educate the public should be utilized.

Source: October 27, 2007 DRAFT Meeting Summary, Negotiated Rulemaking Committee for Dog Management at Golden Gate National Recreation Area

proaches is adopted as the framework, the "recreational" nature of the GGNRA will be reduced and dog walkers will almost certainly be negatively impacted. Even more ominously, House Speaker Nancy Pelosi has proposed a name change for the GGNRA that would call it a national park and thus completely drop the name of "recreational area." The original purpose of the San Francisco holdings would thereby be erased.

## IS DEMOCRACY ALIVE IN WASHINGTON? AN EVALUATION

### Liberty

No matter what the final outcome, one must surely applaud the vibrancy of associational politics on this issue. Dog walkers, by definition "everyman" and from all walks of life, formed several active groups, which developed their own identity and defined themselves not just as advocacy groups on this issue, but as groups with a commitment to the public good. These groups include SFDog, Fort Funston Dog Walkers Association, Crissy Field Dog Group, Ocean Beach Dog, and ProDog, which represents professional dog walkers. While founded in 1976, SFDog formally organized in 1997 in "reaction to the closing of Ocean Beach" to off-leash recreation. In that sense, this organization is a classic political interest group, formed in response to a threat to its members' interests. The group has expanded its mission "to include a variety of programs designed to educate the people of San Francisco about dogs and their place in our culture." Specifically, the group promotes responsible dog ownership and hosts speakers on topics such as search and rescue training. Additionally, it organizes and plugs events to clean up area parks.[32] This group has both an e-mail discussion and announcement list where members can discuss dog-related topics and help one another with canine behavioral issues, lost dogs, and other matters. Likewise, the Funston group was formed primarily to fight the political battle to keep Funston leash-free, but it additionally provides a public service in its promotion of good dog ownership practices, such as "cleaning up after pets, training dogs for voice control, and leashing poorly socialized animals."[33] Both the Crissy Field and Ocean Beach groups cite a similar mission.

Dog walkers, then, organized in response to a threat to their interests. Each of these groups boasts hundreds of members and has organizational sophistication. There are leadership structures in place, regular meetings, and means of electronic communication with members. Such organization indicates a healthy associational life. Significantly, once formed, these organizations themselves then strengthened the bonds of members and their group identity. Evidence of this strengthened bond abounds. There are several clean-up days, rallies, protests, and activities sponsored or promoted by these organizations.

Liberty was alive and well among the off-leash opponents as well. Unlike dog walkers, opponents' interests were not attacked via a policy announcement. Some were undoubtedly unhappy with the status quo before 2001 and were working to close off areas of the GGNRA to dogs, but the dramatic change in policy *favored* their position. As a result, there is not a rash of new groups on this side. Instead, previously established organizations, such as the Center for Biological Diversity, the Golden Gate Audubon Society, the local Sierra Club, the California Native Plant Society, and to some extent, Coleman Advocates for Children and Youth, mobilized their membership and/or resources to limit or end off-leash recreation. In contrast with the dog-walking groups, the missions of these organizations were varied and broader. For example, according to its Web site, the Golden Gate Audubon Society is "dedicated to protecting Bay Area birds, other wildlife, and their natural habitats."[34] Its policy on leashing in the GGNRA is not at all explicit or prominently displayed on its site. Only if you follow links for keeping the city safe for wildlife to the western snowy plover can you click on a television news segment that advocated the leashing policy at Ocean Beach. Likewise, the national Sierra Club cites the exploration, enjoyment, and protection of the wild places of earth, the practice and promotion of responsible use of the earth's ecosystems and resources, and the education and enlistment of humanity to protect and restore the quality of the natural and human environment in its mission statement.[35] The Club's San Francisco chapter cites the following priorities: preservation of Golden Gate Park, toxic reduction and cleanup, transit improvements, open space acquisition and protection, recycling and resource conservation, sustainable job development, wetlands development and protection, and water conservation.[36] While the leaders of this organization have interpreted these priorities as inconsistent with off-leash dog walking at the GGNRA, there is no prominent statement of this position on the chapter's Web site. This is a fairly significant omission if, in fact, the leaders are claiming to speak for their entire membership on this issue. It is not axiomatic that members of this and other environmental organizations would agree with their leadership's position on this issue, and it is curious that such an important issue is not touted more obviously on their Web sites. In fact, some dog walkers formerly belonged to some of these groups and clearly disagreed with the leaders' application of the missions to this issue. That notwithstanding, opponents of off-leash recreation were well organized.

On the criterion of liberty, then, there are positive indications that democracy's health was well. However, the news can never be all good. The admitted infiltration of the SFDog e-mail discussion list during the trial of Michelle Parris was outrageous. Whether the NPS did or did not direct the individual to spy on this group does not matter. The information should not have been used. Remember, this was not the trial of a terrorist, but of someone walking dogs off-leash. Such infiltration has a well-known "chilling" effect on free speech, as members of this *dog discussion list* could never be quite sure again about governmental monitoring. There is simply no way that such a cost could be justified by any conceivable benefit to the prosecution in the Parris case.

Also troubling, we will see, is the disparity in legitimacy of these groups in the eyes that matter, those of the NPS. As a government agency, the NPS has "natural client" groups whose missions coincide with its own. In this case, the NPS is likely to have a relationship with the Sierra Club, Audubon Society, and Center for Biological Diversity. The legal alliance with these groups over the Funston closures, in and of itself, raises questions about the potential for fairness. Ideally, per interest group theory, government agencies should serve to broker fair agreements among fairly equal, competing interest groups.[37] Here, the established groups and the government, at times, were aligned against the newly formed dog-walking groups. That situation should have been avoided. In establishing the negotiated rulemaking process, however, the NPS clearly solicited information and engaged the dog-walking groups. Superintendent O'Neill met with dog-walking representatives prior to the final meeting of the Negotiated Rulemaking Committee. Whether that process and hands-on facilitation compensate for the previous perception of unfairness remains to be seen.

If liberty is to receive high grades across the board, the outcome itself must maximize its practice. While the final outcome, yet to be determined, will speak to the NPS's sense of fairness, the initial decision to end all off-leash recreation in 2001 unnecessarily eliminated all the liberties of one side to the favor of the other. No group, in theory, should walk away with exceptionally high levels of its goals met. Nor should any group be denied all of its key interests, as dog walkers were in 2001. There are times, of course, when illegitimate interests must be denied. If a group wanted to use the GGNRA to dump toxic waste, surely such a claim could be deemed illegitimate. Bird watchers, dog walkers, and plant lovers, however, do not fit that category. The final decision, which is in the hands of NPS, should not elate or devastate any group.

## Equality

To the extent that some groups or animals were "more equal than others," as George Orwell once put it, there are concerns about democracy. Whether they were objectively correct or not, dog walkers did not consider the NPS to be fair or equal in its treatment of groups. In fact, I did not find one dog walker who thought that the NPS was unbiased, though that does not mean there are not such beings. When I asked in written or oral interview questions if the respondent felt that the NPS was neutral among all groups or favored some over others, one prefaced his/her remarks with the quip: "I'll try to treat this as a serious question." That respondent proceeded to highlight the inherent biases of the negotiated rulemaking process in its early removal of large, existing off-leash areas without suggesting alternative areas as replacements, among other things. Another respondent asserted, "Absolutely . . . the NPS was ***NOT*** neutral!!!! They favored those groups who opposed people walking their dogs on NPS lands." In lengthy responses to nine other questions, that particular respondent used an asterisk around only two other words and did not use multiple exclamation marks in any other place. Indeed, more than any other question, this one touched a nerve in dog walkers. It seemed to encapsulate their frustration with the process itself, which in their view was rigged.

The NPS could respond to this frustration with a description of an inclusive and fair process. As required by law, the NPS sought public comment in its Advanced Notice to Negotiated Rulemaking and in the preparation of its Environmental Impact Statement. What is more, the agency had the data analyzed by neutral parties. All comments, with the exception of petitions, were treated equally. If in the proper format, input was tabulated. Such formal adherence to process, though, masks some problematic consequences. On the one hand, the NPS invited public commentary from all, wherever they lived in the United States. Unlike in Connecticut, there were no second-class out-of-towners with a clear stake in the outcome but without a meaningful voice. Participatory democracy favors such an inclusive approach. Yet on the other hand, this approach favored the nationally organized groups, such as the Audubon Society and Sierra Club, which could mobilize their membership. Lacking such a national organization, dog walkers were at a disadvantage but nonetheless managed to dominate public commentary. This disadvantage, though, was not lost on dog walkers. Asked about the inclusion of those living outside the Bay Area, one respondent explained, "Audubon and Sierra Clubs are national organizations and used their nation-wide email lists to generate canned electronic letters opposing off leash recreation. . . . Their comments should be read but given little weight because the people commenting know virtually nothing about the issue. In fact, they know *less* than nothing since they are soaked in misinformation from the anti-dog zealots in the organizations." Recall that out-of-area comments overwhelmingly favored leashing, while local comments overwhelmingly preferred off-leash areas. This is interesting as well in light of the high local membership in these national organizations. The San Francisco Sierra Club chapter claims ten thousand members.[38] If true, there was an underwhelming response from the local membership on this issue, and that possibility hints of a division between the leaders of these organizations and their membership. That notwithstanding, equality in process does not necessarily guarantee fairness, especially when the process itself favors nationally organized groups. The rule of law ensures equality in form, but not necessarily in spirit. The latter requires goodwill on the part of the governmental agency.

To its credit, the NPS distinguished "form" from other letters. Yet the tabulation of commentary and the elaborate process—required by law—of rulemaking fail to capture the intensity of both proponents and opponents of off-leash recreation. Dog walkers were often frustrated with the NPS's claim of fairness and equal treatment despite blatant evidence of overwhelming support for off-leash dog walking. For example, one respondent noted, "Public hearings were held and the vast majority of people who spoke were in favor of off-leash recreation. Each hearing, hundreds of new faces showed up to speak for off-leash recreation. However, the small group who opposed off-leash recreation were always the same few faces. . . . The officials who ran the hearings seemed to treat each side as if they were equal in number and sentiment—That just was NOT the case—ever!"

How well, then, did the NPS do in upholding the value of equality? In negotiated rulemaking, it ensured all stakeholders a seat at the table. Even there, though, dog walkers claimed a double standard in enforcement of protocols or behavioral standards. This dispute centered on the ejection of representatives from the Negotiated Rulemaking Committee, with dog walkers concerned that one of their representatives had been expelled while one of the environmental groups' representatives who had engaged in similar behavior had not. That aside, the equal representation of all stakeholders did not ensure that there was proportional representation of interest group members anyway. In other words, the Committee resembled the Senate where Wyoming and California are "equally" represented with two senators each despite populations of approximately 500,000 and almost 34 million, respectively. In this process, the fact that dog walkers were greater in number simply was not relevant. This form of representation understandably frustrated dog walkers, as they had the numbers and intensity on their side yet received no corresponding level of input.

Once the NPS chose the path of negotiated rulemaking, it adhered strictly to its procedures. In that sense, it treated all interests properly. Again, though, that early decision to revise the 1979 Pet Policy cast a pall on the NPS's sense of fair play. The dog walkers had little trust, as they sensed accurately that the rules of equal representation favored the environmental groups. Rightly or wrongly, the dog walkers also believed that the NPS was upholding only the letter and not the spirit of the law. Given the number of representatives and the complexity of the bureaucratic process, a fair compromise seemed unlikely to the dog walkers. On this point, they were correct, as no compromise with consensus could be reached. In the end, the NPS will make the policy. From one perspective, the bureaucratic process stifled the potential for compromise and extinguished any hopes of a democratic solution to the conflict, a perhaps appropriate ending on the "eastern front."

## Media

Given the conflict surrounding this issue, the media gravitated toward the story. Their coverage, on the GGNRA matter, was most important from the cancellation of the 1979 Pet Policy in 2001 to the taking of the phone survey in 2002. That said, there was extensive coverage of this issue in the media during that period and subsequently. Because of the extent of coverage on television and in print, it is beyond the scope of this work to examine that coverage for bias. A review of only the *San Francisco Chronicle* articles in the period from January 2001 to August 2002 found that proponents and opponents were given voice in the articles, as well as government officials who were supportive of and opposed to the NPS's change in policy. Dog walkers are, though, at times described as "angry" and cast as threatening without a sufficient explanation of the basis for that anger. This issue, as you might expect, is additionally trivialized via the titles of articles and the use of humor throughout them. During this period, the mauling of Diane Whipple also received extensive coverage, as it should have. Nonetheless, the coverage of that tragedy most likely elicited fear among those not familiar with dogs. Recall that the media's reporting of such cases is typically sensational and devoid of context, facts which widen the divide between those afraid of dogs and those who love them. With that said, the phone survey, conducted over a year after the mauling, failed to reveal evidence of such heightened concern for dogs. As noted, that survey was problematic for other reasons, but its impact in this whole process was minimal anyway. Given the negotiated rulemaking process, the development of this policy became a battle among interest groups, some more organized than others, and not one for public opinion.

## Popular Sovereignty

In any democratic evaluation, compliance with popular sovereignty is most important. It is the essence of democracy that people determine legislation and policy. Was this most important criterion satisfied in this case? Recall that it is essential to stipulate that "rulemaking" is done pursuant to law and is theoretically a means of enforcing legislation. The NPS is not an elected body, but part of the executive bureaucracy. Only the top leaders change with presidential administrations. This fact, in and of itself, is problematic in this case. Too many people feel too passionately about this issue for it to be decided in the executive branch by individuals not accountable or responsive to popular control. Legislators, such as Congress, would be better suited to strike a compromise that all sides would consider impartial or fair. To be sure, the NPS is not at fault for its inheritance of this issue. Congress routinely delegates too many contentious issues to the executive branch and thereby insulates itself from the ensuing, divisive politics.[39] Unfortunately, Congress did not intervene in this case, and thus the NPS effectively assumed a legislative role here. While executive rulemaking is not necessarily designed to be "democratic," it is supposed to ensure fairness and a significant role for public input. It is not unreasonable, then, to hold the NPS to those standards.

Unquestionably, the early reversal of the 1979 Pet Policy utterly failed to meet the standards of democracy and the agency's own rules. The impact of this poisonous beginning cannot be overstated. From that point forward, dog walkers considered the NPS biased against them. The decision shifted the onus of change to the dog walkers and therefore objectively placed their interests at a disadvantage. As stated, a federal judge reversed the NPS's decision, but that ruling and the NPS's response did almost nothing to change the already hostile feelings between the NPS and dog walkers. Hiding behind the requirements of "law," when practice had been contrary to such requirements for over twenty years, the NPS started this process with a democratic deficit of gargantuan proportions.

To its credit, the NPS then instituted negotiated rulemaking and made every effort to adhere strictly to the rules of that process. Despite the problems previously highlighted, much public input was sought, obtained, and analyzed professionally. Recall, though, that the change in policy tainted somewhat the results of phone surveys, as questions about the "status quo" were confusing at best. That notwithstanding, the NPS followed its procedures and indeed concluded that it should proceed with negotiated rulemaking. In so doing, it opened itself up to the possibility of leash-free areas in the GGNRA. Yet dog walkers perceived the NPS to be biased against their interests, with one calling the NPS a "dog-hostile advocacy group." The procedures, to which the NPS adhered, favored environmental groups, a fact that dog walkers noticed. What is more, the NPS, the dog walkers knew, had longstanding relationships with those environmental groups. Even if the NPS genuinely tried to apply its procedures as fairly as possible, dog walkers would be akin to gun-control advocates making their case to the leadership of the National Rifle Association. Noticing the NPS's preferences, dog walkers had little trust in this process. Ultimately, of course, when the negotiated rulemaking process failed, the NPS was charged with making the rule.

Without any individual at the NPS being at fault, this decision-making process was problematic. In one version of democracy, usually considered minimalist and less demanding than the participatory model, the government must play the role of a fair umpire among competing interest groups. Because the NPS did not consider all groups to have equally legitimate claims, it would not meet this requirement. This perception of bias is especially problematic given the fallback and now reality that the NPS would make the rule in the absence of compromise. The environmental groups would have little incentive to compromise in negotiated rulemaking, as they would not fear an NPS decision. In contrast, the dog walkers would be under enormous pressure to compromise so as to avoid that outcome. The "NPS fallback" additionally invites cynicism, as some dog walkers considered the whole time-consuming and costly process a sham. The final outcome remains to be seen. If the NPS makes a rule that is clearly a loss to the dog walkers and a victory for the environmental groups, the cynics will be proven correct. That would likely discourage future political participation for all those who took part in this process.

The numbers of participants were indeed impressive. As documented, large numbers of people commented, attended meetings, and joined groups. Given the poor perceptions of the NPS among dog walkers, it is especially impressive that they participated anyway. Further, smaller numbers of people in the dog-walking, environmental, and other groups volunteered to serve on committees that required an extensive amount of their time. They had to please both their own constituents, who could be demanding, and attempt to reach a compromise acceptable to their opponents. On both sides, some such participants endured insults and all of the stress associated with trying to resolve a contentious issue. Without revealing the individuals subject to this harassment, suffice it to say that attacks became personal and even threatening at times. One can only applaud the perseverance of these participants despite the personal toll. Yet such harassment and the perceptions of bias wear people down. Interestingly, some of the leaders on the dog walkers' side have given up the fight, either moving away to more dog-friendly areas or resigning themselves to a hostile relationship with the NPS. A passionate group must either institutionalize its organization and remain vigilant in defense of its interests or face defeat by more organized groups over time. The constancy of this fight, which now dates back over ten years, and reality of this dynamic have unfortunately turned people away from politics. The longer dog walkers have been involved, one dog walker commented to me, the less trusting they are of the NPS and the more wary of the final outcome. Ordinary people, on both sides, should undoubtedly receive high grades for participation, but the process itself seemed to turn people away from politics.

How did the leaders or representatives of groups behave? While there were clearly "hotheads" and those willing to pursue their political goals by any means necessary, the public meetings themselves were civil. It is more difficult to glean the tone of the Negotiated Rulemaking Committee meetings, as the transcripts of those meetings are not publicly available. As noted, the summaries themselves provide some indication of hostility among some of the representatives. The environmental groups, pursuant to their own goals, did not want to identify leash-free areas, and in that sense, they were not eager to work out a compromise. The process, as stated, almost encouraged their resistance. However, the NPS created and enforced protocols of behavior for representatives.

Despite the protocols, the ideal of a deliberative process resulting in a mutually acceptable compromise veered far, far from reality in this case. Repeatedly, dog walkers emphasized extreme frustration with the NPS and environmental groups on this issue. Dog walkers wanted a serious conversation about the environmental impact of dog walking. Citing studies about the matter and contesting the claims of the NPS and environmental groups, they sought evidence and scientific support for the negative and generalized claims made about their recreational activity. The NPS and the environmental groups would not oblige them. While this infuriated dog walkers, it also prevented deliberation, a necessary feature of democratic decision-making in the participatory model.

What is more, the failure to deliberate on this matter resulted in a dichotomous casting of the debate, with dog walkers at sharp odds with bird lovers and environmentalists. Dog walkers vehemently resented this casting and considered it inaccurate, while their opponents accepted this framing of the issue. Importantly, that acceptance of what amounts to an irrepressible conflict between leash-free dogs and the environment might explain the unwillingness of the environmental groups to compromise. Dog walkers believed that leash-free dog walking and a sustainable environment could co-exist. In fact, one leader claimed that in the event of such an outright conflict, s/he would yield to the environment. In the dog walkers' view, the NPS and pro-leash advocates were using "science" in pursuit of their ideological goals and were thereby grossly overstating the negative impact of dog walking. If so, it would certainly not be the first time that pseudoscience was invoked on behalf of a political agenda. Given the critical significance of this issue, it is extremely problematic that neither the NPS nor the environmental groups engaged the dog walkers in a reasoned debate on the matter.

In effect, pro-leash groups, with the aid of the NPS, used birds or the environment as "trump cards." Because all activities at national parks must not have an overall harmful environmental impact, those opposed to off-leash recreation gained political advantage from the assumption that dogs were harmful to the environment. The NPS, on this point, should have engaged in dialogue with the dog-walking groups. Instead siding with the bird and environmental groups, the NPS emphasized anecdotal evidence and selective studies supportive of its view. In so doing, the NPS failed to win the trust of dog-walking groups and missed an opportunity to bridge the differences among these competing groups. One dog walker summed up the resultant view of his/her group, "No one cared about studies or facts. There was no interest in real science." Participatory democratic theorists caution against "trump cards" because they take issues off the table and give some groups advantage over others. In this case, the NPS had to give precedence to environmental concerns, but it need not have cast environmental impact as "a given." That very issue, in fact, was at the heart of the dispute between dog walkers and their opponents. Dog walkers understood this and were, for that reason, furious over this casting. To be sure, an environmental impact statement is prepared as part of the rulemaking process. In its input to that statement, however, the public's role is solely to highlight all possible impacts and not to assess or compare such impacts scientifically. The EIS, in other words, does not compensate for the loss of deliberation on this matter.

Because this critical conversation and resultant deliberation never took place, this issue became the proverbial "elephant in the room" for dog walkers. It colored their perceptions of both the NPS and environmental groups. Because the NPS and these groups would not engage in scientific dialogue but nevertheless made assertions about environmental impact, dog walkers considered such assertions disingenuous, at best, and lies in service of ideology, at worst. Arguably, this "elephant" led dog walkers to have little empathy for their opponents at the GGNRA. Some dog walkers, in fact, distinguished their opponents at the GGNRA with those in city parks. They understood the concerns of elderly citizens and parents who wanted leash- or no-dog zones for children's play areas, but they had mainly animosity for the natural-areas supporters who opposed off-leash walking in the GGNRA. In their view, they were uncompromising and unwilling to engage in an honest conversation about the environmental effects of off-leash dog walking. It is impossible to overstate how much that omission or "elephant" goaded dog walkers, as they resented the antienvironmental label and the lack of respect that was signaled when their arguments were simply ignored.

Despite the high levels of participation, the adherence to legal process, and the outwardly civil behavior by most on all sides, the criterion of popular sovereignty seemed, in this case, to be satisfied only in form, not in substance. There is too much evidence of ill will on the part of the governing agency, perceptions of bias on the part of participants, and animosity toward opponents to consider this a democratic process. Negotiated rulemaking did not bring the competing parties to the table, as theoretically intended that is, for the purpose of working out an acceptable compromise. Perhaps a government agency with no agenda and no history of favoring either side could not have made this process work in this controversial case. With that said, the NPS, which did have a history and was perceived to be in the court of environmental groups, surely could not do it.

# Chapter VII

## All is not Quiet on the Western Front: San Francisco City Politics

The leashing issue in San Francisco's city politics has been every bit as controversial, if not more so, as it has been at the GGNRA. While the national government owns about half of the city's parkland, the city controls most of the remainder. In the late 1990s, the leashing issue at the city parks, many of which are small neighborhood areas, burst onto the political scene. One reporter noted that in her almost two decades of covering San Francisco City Hall, "the debate over whether dogs can be off-leash or on-leash has been by far the most contentious issue. . . . More so than homelessness, pot clubs, development . . . etc."[1] In a debate, Supervisor Mark Leno once claimed that "his office gets more calls about dogs off leash than any other issue."[2] This "western front," then, is as active as the "eastern."

Importantly, the two "fronts" are related. When the NPS began closing sections of Fort Funston and then prohibiting all off-leash activity in 2001, the impact was evident at city parks. Partly because the city would otherwise have the burden of accommodating all off-leash activity, recall that several city supervisors spoke in favor of retaining off-leash recreation at the GGNRA. Officials at the NPS claimed that the GGNRA too experienced increased usage when the city began to enforce leash laws in some parks. Ideally, the two levels of government would have worked together to ensure sufficient space for off-leash recreation in a city with at least 120,000 dogs, while also accommodating its opponents with space of their own. In reality, both levels of government sought to cede as much responsibility for the accommodation of this very popular activity to one another. Divided sovereignty, while protective against tyranny, unfortunately allows such dodges of responsibility. The end result in this case was that dog walkers were fearful of losing space—indeed almost all space—at *both* the GGNRA and city parks. As space for off-leash activity began to shrink in a city with so many dogs, predictable problems arose with other park users. If people are able to exercise their dogs at several locations, there are likely to be fewer dogs at any one location, and therefore fewer conflicts with other uses. Despite that fact, policymakers responded by closing more and more places to this activity. As one might expect, the ensuing politics were explosive.

## CITY PARKS, THE OLD DOG POLICY, AND NEW CALLS FOR ENFORCEMENT

San Francisco's most famous park, of course, is Golden Gate, 1,017 acres of open space, located on the "foggy" (or for non-natives, foggier) side of the city. Described as a wonderland with nine lakes and ponds, this park attracts millions of visitors each year. To create this lush park in what was once a barren area with shifting sand dunes, its developers planted thousands of cypress and eucalyptus trees along with deep-rooted grasses to hold the sand.[3] In addition to Golden Gate, there are several other city parks. Some of these, such as McLaren and Lake Merced, contain hundreds of acres, and others are quite substantial in size as well. In fact, thirty city parks, all with at least ten acres, comprise approximately 2,016 acres of open space, though this includes approximately 450 acres of golf course and a zoo. Certain of these parks, such as Bernal Heights, Buena Vista, and Dolores, are popular places to exercise dogs off-leash. Further, there are multiple neighborhood parks under ten acres in size. Some of those parks, such as Duboce, Sunnyside, and Noe Courts, are popular multiuse areas, with off-leash dog walking one of those activities.

Several of the parks with a history of contention are in or near the Mission and Noe Valley, in the center of the city, which is a heavily populated area. This area is filled not just with humans, but also claims the "highest density of dogs" in the city.[4] The Noe Courts, Duboce Park, and Corona Heights are in that area, fairly near the famous Castro Street, which is "practically synonymous with San Francisco's gay community," and Haight-Ashbury, once populated by hippies but now much more gentrified albeit with vestiges of its past in evidence.[5] Approximately one acre in size, the park called Noe Courts is the scene of much controversy between dog walkers and parents of young children. Duboce, we will see, was the object of intense and long-lasting controversy, while Corona Heights was the subject of an early skirmish. Dolores, a wide open park with lots of people, with and without dogs, peacefully

*Dolores Park.*

coexisting on the grass, is fairly close to Castro Street as well. Dog walkers are so attached to this park that they formed their own organization, Dolores Park Dogs, in 1997, to ensure that it remained "dog-friendly."[6] While also in the Noe Valley, Bernal Heights is a good distance from these famed neighborhoods of Castro and Haight-Ashbury. The larger parks, such as McLaren, Stern Grove, and Lake Merced, are more to the south and/or west. For the most part, the western, ocean side of San Francisco County has the largest parks, with the exception of McLaren.

Like many other municipalities, San Francisco passed a citywide leash law in 1968. In law, dogs were to be leashed in all public spaces, with the only exceptions in the form of fenced, off-leash areas at eighteen city parks. According to the San Francisco Recreation and Parks Department itself, these areas were "out of the way and in poor shape."[7] The space was so inadequate for dog walkers, who estimate themselves to comprise 60 percent of all park users, that people sought other options.[8] That was a possibility because San Francisco's leash law, like many others elsewhere, was not strictly enforced. As a result of that lax enforcement, in fact, people could exercise their dogs off-leash at multiple city parks. In many of these parks, dog walkers formed friendships with others and established daily routines. Just as they did at Fisher Meadows in Connecticut or Fort Funston, people became attached to both their friends and the land. The attachment might even have been stronger, as these groups were, in some cases, truly neighborhood ones.

Beginning in the mid-1990s, city officials began to call for enforcement of the 1968 law. As noted, the city crackdown on off-leash walking coincided with a changing philosophy at the GGNRA, which would result first in reduced space for dogs and then a complete prohibition of off-leash walking in 2001. City officials undoubtedly worried that their parks would experience increased usage because of the GGNRA's restrictions, but that was not the only reason for the city's decision to regulate off-leash use. San Francisco was by no means exempt from the familiar pressures that instigate these disputes. At the city level, children's supporters, such as the Coleman Advocates for Children and Youth, objected to the presence of off-leash dogs in or near children's play areas and to dog litter in playing fields. Indeed, that group issued a "report card" for parks in 1998 that named dogs as a problem. As Crawford notes, these two groups, dog walkers and parents, were "vying for space in the Bay Area's overtaxed local and federal park systems."[9] Undoubtedly, the gentrification of the city led to a surge in the number of people who spent time in parks as well. There were instances in the 1990s when conflict among user groups erupted and caught the public's attention. For example, off-leash walking was restricted at Corona Heights and Grattan Park in response to the demands of opponents after political struggles.

In the economic boom of the 1990s, the city was also able to devote resources to the improvement of its parks. Because of previous budgetary constraints, many city parks were at this time in a state of disrepair. In fact, Harnik reports that by 1996, "Playgrounds were in shambles, virtually every recreation center had a leaky roof, playing fields were pockmarked with ruts and bumps, tree planting had almost ground to a halt, and as many as 1,000 homeless persons had set up semi-permanent encampments in various parks, particularly Golden Gate Park."[10] In that dire state of affairs, the enforcement of a leash law would not exactly be a top priority. As an effort was made to improve the condition of parks, though, dogs would not escape notice. With the city's effort to clean up its parks, natural-areas supporters turned their attention to them as well. In 1997, the Recreation and Parks Department (RPD) established a citywide natural areas program for purposes of preserving and restoring ecological habitat within the city. Once such areas were identified, especially if they contained sensitive habitat areas, off-leash dogs and probably on-leash dogs would almost certainly be excluded from them. As it did at the GGNRA, the program, for all of its benefits, had the effect of reducing *recreational* space in a densely populated city.

Propelled by restrictions at the GGNRA, a change in environmental philosophy, gentrification, an increased attention to its own parks, and disputes at local parks between children's advocates and dog walkers, the city waded into the politics of leashing via calls for enforcement of its 1968 law. When it did so, dog walkers, not surprisingly, reacted with alarm. That old law provided them with virtually no acceptable place to exercise their dogs when they had been accustomed to free access to most city parks. The shift in policy from almost no enforcement to total enforcement, then, would represent a major loss to dog walkers. To be sure, the city promised to increase the number of dog-play areas (DPAs) and to improve the current ones, but with its track record, such a pledge was not really credible in the 1990s. Dog walkers imagined that they would be relegated to run-down areas in unpopular parks. Opponents of off-leash walking, of course, stood to gain from enforcement. As in other disputes, opponents had the advantage of simply being able to demand enforcement of a preexisting law, and dog walkers had to challenge the law itself. Cast in such dire terms of total or no enforcement, this debate was framed to be a bitter one.

## WHO IS IN CHARGE HERE?

Since 1856, San Francisco has had a combined or consolidated city-county government, the only such one in the state of California. As a result, city and county officials are one and the same, and their jurisdiction reaches beyond city limits, covering an area of forty-seven square miles with an approximate population of 740,000 in 2005.[11] While called a county, this is the area that outsiders equate with "San Francisco." The area terminates in the north, once one crosses the Golden Gate Bridge, and in the south, right after Candlestick Point State Recreation Area. There is almost a natural division between San Francisco and its southern boundary in the east in the form of San Bruno Mountain State Park. In addition to the downtown area close to the bay, the county includes the oceanfront and famed Cliff House and former Sutro Baths as well as the zoo near the southwest corner.

The city/county government itself is structured familiarly with the three branches of executive, legislative, and judiciary. Headed by an elected mayor, the executive branch includes appointed and elected officials as well as a sizable civil service. The legislature consists of an eleven-member Board of Supervisors, which presides over an independent branch that includes several offices, such as clerk, budget analyst, and others. This Board is charged with passing legislation. Once passed, legislation is sent to the mayor who has ten days to sign it. In the event of a mayoral veto, the Board can still pass the legislation via an override provided that eight of the eleven members vote to do so. Since this is California, citizens can also pass legislation using direct ballot initiatives.

Each supervisor represents a distinct geographic district, and a few have been sympathetic and helpful to dog walkers. Like the mayor, they are elected using instant runoff voting. If a candidate receives a majority (or 50 percent plus one) of the vote in this system, s/he wins the office. However, if no candidate captures a majority of the vote, the voters' second and possibly third preferences are automatically invoked to simulate an actual runoff vote and elect a winner. For example, if a voter's top candidate had been eliminated, his/her second or possibly third preference would then count for the remaining candidates. The goal of such a system is to ensure at least majoritarian support for elected officials and avoid an outcome in which a candidate is elected with, say, 30 percent of the vote when that candidate is the last choice of the remaining 70 percent, which split its vote among other candidates. San Francisco was the first major city in the country to adopt this electoral system in 2002, a fact that demonstrates the city's commitment to fair democratic processes.

There have been forty-two mayors of San Francisco, including Willie Brown—who served during the formulation of the new dog policy, from January 1996 until January 2004—and his successor, Gavin Newsom—who took office in January 2004 and is still serving as of 2010. Because Brown hired Elizabeth Goldstein as the general manager of the Recreation and Parks Department (RPD), he was not quite the darling of dog walkers. Goldstein, for her part, was responsible for the development and presentation of the new dog policy, which dog walkers, we will see, considered anathema. Newsom, in contrast, had the support of DogPac, the financial-giving arm of some dog-walking groups, in his bid for his seat on the Board of Supervisors in 2002. Given that Newsom had once said that "dog rights" will eclipse all other issues to become "the single most important issue in San Francisco," it is no surprise that he won the support of dog walkers. At the meeting on January 23, 2001 about the discontinuation of off-leash recreation at the GGNRA, Newsom additionally made a passionate appeal on behalf of dog walkers.[12] It is fair to say, then, that he is a better friend to dog walkers than his predecessor.

Supervisor Leland Yee, though, is perhaps an even dearer friend. Yee proposed an ordinance to overrule the new dog policy, with the goal of expanding off-leash opportunities. Other supervisors, such as Bevan Dufty, have inserted themselves into this issue in an effort to strike compromises among competing users at local parks. Given the number of dog walkers and the popularity of off-leash walking, elected supervisors simply cannot ignore the issue or deem the activity illegitimate. With that said, there are those, such as Yee, who champion the dog walkers' cause, and others who tepidly admit the popularity of the activity.

It is the mayor who presides over the administration of the Recreation and Parks Commission. Consisting of seven members, all of whom are appointed by the mayor to four-year terms, this Commission governs the ever-important—to leashing issues, at least—RPD. Indeed, it is the policymaking body for the RPD. According to the City Charter, Commissions, including this one, are to "formulate, evaluate and approve goals, objectives, plans and programs and set policies consistent with the overall objectives of the City and County, as established by the Mayor and Board of Supervisors through the adoption of City legislation."[13] All new policies and any changes to existing ones, in other words, must be consistent with the Charter and ordinances. Before any such changes can be made, public hearings must be held, and such hearings must be publicly noticed at least ten days in advance. While closed sessions of the Commission's meetings are allowed in some instances, the rule is for its business to be open to the public. The Charter specifically states that the Commission should encourage the participation of all interested parties. Records, including voting ones, are to be available to the public as well. For a new policy to pass, a majority of the Commission's members, in this case four, must vote to approve it.

Pursuant to the policies set by the Commission and under the direction of its general manager, the RPD manages and directs all of the city parks, including Golden Gate. It is the enforcement agency and therefore includes park rangers or "police." If tickets were to be issued to errant dog walkers, this would be the agency to issue them, though city police could do so as well. Whether formulated internally or by a task force, any plan or proposal of the RPD must win the approval of the Recreation and Parks Commission. Such policies must be consistent with legislation. Indeed, legislation or an ordinance, passed by the Board of Supervisors and approved by the mayor or via direct initiative, could trump, overrule, or change any Commission policy. Further still, the Board of Supervisors and the mayor must pass a budget that allocates money to enforcement agencies. The agency itself, such as RPD, then must decide which policies require the most attention and enforcement. With respect to the leash law, of course, the issue of enforcement has been almost as important as the substance of legislation itself.

The city's Animal Care and Control (ACC) bears some responsibility for the enforcement of leash laws as well. However, that agency's mission highlights its responsibility for "stray, injured, abandoned, neglected and mistreated animals."[14] In a city as populated as San Francisco, that task alone would consume a good deal of the agency's resources. This agency reports to the director of general services or the city administrator, who is appointed by the mayor to a five-year term. Additionally, the San Francisco Board of Supervisors oversees a separate Animal Control and Welfare Commission. This advisory Commission can hold hearings, study a matter, and make recommendations to the Board of Supervisors. It does not have legislative or regulatory power. Comprised of seven voting members, who are appointed by the Rules Committee and approved by the mayor for two-year terms, and four non-voting members, the Commission addresses any issues of "animal abuse, cruelty, nuisance or any conditions that may directly or indirectly affect animals."[15] While the RPD has been by far the more significant player in leashing issues, these two entities have had some involvement at times.

## POLICY FORMATION

Supervisor Amos Brown officially activated the "western front" when in February 1998, he "vowed to crack down on those who openly defy the city's leash laws" and called for a hearing on this issue before his new Parks and Recreation Committee.[16] Prior to this time, the Animal Control and Welfare Commission had been trying to resolve the leashing issue but had not been successful. To develop a comprehensive plan, Brown formed a fourteen-member task force that included dog owners, child advocates, and city officials. Brown was clear that his priority was to enforce the current leash law so as to protect families and children, though in creating this Advisory Dogs Off-Leash Task Force, he acknowledged the need for an assessment of off-leash areas that could potentially increase their numbers. Nonetheless, Brown charged this Task Force to operate from the assumption that all park areas would have enforced leash laws with only select areas to allow off-leash walking. Dog walkers, who could run their dogs at several parks, thus stood to lose tremendously from this assumption.

After a six-month study of the issue, the Task Force recommended increasing the number of off-leash areas from eighteen to thirty-seven in April 1999. Not surprisingly, there was controversy over the specific recommendations and omitted sites, most notably Grattan Park, which was a popular dog-walking area. Over one hundred people, mostly dog walkers, attended the Task Force's meeting, with the hope of persuading the members to increase the number of off-leash sites. While they were unsuccessful in that quest, children's advocates were unhappy as well with some of the sites included on the list, such as Sunnyside Park. In their view, the Task Force was biased toward dog owners.[17]

Despite the Task Force's unanimous approval of the recommendations, the city attorney declared the new rules invalid. The Task Force had failed to take public commentary on the proposed additions to off-leash areas, as was required by law. As a result of that and other factors, these recommendations never became law. However, they were forwarded to the RPD, which ultimately used them as the starting point for its own proposed policy. It was not until June 2001, approximately two years after the Task Force's proposal, that RPD first recommended a general policy at a press conference.

Undoubtedly, the brand new leashing requirements at the GGNRA, together with the fatal mauling of Diane Whipple earlier that year, motivated the RPD to take action on this issue. What is more, the RPD had been unable to resolve leashing disputes at individual parks and thus had an institutional incentive to provide a comprehensive framework to deal with such controversies. While those reasons are valid, dog walkers correctly perceived their activity as under attack at *both* the GGNRA and city parks. They also well understood that the underlying framework of the city's new policy was that of Amos Brown's Task Force and therefore, not one friendly to their interests.

General Manager Elizabeth Goldstein asserted that the RPD worked on the draft policy for a "long time," studying policies of other urban areas and hearing input from "various institutional stakeholders."[18] According to the *San Francisco Chronicle*, park officials placed "park advocates and dog lovers in two separate rooms and asked for their suggestions."[19] The draft policy was presented on June 12, 2001, and the public then had approximately five weeks to comment upon the proposal. The public response was overwhelming, with over 2,700 comments submitted. While General Manager Goldstein represented that a team of eight people read and discussed each and every comment, no formal analysis of the commentary was completed. In response to the commentary, the RPD discussed and somewhat revised the policy with stakeholder groups in the fall of 2001. After those discussions, a final draft was publicized on February 25, 2002 and presented to the Recreation and Parks Commission at a special public meeting on May 8, 2002.

As we will see, dog walkers roundly denounced the policy. In their view, it grievously harmed their interests. While the RPD claimed that the policy was a compromise, only opponents of off-leash walking considered that to be true. Indeed, dog walkers held the city's first "Critical Mutt Rally" in protest of this policy on August 3, 2001. Over five hundred persons, some with dogs who were dressed in "necklaces, T-shirts and reindeer antlers," descended upon City Hall to oppose this policy, which they labeled a "Dog Pen" one.[20]

## THE POLICY

The proposed dog policy was based largely on the assumption that dog-play areas (DPAs) or off-leash areas had to be separated from all other park activities. While fencing was not necessarily required, some physical boundary was mandated to delineate these off-leash areas clearly. When not in these "designated exercise areas," all dogs were to be "leashed or tethered."[21] The RPD promised enforcement of this policy as well. From the perspective of dog walkers, this policy would end the time-honored ritual of walking one's dog in open space. City officials, in contrast, stressed the increase in off-leash areas, alternatives to fencing, and the trend of confining off-leash activity to "dog parks," translated in this case to DPAs.

The policy classified city parks into three groupings based on their size. For parks over thirty-five acres in size, "soft barriers," such as "language posts or field markers," could define the DPA. However, "hard barriers," such as fencing, would be required in these parks if the DPA was adjacent to an area with a conflicting use or a "sensitive habitat area."[22] According to this policy, sensitive habitat areas, which constituted approximately 125 acres of those natural areas available for recreational use, were those that supported locally important, rare, threatened, or endangered species. The identification of sensitive habitat and natural areas was not settled when this policy was proposed and continues to be an issue in San Francisco politics. Because dogs were to be excluded from sensitive habitat areas completely, this unknown variable made the policy all the more ominous for dog walkers. Depending upon the placement of these areas, space for dogs could shrink at large parks or such space could be fenced. Additionally, even at these large parks, the policy stipulated that "all park users must be able to access the facility without encountering off-leash dogs."[23] Still, the most desirable DPAs were in these large parks, as they were the most likely to blend with other uses and appear less segregated than those in smaller parks. Excluding a golf course and a zoo, the city has ten parks over thirty-five acres in size. Among these are McLaren Park, Lake Merced, and Golden Gate.

In the second classification were large parks, those between ten and thirty-five acres in size. Nineteen parks, including Bernal Heights, Corona Heights, Douglass, and Dolores, fit this category. For these parks, the policy notes that "unfenced DPAs are possible as long as paths, boundaries, signs, topographic features, landscaping and/or other use separation features can reasonably define areas." Once again, hard barriers, such as fencing, would be required if adjacent to a sensitive habitat area or playground. The policy stipulates a minimum size of thirty thousand square feet, which is equivalent to "approximately four tennis courts," for DPAs in these parks.[24]

Finally, and most controversially, were the hundreds of neighborhood parks that are under ten acres in size. For these parks, DPAs had to be physically enclosed and could be as small as ten thousand square feet (approximately 1.4 tennis courts per the policy). Dog walkers considered these "runs" most undesirable. Given the city's history with upkeep of these areas or, more accurately, lack thereof, dog walkers feared the worst: run-down, out-of-the-way ghettos.

While the RPD stressed the possibility of non-fencing alternatives especially at parks larger than ten acres, the policy itself emphasized the need for barriers. The policy represented a major shift from multiuse parks, where dog walkers blended with others, to dog parks, fenced or separated. It further encouraged the RPD to partner with private groups to "share the responsibility for maintaining and monitoring DPAs."[25] On this score, the policy rightly vested responsibility for the monitoring of compliance with a government agency, the RPD, and did not formally expect ordinary citizens to perform that function. Private partners had mainly a stewardship role, though they could engage in fundraising to supplement city monies.

Additionally, the policy established a Dog Advisory Committee (DAC), which would be comprised of eleven members. While three of those members would speak for governmental agencies, the other eight would represent "the DPA community, children's groups, environmental groups, [and] other park users."[26] This advisory committee was tasked with several varied responsibilities, including the organization of educational events (e.g., obedience classes), the identification of partnership opportunities for DPAs, and the promotion of community relations. Perhaps more importantly, the Committee was to assist in the review of DPAs, establish a formal complaint and evaluative instrument for them, and act as a liaison among users, local residents, and citizen associations. It would also make recommendations about new DPAs. Needless to say, this Committee, which was staffed with natural adversaries and was to meet bi-monthly, had a challenging agenda.

The policy created procedures for the proposal and creation of new DPAs, which, we will later see, involved several layers of approval. This turn from lackadaisical enforcement to bureaucracy and formality signaled a transformation in park-use philosophy, and it elicited frustration and indignation from dog walkers. On its own terms, the segregation of off-leash dog areas, the policy was not unreasonable. It was those terms themselves and the monumental shift that they represented that upset dog walkers.

To be sure, this policy had been slightly adjusted in response to commentary and negotiations. Most significantly, the "Gold Bone Program," in the original draft, was now excluded. That program would have granted dogs who had received training and certification in voice control greater off-leash privileges. In other words, if a dog truly was under voice control, s/he could be off-leash outside the DPAs. Citing concerns about accessibility to such training and the creation of a double standard, dog walkers objected to this program. Pro-leash advocates voiced skepticism about it as well, fearing both that certified dogs would not always respond to their people and that non-certified dogs would be more likely to stay off-leash if there were such exceptions. Otherwise, language was changed to accommodate concerns on both sides, but the essence of the policy remained consistent from its initial formulation to its completion. In fact, the lack of substantive change despite overwhelming objections to the first draft angered dog walkers. SFDog and other off-leash advocates worked diligently to offer alternative solutions aimed at accommodating both dog walkers and those who wanted to avoid dogs. For example, they suggested timed-use, or certain off-leash hours, at smaller parks instead of enclosed runs, which very few seemed to want. The final policy charged the DAC with studying this matter further, but codified the barrier rules for all parks.

## THE RESPONSE

Because the Recreation and Parks Commission had received over 2,700 public comments on this issue, it held its special meeting to hear oral comments and vote on the policy at City Hall. The Commission typically meets in a building that can accommodate only sixty people. On this night, according to the *San Francisco Chronicle*, "nearly 1,000 people filled the chambers and an additional over-flow auditorium downstairs which was equipped with a large screen broadcasting the meeting. They appeared to be about 3-to-1 in favor of looser regulations for dogs."[27] That ratio, at least, accurately depicted those who had the opportunity to speak publicly at the meeting. Of the 153 speakers from the general public, 103 were opposed to the dog policy, 35 were in favor, and the remaining 15 did not articulate a clear position on the matter. However, public comment was closed out of the necessity of time before all who wanted could speak. Even with the cutoff, the meeting lasted over five hours.

Significantly, all those who spoke against the policy were off-leash advocates, either dog walkers or people who favored off-leash recreation. This group did not consider the policy to be a compromise, but a total loss. In contrast, virtually all those who spoke in favor of the policy wanted to limit off-leash recreation or spoke for other interests, such as the environment or children's playgrounds. These advocates depicted the policy as a compromise. When the policy passed, these advocates were "pleased with the decision." On the other hand, "most audience members" or off-leash advocates "left unhappy."[28] When sides are drawn so clearly, with all of one side denouncing a policy and all of the other supporting it, a "compromise" has not been reached. By definition, a compromise should split advocates into purists and pragmatists on both sides of an issue. Few should be left totally unsatisfied, as off-leash advocates were in this case.

Why did dog walkers object to this plan? Based on the verbal commentary at the meeting, off-leash advocates objected vociferously to the lack of fairness in the decision-making process. At least twenty-five people cited procedural problems in their objections to the policy. Not surprisingly, off-leash advocates cited the obvious fact that they outnumbered their opponents at all public meetings and in commentary. For example, a commenter named Mr. Swan observed, "you don't need to be a weatherman to tell which way the wind blows here. . . . if you put [the cards of people seeking the floor which note their positions] in stacks, it'd be the same results as I've seen in countless of these meetings that I've attended, cause it's about one for the policy, six against. You just need to do the numbers." On this point, commenter Mr. McAllister also took the Sierra Club and Audubon Society to task for claiming the support of their general membership numbers, some of whom might very well oppose this policy. He explained that "There are many environmentalists in both these clubs who support off-leash recreation" and cited a letter in support of off-leash recreation at the GGNRA that had the signatures of forty-seven local Sierra Club members.[29]

Beyond the numbers, off-leash advocates criticized the RPD's lack of adherence to the spirit of the law, which requires public commentary. That commentary is supposed to be considered and possibly reflected in the final policy. According to one commentator, Mr. Cockrell, the policy "does not take into consideration the overwhelming public comment against . . . [it], the largest public comment in RPD history, much of which was never read or analyzed." Another commentator, Ms. Arnold, noted that the vast majority of comments at the August 7, 2001 Board of Supervisor's Recreation and Parks Committee meeting were against the policy. Then, she claimed, "I did not hear any compelling reason to ignore those comments but that is essentially what has been done." This complaint was a refrain in the commentary, with another observing that "input that is ignored is not really communication," and yet another simply concluding, "we still haven't been heard."[30] Off-leash advocates seemed to surmise that the RPD went through the legal motions so as to pass its original proposal with only minor modifications.

As they were with the NPS, off-leash advocates were frustrated with the lack of evidence upon which the city based such a dramatic change in policy. For example, a commenter named Mr. Daley exclaimed, "if you haven't made a survey of how a park is used, I don't know how you can formulate a policy to exclude dogs from such a park." Further building upon this argument, commenter Ms. McKay not only highlighted the RPD's lack of objective data to support the existence of a problem with dogs at parks, but additionally cited evidence to the contrary of such a claim. She noted, "In 1997 the San Francisco Partnerships for Parks interviewed people at Golden Gate Park, over three hundred people, sixty one percent of them said they did not feel safe in the park at all times. . . . Not one of them named a dog as a reason for feeling unsafe."[31] Instead of relying upon data and analysis, the RPD, in the view of off-leash advocates, exaggerated the controversy and used dogs as a convenient scapegoat for problems attributable to humans and the poor maintenance of parks.

Dog groups had no ownership of this policy since they were not present during its formulation. As commenter Mr. Day explained, "I am opposed to this policy primarily because it was not drafted by dog groups, it was drafted by anti-dog groups. It's rather like having a playground policy created by anti-child groups. I feel that there could be a policy drafted that would be successful but there won't be success with this policy because we were excluded." What was worse, observed Mr. McAllister further, "its implementation is put in the hands of an advisory committee that could be composed entirely of organizations that are opposed to all forms of off-leash recreation outside of pens with 'impenetrable barriers' in their words."[32] Whatever the claims or perceptions of the RPD, dog walkers did not consider themselves fully included or even acknowledged in this process.

The number one objection to the proposal on substantive grounds was the loss of a multiuse park, replaced with an undesirable, segregated "pen" for off-leash exercise. At times, off-leash advocates referred to the policy as the "dog pen policy." One commented that "The keystone of it seems to be dog pens and enforcement." Another cautioned, "these pens are smelly and dangerous to children and the elderly. Please don't put up pens." More than anything, this certainty at small parks and possibility at others defined the plan for dog walkers. It spelled their expulsion from a broader community almost in a punitive way, as they were defined as threatening and in need of confinement. Several commentators expressed dismay at this segregation from other users and the loss that would entail. For example, commenter Ms. Sire stated, "I would like to affirm the sense of community that comes from our park, McLaren Park, when there are dog walkers, elderly tai chi exercisers, and other people enjoying the morning." Another commented, "I urge you to visit Dolores Park to see that multiuse is possible. . . . The dog policy would separate and promote intolerance and miscommunication. . . . It is important to keep people together." The policy threatened the social bonds among dog walkers as well. As commenter Ms. Patterson put it, "the dog scene in the dog community is beautiful."[33] This policy would disrupt that scene.

Even on its own terms, this policy shortchanged dog walkers. Given the numbers of people who partake in this activity, the allotment of space itself was sparse. Several commenters noted that dog walkers are primary and legitimate users of parks, and it followed that they were entitled to a greater share of space if there was to be this unwanted segregation. For example, a commenter named Ms. Franklin highlighted that "We have approximately 125,000 families with dogs in the city and it is not fair and equitable treatment to give us less than 1% of the City's Parkland, especially when there are 555 acres of golf courses, 100 acres of archery ranges and all the sports fields." Providing evidence to substantiate this disparity in treatment, commenter Ms. McKay reported, "In 1998, RPD did a survey and in their own words they were impressed and almost overwhelmed by the response of the dog owners. When the strategic plan was published based on the survey there was no mention of us as a recreational user in the park. We were completely whitewashed out."[34] In Orwellian terms, even if this is the "western front," dog walkers were not as equal as other park users.[35]

In their statements against the policy, dog walkers made several other points. The reduction in areas for off-leash exercise would require people to travel greater distances, which, in turn, could reduce or eliminate access for disabled individuals and those without automobiles. Car owners would have to drive greater distances and thereby have a negative impact on the environment. Several commenters noted the pleasure that humans experience from watching off-leash dogs play and the resultant reduction in stress for those humans. As a commenter named Ms. Inderdohnen pleaded, "Many people with or without dogs come to the Park only to watch dogs play together. It is a remarkable sight and certainly a stress reliever. Please do not take away the pleasure of watching dogs running free that gives both pleasure to dogs and observers." Others explained that the exercise needs of dogs would not be met under this policy. More commonly, though, several—at least seventeen—emphasized dog walkers' beneficial impact on safety at parks. With this policy, they argued, parks would become less safe. As commenter Mr. Looman maintained, "The plan will significantly diminish the recreational opportunities for the largest single group of Park users and by de-populating the non-dog parks it will enlarge opportunities for drug dealing and other crimes." A non-dog owner and jogger, who was opposed to this policy, added, "I like to jog in parks where I feel safe. I feel safest in parks where there are other people. I am afraid that if dogs are required to be on leash less [sic] people will go to the Parks to walk their dogs."[36] For all of these reasons and others, virtually all dog walkers who commented objected to this policy.

Interestingly, advocates of the policy most frequently cited environmental reasons in their verbal comments. Sixteen commentators cited such reasons, while only seven expressed concerns about children's interests. That fact provides some indication that the issues and divisions at the GGNRA were playing out at the city level as well. At city neighborhood parks, one would typically expect more noise from children's advocates than environmental ones. Representatives of the California Native Plant Society and the Golden Gate Audubon Society endorsed the policy, as did others who specifically cited environmental concerns. For example, commenter Ms. Gravinos explained, "We also need to consider the needs for other park users and . . . one very important group of park users, the non-humans and it is essential that we have a process that takes into account the needs of wildlife of all different kinds." Another commenter said simply, "I support the dog policy and I especially support the preservation of natural areas in parks."[37]

Additionally, proponents made substantive arguments about the positive impact on children's interests and public safety generally. For instance, a commenter named Mr. Murphy complained that "The present situation is intolerable. . . . aggressive, barking, snarling dogs with owners far in the distance are not what I go to the park for. They are a constant threat to anyone who uses our Parks." This policy, in his view, would improve matters. Expressing concerns for children's interests, commenter Ms. Elmansoumi reported, "I'm disheartened when I hear the children tell me they don't like a park because there are too many dogs. . . . In addition it is very difficult to find a place in parks where the kids can sit and have their snack because of the smell from dogs." Marybeth Wallace, a representative from Coleman Advocates for Children and Youth, went on record as a supporter of this policy as well.[38]

Several proponents, at least ten of the thirty-five who spoke, responded to dog walkers' complaints about the process. In their view, there was sufficient deliberation and a fair compromise. As Wallace argued, "This has been an open policy from the beginning, anti-leash activists have participated every step of the way." Indeed, according to proponents, the concerns of dog walkers were reflected in the final policy. As commenter Ms. Darrah explained, there has been "a long and difficult process of developing a policy that serves the off-leash community as well as protecting other park users. . . . Many concessions have also been made on matters of grass turf, no fences, and no user fees. . . . The policy remains a . . . fair compromise." Others noted that this policy would provide a necessary framework within which to resolve heated disputes over local park use. Overwhelmingly, the proponents considered the policy to be a compromise.

In recognition of their smaller numbers at this meeting and others before it, proponents invoked the notion of a silent majority. One commenter explained, "This has been over a three-year process, with unfortunately the loudest voices heard by dog owners. . . . It's really important for you to understand too that my friends are at home with their children and they would very much like to be here." Another commenter, more bluntly, petitioned, "I hope you hear what most of the people who are not here tonight are saying."[39] In the view of proponents, the majority of citizens supported their position. In this case, however, there was no polling or other data to support that or the opposite position.

The majority of speakers on both sides refrained from attacking their opponents. Of course, there are always a few given the nature of this controversy. Just two proponents directly insulted dog owners. One of those sarcastically asked, "Are dog owners a class of citizens who have suffered discrimination due to race, gender or are they part of an economically disadvantaged group thus deserving of special treatment in San Francisco, no . . ." A few other commenters invoked the "parks for people" argument, which, of course, denies the interests of the humans with dogs, and another commenter set a completely unrealistic bar for dog ownership in a city. The latter individual noted that "As a guardian of my three dogs I purchased a home with a front yard, back yard and a driveway . . . before I became a dog owner, I think that is part of being a responsible dog owner."[40] That financial prerequisite would prevent most city dwellers from obtaining the benefits of canine companionship. These voices, though, were in the minority among proponents, as most did not attack or insult dog owners.

On the other side, just one person insulted the proponents of the policy. That individual argued "that the people who are most in favor of fencing the dogs off actually constitute the special needs group here. . . . Why don't we fence off the areas . . . that they want?"[41] However, the *San Francisco Chronicle* described the meeting as boisterous. Specifically, the article stated, "People cheered and boo'ed so vociferously after each speaker, the commission's President, John Murray, had to repeatedly warn them to quiet down."[42] The crowd was overwhelmingly opposed to the policy and in favor of off-leash recreation.

Not captured on the record are the off-handed remarks that both proponents and opponents of the policy made to one another. Given the intensity of this issue, it is not surprising that each group would have insulting nicknames for one another, such as "plant Nazis," to describe some proponents, or "fringe lunatics," to describe opponents. There is also some resentment among on-leash proponents about the prominence of this issue. They do not understand why people care so passionately about it and sometimes conclude that dog walkers "don't have lives."[43] For their part, dog walkers occasionally equate the most stringent anti-dog zealots with all pro-leash advocates, some of whom have legitimate concerns and are willing to compromise. The casting of this issue into such dire terms arguably exacerbated this "us-versus-them" attitude and the vitriol on both sides.

## THE DECISION

After the public comment, the Commissioners discussed the policy, amended it, and unanimously approved it. For dog walkers, the framing of the decision was highly problematic. On the one hand, as Commissioner Newhouse Segal highlighted, "the alternative would be . . . strict enforcement of the dog policy as it stands now. Which would be a lot less than what is being proposed tonight in terms of additional areas for recreation with dogs." The default, then, was not the status quo, but enforcement of the city's leash law. Yet in reality, Commissioner Murray acknowledged that "We've in effect had no rules in our parks for 10 years with regard to how dogs live in them." Similarly, Commissioner Chin highlighted, "as it is right now we have de facto dog play areas all over the City. All day 24/7." "Right the entirety of every park," Commissioner Murray agreed.[44] The current alternatives did not include this status quo, but the new policy or enforcement of the old, draconian law. The unwillingness to work from the de facto blueprint of leash-less freedom rather than the de jure requirement of leashing everywhere disadvantaged and frustrated dog walkers. They literally could not win this debate.

With that said, the Commissioners clearly acknowledged the legitimacy of off-leash walking as a form of recreational park use. Commissioner Chin, who was the strongest in his support for this interest, noted the need for more space for off-leash dogs, "both in number and in terms of acreage." Additionally, he suggested "greater flexibility in terms of the criteria enabling a particular neighborhood to look at hours and timed use alternative." That idea of timed-use, instead of pens, was much more appealing to dog walkers. While Commissioner Chin attempted to amend the policy to allow for this option, Commissioner Murray and General Manager Goldstein persuaded him and the others to settle for a study of the timed-use alternative. In the approved policy, following amendment, the DAC was to "prepare and deliver a report to the Recreation and Park Commission no later than October 2002 on timed use."[45]

Somewhat shockingly, General Manager Goldstein did not have the most confident answer to concerns about enforcement. When the issue was broached, Goldstein responded, "Well, we have worked with Animal Care and Control, and the Police Department in advance of this meeting . . . to talk about ways that we could work together to do enforcement."[46] Given the structure of city government, this is not an easy issue. Yet enforcement was missing in the old policy and the underlying assumption of this one. If that was not certain, one wonders why so many people, on both sides of this issue, were put through this grueling process. The RPD presumably reasoned that once a workable policy was in place, enforcement could follow later as the budget permitted.

## THE AFTERMATH

Pursuant to the dog policy, the newly formed DAC met for the first time on September 5, 2002 and included representatives from the San Francisco Police Department, San Francisco Department of the Environment, ACC, Golden Gate Audubon Society, California Native Plant Society, Environmental Quality for Urban Parks (EQUP), SFDog, San Francisco SPCA, PAWS, Coleman Advocates for Children and Youth, and the San Francisco Veterinarian Medical Association. In one of the early meetings, on July 22, 2003, the representative from SFDog inquired about the qualifications of organizations on the Committee, especially EQUP. At that point, the representatives from EQUP and Golden Gate Audubon Society left the meeting, causing the Committee to lose its quorum and cease its business. Other than that incident and the occasional public complaint about the Committee's composition, the minutes, which are spotty at times, do not report much discussion about the propriety of the Committee itself. Instead, the Committee seems to conduct its business.

Foremost on its agenda was the approval of proposed DPAs. When a group requests a DPA or a modification to one, the RPD has sixty days to evaluate the request and make a recommendation to the DAC. There must be public notification and an opportunity, usually in the form of a community meeting, for the public to comment. The contentious debates, for the most part, play out at these community meetings. The RPD reports back to the DAC about the sentiments of people at these community meetings. At times, a few options, with varying levels of support, might be presented to the DAC, which, in turn, can approve one or none. If the DAC approves a new DPA, City Planning next reviews the proposal. Then, it is "presented to the Parks and Planning Committee of the Recreation and Park Commission and then onto the full Commission for final determination."[47]

Despite the layers of bureaucracy, communities were able to reach agreement and gain final approval for several DPAs. In some cases, the process proceeded rather quickly. For example, DPAs were soon established at Jefferson Square (though not the option preferred by dog walkers), Crocker Amazon, Douglass, and Upper Noe Parks. Others were much more controversial and involved a long negotiating process. Duboce would be a case in point. About Duboce, San Francisco reporter Lelchuk wrote, "After dozens of heated community meetings and at least two rejected plans for a dog area, Supervisor Bevan Dufty . . . stepped in to mediate at Duboce. The result was another plan that will be reviewed by the City's Dog Advisory Committee."[48] Ultimately, a compromise was reached on Duboce and approved by the DAC on December 13, 2005 and the full Commission in January 2006. About the final approval, a reporter commented, "In the expansive volume that could be the history of dog relations in San Francisco, at least a few officials would like advocates to take a look at the chapter that is Duboce Park. At Thursday's Recreation and Park Commission meeting, a measure sectioning Duboce Park into three usage areas—no dogs, dogs on leash and dogs off-leash—sailed to approval with barely a peep of opposition."[49]

Clearly, this system functioned with some level of success. By 2005, there were twenty-six approved DPAs, an increase of seven from the original nineteen when the policy was approved.[50] What is more, the DAC met fairly regularly from April 2003 until February 2006. After that, it met sporadically and agreed to sunset itself in February 2007. At these meetings, public commentary, limited though it was, hinted at some problems with this system. Enforcement remained a problem, which concerned on-leash advocates, while dog walkers inquired about timed-use and more trail DPAs.

Recall that the pre-dog policy days had such lax enforcement of leash laws that it was as though they did not exist. This policy promised more and better off-leash areas and enforcement in on-leash areas. That is not what happened. On March 8, 2005, almost three years after the policy passed, Dan

McKenna, representing the RPD, presented to the DAC a proposed enforcement program. About existing conditions, the program stated, "Many parks with or without DPAs are experiencing a lack of compliance with existing leash laws." A "partial list" of parks with such problems included thirteen sites. Available city personnel to enforce the leash law included four *part-time* RPD park patrol officers and perhaps staff from ACC and the San Francisco Police Department, which, the report indicated, did not consider enforcement of the leash law its "highest priority."[51] The ACC had more dismal levels of funding than RPD. With only nine deputy animal control officers citywide in July 2005, the ACC had to attend to many other functions. Representing that agency, Carl Friedman announced in October 2006 that "RPD rescinded funding from Animal Care and Control for Animal Control Officers to cite off leash violations, so enforcement of leash laws is not a departmental priority."[52] This fiscal reality frustrated supporters of the dog policy. It also implied that enforcement was dependent upon self-policing and education. Indeed, the enforcement policy relied heavily on those ingredients, though it also included plans to deploy resources strategically to "hot spots," expand ranger forces, and increase fines for noncompliance. Despite not winning the approval of the DAC, the RPD planned to bring this enforcement policy to the full Commission.[53] This whole exercise seemed somewhat futile, as an RPD representative acknowledged in November 2006 that the Department needed to rely on peer enforcement given its poor resources.[54]

For such an approach to be successful, dog walkers had to be invested in it. The original dog policy never had their consent. As a result, the RPD in 2005 called for "system-wide planning" to replace the DAC. Instead of relying upon communities to propose DPAs, which fewer were doing since there was little enforcement, the RPD would determine where de facto off-leash use was taking place, investigate if legalization in that area was possible, and identify conflicts and possible resolutions. Additionally, the RPD would consider the protection of natural areas, which had become an increasingly contentious issue in San Francisco. Ultimately, this systemic approach would replace the DAC, but the transition was slow. At the October 2006 meeting, Scott Reese of the RPD estimated an eight-month planning process.

Ironically, the RPD returned to the dog walkers' 2002 suggestion to consider timed-use. RPD staff, with the help of a subcommittee of the DAC, completed a report about the timed-use option in September 2006. Based on a review of current policies and a study of several recreation and park departments that currently have timed-use, the report concluded that it was a "viable management and park use option when the proper conditions for planning, design, management and enforcement are present."[55] The report identified seven rationales for a timed-use policy, including the needs to maximize the recreational use of available park space, to increase off-leash DPAs in some communities, to avoid conflict among different park users, and to reduce costs related to the construction of formal DPAs. Negative impacts, such as safety and health concerns, were also stipulated. The safety concern of dog bites were said to be "extremely infrequent in San Francisco." The report did not deem health concerns, which were related to the presence of dog feces, significant in the cities with a timed-use policy. However, these concerns were reflected in the report's emphasis on the need to return timed-use areas to their original state after dog exercise periods.

Additionally, the report stated criteria for the specific identification of possible timed-use areas and time allocations. Among these criteria were the size and density of the dog population, the size of the area, the area's proximity to significant natural areas, and the impact on children/community play spaces. A timed-use area, per the report, would have one to four sessions per day, which would be scheduled to avoid conflict with other uses. Perhaps to ensure consistency with the existing dog policy, the report recommended that bona fide community organizations obtain permits and thereby assume responsibility for the use of these areas. Such areas would be another tool for the RPD to invoke in the general management of park user needs. Ultimately, the RPD and the Commission would determine which parks would be eligible for timed-use. Importantly, the amended dog policy, in draft form, states that "Permanent fencing will not be required to define Time Use DPAs," and that is true even at small parks.[56] If this option is successful, dog walkers would be accorded a real concession and one that addresses their greatest concern, the relegation to "pens."

## GRADING THE CITY

### Policy Formation and Approval in 2002

It is difficult to fault the formal rules and decision-making structures in San Francisco, as they are open and democratic. Those rules require public notification of rules changes, opportunity for citizens to comment, and the inclusion of stakeholders. As we saw with the GGNRA, however, formal procedures cannot deliver a democratic outcome unless individuals with decision-making authority conform to the *spirit* of those procedures. There is a world of difference between the letter and spirit of law.

At the May 2002 special meeting of the Recreation and Parks Commission, dog walkers did not believe that they had been heard or that their concerns were taken seriously. There was clearly a great deal of frustration with General Manager Goldstein and the RPD's policy formulation. Proponents of the policy were satisfied with the procedures. That stark disagreement raises a red flag, as one side considered the policy unacceptable and therefore, had no investment in it. One side "won" and the other "lost," a casting that is usually not indicative of the most democratic result. A minimalist, concerned mainly with formal procedures, would approve of this process, while a participatory democrat, concerned with the actuality and use of the procedures, would disapprove.

The commissioners themselves heard public testimony on the policy and in their discussion, took the concerns of both sides seriously. Although it is understandable that the commissioners would give heavy weight to the RPD's recommended policy, the commissioners could be faulted for not taking a more proactive role in this case given the myriad objections, volume of commentary, and controversy. According to the Charter, the Commission is, after all, the policymaking body for the RPD. Especially in light of the complaints about the process of policy formulation itself, the Commission might have opted to delay its vote and insert itself more directly in that process. Instead the Commission basically deferred to the RPD's judgment on this matter. As an unelected, executive body, whose members are appointed by the mayor to four-year terms, the Commission is institutionally unlikely to be as responsive to public pressures, no matter how intense, as a legislative body. Add to that a close to zero probability of a Republican being competitive in a San Francisco mayoral contest and it is evident that the commissioners had little incentive to fear public opinion. With that said, the commissioners were not at all dismissive of dog walkers' concerns, and they ordered a study of timed-use, the preferred option of dog walkers.

The framing of this issue, as previously noted, worked against dog walkers. Because there was a leash law already on the books, the venue for policymaking was in the executive, not legislative, branch. By definition, that ensures a less democratic process. Further, the law, which had not been previously enforced, was extremely detrimental to dog walkers' interests. Casting that as the fallback position if the new policy did not pass, both the Commissioners and the RPD placed dog walkers in an almost impossible negotiating position.

Despite that, there was record-breaking participation on this issue. RPD received over 2,700 comments on the policy, and meetings were well attended. While a participatory democrat would applaud this engagement, he or she would additionally require that the input receive due consideration. RPD General Manager Goldstein represented that all public commentary had been read, however, there was no proof of that claim. No formal analysis of the commentary was performed, as it had been on the federal level. Nor was any polling done, which made any claims about majoritarian support unfounded. This omission arguably contributed to dog walkers' perceptions that their case had not been heard. To be sure, the RPD did not have the financial resources of the NPS, which was able to hire outside social scientists. However, the RPD could have completed and made public a rudimentary, in-house analysis of the commentary. Among dog walkers, there was, perhaps as a result of this omission and other factors, a poor opinion of the city's professionalism. The policy appeared to them as arbitrary and unnecessarily hostile to their interests.

At the meeting, most of the speakers on both sides of the issue did not insult their opponents. The forum and its format, however, were not constructed to facilitate deliberation. Speakers each had a very short time to state their positions and attempt to persuade the commissioners to pass or reject the policy. Ideally, the RPD would have facilitated deliberation among stakeholders prior to this meeting at which it was seeking the Commission's approval of what it considered a final policy. The stark division between dog walkers, who opposed the policy almost unanimously, and the other park users, who approved the policy almost unanimously, strongly hints that no such deliberation occurred before this meeting. This was certainly not a community-building event, as people left the meeting angrily. The policy, to state the obvious, was not the product of consensus politics, but rather conflict politics.

Given that San Francisco's government is a combined city/county one, geographic inclusiveness did not present a problem. Park users were not divided into taxpaying residents and outsiders. However, one commentator raised the issue of gender equity, noting that "Off leash recreation is one of the few outdoor activities in which women are the majority."[57] Others urged the Commission to consider the needs of the elderly, disabled, and those without automobiles, all of whom needed space to exercise their dogs within a fairly short distance from their residences. Yet because the policy did not specify the future locations for off-leash recreation, the commissioners could conclude that such concerns would be addressed adequately within the policy's framework. Importantly, proponents of the policy cited these same groups in their advocacy of leashing.

Freedoms of speech and association were alive and well in this controversy. Rallies were held, people on both sides attended meetings and spoke, and people wrote thousands of letters. Organized groups were active as well.

Once again, those groups seeking to limit off-leash walking had preexisting organizations dedicated to broader or alternative goals, such as birds, nature, or children. The dog walkers, who had recently organized groups to defend their interests at the GGNRA, now utilized those and other neighborhood groups to confront this new threat.

If the city was to be evaluated solely on the formation and approval of the policy itself, its participatory grade would nonetheless be poor. It easily could have opted for a more consensual approach that incorporated options more acceptable to the dog walkers. Cast in mutually exclusive terms, the issue produced winners and losers, with the latter possibly concluding that their participation did not matter and that the process was unfair. The city's involvement did not end with the passage of the policy, however, and it did redeem itself somewhat in the aftermath.

## Grading the City under the New Policy

Dog walkers feared that this policy would lead to "pens" and substantially reduce their access to parks. In contrast, the city promised that there need not be pens in many places and that the policy could work to everyone's benefit. What was the reality? How democratic was the framework that this policy created?

Unquestionably, the RPD could point to some success stories. There were indeed instances when, under this rubric, diverse interests, including dog walkers, came together and struck workable compromises. The DAC itself brought representatives of several groups together on a regular basis to evaluate DPA proposals and to address related issues. In short, the dog policy was not the nightmare envisioned by dog walkers, but neither was it what the RPD promised.

The dog walkers' nightmare was averted largely because enforcement remained lax. If the RPD had aggressively enforced this policy, it would have been extremely detrimental to the interests of dog walkers. There simply were not enough DPAs to accommodate the demand, but the RPD's tacit acceptance of some "de facto" DPAs and its loose enforcement kept the situation tolerable for dog walkers. Proponents of the policy, on the other hand, were disappointed and somewhat frustrated that the adoption of this policy did not signal the end of the status quo ante or lax enforcement. Interestingly, the RPD's lack of resources arguably pushed it to develop a policy more acceptable to dog walkers or grounded in compromise. Given the Department's need to rely on self-policing to some extent, it was essential that dog walkers have a stake in the success of the policy. With the possible adoption of timed-use, a suggestion originally touted by dog walkers, and a system-wide approach, the

RPD is now trying to make the policy more palatable to off-leash advocates. While this new approach is commendable, it is a bit difficult to applaud the RPD's change of heart, which seems to have resulted more from economic necessity than from any desire for inclusion and equity. Despite the motivation, the RPD is pushing for an amended dog policy that now includes the possibility of timed-use, and at this writing there has not been a punitive enforcement policy in areas that lack DPAs. The battles continue, but dog walkers are now at the table in city politics, even if they have to beg for scraps at times.

# Chapter VIII

## Conclusion

The case studies of Avon, the GGNRA, and the city of San Francisco should concern both participatory and minimalist democrats. The results should also alarm off-leash advocates, as it is clear that even in San Francisco, the one-time best city for dogs, their interests are not quite as equal as everyone else's. At the least, dog walkers in populated areas should be put on notice that they might find themselves on the defensive. However, the news is not all bad, as off-leash dog walkers have been able to claim significant accomplishments in the forms of dog parks and official recognition. From these success stories and importantly, from failures such as Avon, off-leash advocates as well as governmental officials can learn much.

### DEMOCRACY AT RISK

The resolutions of leashing conflicts in the three case studies ultimately send mixed signals about the health of democracy. On the criteria of civil liberties and equality, the signals were more encouraging than they were on the criterion of popular sovereignty. Because popular sovereignty is the defining feature of democracy, this might be a bit like saying a team was outstanding in practice, just not so good in games. Perhaps these results are not too surprising given the American priority on individual rights and the Constitutional bulwarks against "majority tyranny." Even though the Founding Fathers were not exactly enamored with democracy, one would still expect better in the late twentieth and early twenty-first centuries, especially at the local level where citizens allegedly should have their greatest influence on matters that obviously concern them.

## Liberty

While there were indeed minor concerns about liberty, such as the federal infiltration of a dog discussion list, the formation and use of associations on both sides of this debate attest to liberty's health. Free speech was evident at public meetings where advocates of leash laws would make their case, in some instances even insulting dog walkers, despite being vastly outnumbered. Rallies in support of off-leash recreation became commonplace in San Francisco as well. A minimalist would therefore offer a high democratic grade on this count. While participatory democrats would be pleased with these signs as well, they would lament the lack of restraint in the use of governmental authority in Avon and also in the NPS's 2001 decision to end all off-leash recreation at the GGNRA. The NPS would surely be cited in violation of this maxim given that a federal court ultimately ruled this decision to be illegal. When consensus or compromise cannot be reached, participatory democrats prefer that the governing bodies tread lightly with their power. Obviously, that was not the case in Avon and the GGNRA.

## Equality

Minimalists would award satisfactory grades for the criterion of equality with some caveats, while participatory democrats would again be more critical. In San Francisco, the NPS and the city's Recreation and Parks Department went to much effort to ensure all stakeholders a seat at the proverbial table. Both minimalists and participatory democrats would applaud those efforts. While the Avon Town Council excluded out-of-towners with its decision to call for a referendum, it was legally entitled to do so. All citizens of Avon had the opportunity to vote and on this criterion of equality at least, that fact would satisfy a minimalist. Participatory democrats would be more inclined to recommend the inclusion of all stakeholders in such an important decision.

A greater threat to this criterion was the partisanship or advocacy of both the Avon Town Council and the NPS. Neither governmental body was perceived as anything close to a neutral arbiter among interest groups, as both treated the interests of dog walkers as either completely illegitimate, in the case of Avon, or not quite as equal as other ones, in the case of the NPS. The city, in acknowledging the need for an increase in off-leash areas, recognized the legitimacy of the dog walkers' interests, even if its relations with them were not the best. The formation of the Dog Advisory Committee and the city's involvement in local disputes, such as the one at Duboce, attest to its willingness to view this interest as legitimate. Both minimalist and participatory democrats would applaud such engagement with all interests. On the other hand, even a minimalist would object to the lack of neutrality in the other two cases. Overall, the "score" on the criterion of equality would fall short of the one on liberty but not be quite as wanting as the rating for popular sovereignty.

## Popular Sovereignty

Indeed, the greatest violations of democratic theory were by far in the area of popular sovereignty. Even the minimalist's desire for competitive elections was not met in Republican-dominated Avon, Democratic-dominated San Francisco, or the unelected NPS. The failure of Avon and the NPS to substitute the competition of interest group politics and instead to advocate against the interests of dog walkers would doubly condemn those two cases on this criterion. If Avon and the NPS failed to meet a minimalist's standards for popular sovereignty, they certainly failed to satisfy the more demanding standards of a participatory democrat.

To be sure, participatory democrats would be pleased with the extraordinary levels of participation in Avon and San Francisco, including well-attended meetings, letter writing campaigns, public speaking, and voting. Yet in the cases of Avon, the NPS, and even the special meeting in San Francisco to approve the dog policy in 2002, the decision-making structure did not foster deliberation. Because the Avon Town Council and the NPS made decisions that significantly advantaged opponents of off-leash walking prior to any democratic process, such opponents had no incentive to compromise or engage the other side in a deliberative discussion. The format of public meetings, and indeed lack of space in the case of the NPS, did not exactly encourage discussion either. San Francisco did slightly better on the matter of deliberation, as there was at least one member of the Recreation and Parks Commission who heard the concerns of off-leash advocates and responded with a meaningful concession, though it did not pass. The differential is only slight, however, as dog walkers were extremely frustrated with the lack of deliberation in the formulation of the city's policy. To be sure, the city later improved its efforts to establish a dialogue via the creation of the Dog Advisory Committee and ultimately, the turn to system-wide planning.

The NPS, of course, also tried to create a deliberative result with the negotiated rulemaking process. Yet its early advocacy against off-leash recreation, evident in its illegal rescission of the 1979 Pet Policy, its closures at Funston, and its resultant identification with groups aligned against dog walkers, such as the Golden Gate Audubon Society, undermined the agency's standing as a neutral arbiter. What is more, the NPS asserted "trump cards," or assumptions that could not be questioned. These are unacceptable in participatory theory, and these trump cards weighed heavily against the interests of dog walkers. Most significantly, the dog walkers were never granted a genuine conversation about the ecological impact of their recreational activity. The NPS did not satisfactorily respond to their arguments that off-leash recreation did not cause significant harm to plants and wildlife.

The Avon Town Council shunned the very idea of deliberation in 1998, as it would have subjected its decision to scrutiny and amendment. In this case, a final decision *preceded* public input and deliberation. That decision eliminated off-leash recreation on all town property, and thus any input from those seeking to retain this activity was unwanted and ultimately ignored. Since off-leash advocates cared so deeply about their loss and pursued the only option available to them in the form of a special town meeting, the Town Council cleverly responded with a political solution that would void any decisions made at that meeting. It put the issue to the voters of Avon in the form of a referendum. In so doing, the Town Council minimized the impact of the dog walkers' intense feelings and eliminated all potential for compromise or deliberation. Yet it could claim the "democratic" high road, as a vote, after all, is a vote. This format, which guaranteed winners and losers, poisoned communal relations in Avon. Divisions in the town were magnified, not soothed. Years later, the "losing" side still feels bitter toward the Town Council and a sense of alienation from Avon. A participatory democrat would accordingly fail Avon on the criterion of popular sovereignty despite its superficial claims to democracy.

Clearly, Avon's policy did not incorporate the concerns of off-leash advocates because of the timing of its announcement. In contrast, the NPS was diligent in its solicitation and study of public input, as was required by federal law. It cannot be said that the NPS ignored public input since it was the basis upon which it launched the negotiated rulemaking process. Yet any agreements that emerged from that process would not have been binding given the environmental planning piece and the NPS's discretion. With no consensus reached on the areas most important to dog walkers in San Francisco, the NPS must make the policy. Whether the NPS will treat the interests of dog walkers seriously remains an open question. Indeed, with a current effort to rename the GGNRA a national park, the NPS seems to be setting the stage to reduce recreational use, an outcome that would severely harm the interests of off-leash advocates.

Ironically, the city, which failed to analyze the input from dog walkers in 2001, ultimately did better in incorporating the concerns of dog walkers into its substantive policy. Perhaps because of economic necessity, the city heeded dog walkers' desires for timed-use options and a lack of "pens." Of the three, the Avon Town Council, the NPS, and the city, the latter, after a very rocky start, came the closest to satisfying the requirements of participatory democracy. The NPS, while striking the proper appearance with its formal studies, came up short substantively on these admittedly difficult criteria. The Avon Town Council did not even attempt to meet these criteria. It is interesting that the most financially strapped of the three governmental bodies received the highest grade. Sadly, that democratic outreach was motivated, at least in part, by a financial inability to enforce a more punitive policy. The city basically had little choice but to work out a compromise with off-leash advocates, while Avon had the resources to enforce a punitive policy.

## LESSONS FOR GOVERNMENT

It is perhaps not too presumptuous to speculate that officials in Avon, the San Francisco RPD, and the NPS did not exactly enjoy their brushes with leashing politics. While the occasional anti- or pro-leash zealot secures a spot on a decision-making body, most governmental officials would probably prefer to avoid the spectacle that accompanies such divisive issues. Yet ironically, and most especially in Avon and the NPS cases, governmental officials not only triggered, but seemed to fan the flames of the leashing controversies. What can other officeholders, who might yet confront this issue, learn from their experiences so as to resolve the issue in a more democratic and equitable manner?

### Rise Above the Fray

When constituents are aligned against one another on an issue of great concern to them, governments should not align with one side and become a partisan in the fight. When governments do that, as Avon and to some extent, the NPS did, they infuriate those citizens on the "other" side. They transform the already contentious issue of leashing into a multifaceted debate about fairness, objectivity, inclusivity, access, and a host of other emotionally-charged concerns. The "losing" side becomes doubly angry, both at the substantive resolution and the political process.

Instead, in leashing disputes, government officials should first and foremost validate the concerns on each side. Whatever their own personal views, officials should acknowledge the legitimacy of a citizen's preferences on his or her own terms. A government official is not there to judge those preferences in such cases. Remember that this policy dispute does not involve ethically inviolable principles, but concerns the competing uses of recreational space. It is nonetheless extremely important to people and that importance should be acknowledged.

If government officials accorded such respect to the advocates and opponents of leash laws and appreciated the passion on each side, it is almost certain that they would seek a compromise. Importantly, they should let that goal be known from the start so that both sides have an incentive to work with authorities and their opponents. People behave with much less restraint when they do not think there is anything to lose. If one side is favored, that too poisons any hopes of negotiation with the other. The government, which rises above the fray, validates the concerns of all participants in the debate, and firmly and consistently insists on compromise, has the best chance of resolving this issue equitably and without spectacle.

## Do Not Be Rash

Given how important this issue is to people, it is imperative that governments not act hastily. Decisions should be made after public input and should be supported, when at all possible, with evidence. In these cases, dog walkers were especially incensed with decisions made without their input and on the basis of anecdotal and/or controversial evidence. When people are consulted and presented with arguments, which are substantiated, they are inclined to respond reasonably. Alternatively, when someone is told their recreational activity is to be banned without any prior consultation or supporting data, that person is likely to become indignant.

Governmental deliberation will not only yield a more reasonable response from partisans in this debate, but it will very possibly generate new ideas. Because off-leash recreation is so popular and important to people, its advocates are likely to develop creative ideas about how to accommodate their needs without infringing upon the interests of others. Once people feel "safe" or believe that the government is truly unbiased and committed to compromise, they will almost assuredly become a part of the solution.

## Keep in Touch

When a compromise is secured, governmental officials should retain open lines of communication with off-leash advocates and opponents. Ideally, off-leash advocates, as they have done in San Francisco and so many other places, will have organized groups with a leadership structure. If complaints or problems arise, governmental officials can contact leaders, who can attempt to resolve the matter before it escalates. This approach would build a constructive relationship among dog walkers, opponents, and the government, as its implicit assumption is the accommodation of all interests. Compare that approach to one in which a government accumulates complaints, never attempts to alleviate the situation or inform dog walkers about them, and then uses those complaints to ban off-leash walking. That type of approach is sure to generate anger and frustration, while open lines of communication build trust.

---

When leashing issues arise, governments will be challenged. However, it is possible to deal with these issues in a manner that brings out the best in people, builds community, and satisfies all but the most zealous. To do so, a government must accept the significance of this issue and have the will to resolve it fairly.

## LESSONS FOR THE MULTIUSE FIGHT

As these three cases document, dog walkers cannot count on governments to have that will. To the contrary, the cases unequivocally illustrate that dog walkers lose at times and do so in ways devastating to their interests. In these cases, they—people looking to run their dogs—were cast as a "special interest," with all the negative imagery that implies. Other recreational interests are rarely, if ever, cast this way, even if some interests, such as downhill skiing or golf, are practiced by a smaller and probably wealthier segment of the population. To be sure, dog walkers, unlike skiers and golfers, were trying to retain access to multiuse areas, places shared with other types of users. That is an increasingly tough fight and yet, given the decrease in open space and the need for community-building, it is a cause worth the effort. Such multiuse areas bring different types of people together and importantly, they define dog walkers as a part of the community. To be sure, dog parks, or exclusive-use areas, are needed and provide much enjoyment for many people and their dogs. Alone, however, it is highly unlikely that they can serve the enormous demand for off-leash recreation. Access to multiuse areas, whether in the form of timed-use or without restriction, allows dog walkers to continue the centuries-old tradition of *walking* with their dogs.

### Organization

If in real estate the mantra is location, location, location, in politics it is organization, organization, organization. The importance of organization simply cannot be overstated. In San Francisco, dog walkers clearly obtained better results once they created permanent advocacy organizations. When any group's interests are attacked frontally, as they were in 2001 and 2002 in San Francisco and 1998 in Avon, people will come together, attend meetings, and organize. Much effort must then go into the maintenance of the organization during ordinary times. Without an organization, attacks can go unnoticed until it is too late to do anything about them and there can be a steady erosion of off-leash recreation. Each decision might appear minimal and therefore not result in outrage, but a group of such decisions can collectively harm the interests of dog walkers severely. A permanent organization remains vigilant in its group's defense and additionally negotiates with other groups and the government. In so doing, it gains legitimacy for the activity itself.

Dog walkers in San Francisco, Seattle, Denver, Boulder, New York, and so many other places have built and nurtured such permanent organizations. Why not take the next step and create a national organization that enables these groups to retain local independence but provides the benefits of numbers and unity? The Golden Gate Audubon Society was able to tap into a national organization to the detriment of dog walkers in San Francisco. Surely, San Francisco dog walkers could have called upon such a national network, had one existed, to solicit thousands of comments about the need for off-leash walking at the GGNRA. What is more, a national organization could assist local groups of citizens in the early stages of formation, sharing strategies and useful information.

Dog walkers, if sufficiently organized, would have significant political clout. They would have a huge grassroots membership, which could flood Congress with e-mails, letters, and phone calls when necessary. Additionally, the group would not lack financial resources, as at least a portion of this group has demonstrated a willingness and ability to donate financially to this cause. Finally, the organization could appeal to its membership to vote on the basis of a cross-cutting issue, or one that does not divide along party lines. A national organization could give dog walkers a voice with real power, much like other interests have. Consider, for one impressive example, the political power of the American Association of Retired Persons.

## Public Image

It is essential that dog walkers are mindful of their public image and take a proactive approach to ensure that it is positive. In 1998, the Avon Town Council successfully painted a horrific image of dog walkers as selfish, angry, obnoxious, and even dangerous individuals, using that stereotype to win the referendum. It is all too easy to depict dog walkers this way once a government has attacked their interests and taken something of great value from them. Dog walkers must be careful not to fall prey to such traps. Otherwise, they become like the little brother who hits an innocent-looking, older sibling who, unbeknownst to all, had just secretly pinched him.

Organized groups, such as SFDog, can humanize dog walkers and explain the benefits of off-leash recreation. Many of these groups have done a great job with the latter task and arguably, need to pay attention to the former goal as well. People—thousands upon thousands of them—love this activity and draw happiness from it, while simultaneously benefiting another species. That *human* joy needs to be communicated in a way that does not require listeners to accept dog people's assumptions about dogs. Consider an analogy. I fully understand that people truly love golf and obtain great enjoyment and benefit from it, yet I have absolutely no comprehension of the explanation for that. Nonetheless, I respect the reality and am totally supportive of the creation and maintenance of golf courses, including public ones. Dog walkers similarly need to convince humans—non-dog people, that is—of *their* love for off-leash recreation without getting into a controversial discussion of why they love it. Dog walkers are no more or less selfish than anyone else. Yet they are depicted at times as selfish when golfers, bikers, surfers, and others are not. Even hunters have cultivated a better reputation. Those facts are indicative of an image problem, one dog walkers need to address via outreach and education. Above all, they must never allow themselves to be goaded into angry spectacle, no matter how outrageous the provocation.

## Common Cause

Dog walkers should offer the proverbial olive branch to their adversaries, and if organized nationally, they could do so. Yes, I am aware that no good deed goes unpunished and that the branch might very well be thrown back in the form of a stick or worse. Nonetheless, it is worth the effort. How, in the name of good sense, can the Sierra Club be the enemy of people who love to hike with dogs? One of the goals of a national organization or even a statewide organization could be to create *more* trails and to preserve open space. If the organization directed some of its lobbying efforts to those ends, it would obviously have common cause with groups, such as the Sierra Club and possibly other environmental collectives. In seeking a common cause and advocating for the public good, dog walkers would improve their public image as well.

Indeed, many dog walkers in San Francisco found it painful that the Audubon Society and environmental groups were aligned against them. Many, many dog walkers love birds, and many, many bird watchers love dogs. Often, a close relationship with one animal leads to an appreciation of other species. Recall that some opponents of off-leash walking might resent the threat to the human-animal distinction that a close relationship with a dog poses. Those opponents are unlikely to support any wildlife groups or objectives. Dogs, in demonstrating the value of another species, sometimes make animal lovers and environmentalists of their unsuspecting keepers. Why not build on that bridge? Why not reach out to those in other animal-loving groups who have no disdain for dogs? If *all* animal-lovers and environmentalists made common cause, the range of their accomplishments could be vast.

Dog walkers might additionally bring a healthy dose of pragmatism to the legislative table and be well positioned to appeal to both sides of the political aisle. After all, they are necessarily adept at begging for scraps and seeking compromises. On the issue of open space, they could position themselves between extremists who, on one side, want to exploit public land for commercial profit, and on the other side, will not allow any recreational uses of public lands. Given the problem of obesity in the United States and the health benefits of exercise for virtually everyone, an organization that advocated for the maintenance and expansion of *recreational* space could win over hearts and minds, and it could do so in a way that would be acceptable to environmentalists and animal lovers.

## MAKING THE FUTURE

As these cases illustrate, dog walkers can and have lost access to places very dear to their hearts. Such outcomes do not at all detract from the extraordinary achievements of organized dog walkers in the span of just over a decade. Given the *lack* of national organization, the spontaneous emergence of so many grassroots groups is astounding. There has been nothing short of an explosion of local organization, and there are now over 1,600 off-leash areas to claim as a result. That is good news indeed for dog walkers. And yet, they cannot be content with these accomplishments.

A "victory," such as the establishment or maintenance of an off-leash area, is never permanent, particularly if it is multiuse. Ironically, as the activity of off-leash dog-walking *increases* in popularity, it has been more likely to come under attack. People seek to eliminate it, citing its very popularity or "too many dogs." The proper response to signs of an increasingly popular activity, which is healthy and enjoyable, is to find *more, not fewer* places in which to engage in the activity. While dog parks certainly help to fulfill the demand, multiuse areas are also needed and are symbolically important. They were historically the *only* type of places to walk dogs or engage in other forms of recreation. It is those areas, true gems in populated cities and anonymous suburbia, which are most often endangered. Such places will only be retained with persistence, humor (lots of that), friendship, and above all, organization.

# Selected References

Aberbach, Joel D., and Bert A. Rockman. *The Web of Politics*. Washington, DC: Brookings Institution, 2000.

American Veterinary Medical Association. *U.S. Pet Ownership and Demographics Sourcebook*. 2007 ed. Schaumburg, IL: American Veterinary Medical Association, 2007.

Anderson, P. Elizabeth. *The Powerful Bond between People and Pets: Our Boundless Connections to Companion Animals*. Westport, CT: Praeger, 2008.

Arblaster, Anthony. *Democracy*. 2nd ed. Minneapolis: University of Minnesota Press, 1994.

Barber, Benjamin. *Strong Democracy: Participatory Politics for a New Age*. Berkeley: University of California Press, 1984.

BARK Editors, ed. *Dog is My Co-Pilot: Great Writers on the World's Oldest Friendship*. New York: Three Rivers Press, 2003.

Barker, Malcolm E. *Bummer and Lazarus, San Francisco's Famous Dogs: A True Story, as Reported in the Newspapers of 1861-1865*. San Francisco: Londonborn Publications, 2001.

Battiata, Mary. "Lassie Go Home: Dogs and Humans have belonged to a mutual admiration society for thousands of years. So why, suddenly do dogs seem so annoying so much of the time?" *Washington Post*, May 30, 1999.

Beck, Alan, and Aaron Katcher. *Between People and Pets: The Importance of Animal Companionship*. Rev. ed. West Lafayette, IN: Purdue University Press, 1996.

Bekoff, Marc. *The Emotional Lives of Animals: A Leading Scientist Explores Animal Joy, Sorrow, and Empathy—and Why They Matter*. With a forward by Jane Goodall. Novato, CA: New World Library, 2007.

Bellah, Robert N., Richard Madsen, William M. Sullivan, Ann Swidler, and Steven M. Tipton. *Habits of the Heart: Individualism and Commitment in American Life.* New York: Harper and Row Publishers, 1985.

Benhabib, Seyla, ed. *Democracy and Difference: Contesting the Boundaries of the Political.* Princeton, NJ: Princeton University Press, 1996.

Bennett, Lance. *News: The Politics of Illusion.* 7th ed. New York: Longman, 2006.

Blaug, Ricardo, and John Schwarzmantel, eds. *Democracy.* New York: Columbia University Press, 2000.

Brandow, Michael. *New York's Poop Scoop Law: Dogs, the Dirt, and Due Process.* West Lafayette, IN: Purdue University Press, 2008.

Broder, David S. *Democracy Derailed: Initiative Campaigns and The Power of Money.* New York: A James H. Silberman Book, Harcourt, Inc., 2000.

Coile, D. Caroline. *Barron's Encyclopedia of Dog Breeds.* Hauppauge, NY: Barron's Educational Series, Inc., 1998.

Curnutt, Jordan. *Animals and the Law: A Sourcebook.* Santa Barbara: ABC-CLIO, 2001.

Dryzek, John S. *Deliberative Democracy and Beyond: Liberals, Critics, Contestations.* New York: Oxford University Press, 2000.

Duany, Andres, Elizabeth Plater-Zyberk, and Jeff Speck. *Suburban Nation: The Rise of Sprawl and the Decline of the American Dream.* New York: North Point Press, A Division of Farrar, Straus and Giroux, 2000.

Fallows, James. *Breaking the News: How the Media Undermine American Democracy.* New York: Vintage, 1997.

Fishkin, James. *Democracy and Deliberation: New Directions for Democratic Reform.* New Haven, CT: Yale University Press, 1991.

Fowler, Robert Booth. *The Dance with Community: The Contemporary Debate in American Political Thought.* Lawrence, KS: University Press of Kansas, 1991.

Gormley, William T., Jr., and Steven J. Balla. *Bureaucracy and Democracy: Accountability and Performance.* Washington, DC: Congressional Quarterly Press, 2003.

Gutmann, Amy, and Dennis Thompson. *Democracy and Disagreement: Why Moral Conflict Cannot be Avoided in Politics, and What Should be Done About It.* Cambridge, MA: Belknap Press of Harvard University Press, 1998.

Harkin, Peter. *Inside City Parks.* Washington, DC: Urban Land Institute, 2000.

Heclo, Hugh. *A Government of Strangers: Executive Politics in Washington.* Washington, DC: Brookings Institution, 1977.

————. "Issue Networks and the Executive Establishment." In *The New American Political System*, edited by Anthony King. Washington, DC: American Enterprise Institute, 1978.

Held, David. *Models of Democracy*. 3rd ed. Stanford, CA: Stanford University Press, 2006.

Hobbs, Frank, and Nicole Stoops. *Demographic Trends in the Twentieth Century*. US Census Bureau, Census 2000 Special Reports, Series CENSR-4. Washington, DC: US Government Printing Office, 2002.

Hudson, William E. *American Democracy in Peril: Eight Challenges to America's Future*. 5th ed. Washington, DC: CQ Press, A Division of Congressional Quarterly, Inc., 2006.

Kahane, David. "Pluralism, Deliberation and Citizen Competence: Recent Developments in Democratic Theory." *Social Theory and Practice* 26:3 (Fall 2000): 509-25.

Kerwin, Cornelius M. *Rulemaking: How Government Agencies Write Law and Make Policy*. 3rd ed. Washington, DC: Congressional Quarterly Press, 2003.

Klein, Herbert S. *A Population History of the United States*. New York: Cambridge University Press, 2004.

Lowi, Theodore. *The End of Liberalism: The Second Republic of the United States*. 2nd ed. New York: W. W. Norton and Company, 1979.

Macedo, Stephen, ed. *Deliberative Politics: Essays on Democracy and Disagreement*. New York: Oxford University Press, 1999.

MacPherson, C. B. *The Political Theory of Possessive Individualism: Hobbes to Locke*. New York: Oxford University Press, 1962.

Mahtesian, Charles. "The Trouble with Dogs." *Governing* (March 1999). http://www.governing.com/archive/1999/mar/dogs.txt. Accessed August 5, 2003 (link discontinued).

Manning, Kathleen, and Jim Dickson. *Images of America: San Francisco's Ocean Beach*. San Francisco: Arcadia Publishing, 2003.

Mansbridge, Jane J. *Beyond Adversary Democracy*. New York: Basic Books, Inc., Publishers, 1980.

Masson, Jeffrey Moussaieff. *Dogs Never Lie About Love*. New York: Three Rivers Press, 1997.

Mill, John Stuart. *Utilitarianism, On Liberty, and Considerations on Representative Government*. Edited by H. B. Acton. London: J. M. Dent & Sons, 1972.

Miroff, Bruce. *Icons of Democracy: American Leaders as Heroes, Aristocrats, Dissenters and Democrats*. New York: Basic Books, 1994.

Morrell, Michael E. "Citizens' Evaluations of Participatory Democratic Procedures: Normative Theory Meets Empirical Science." *Political Research Quarterly* 52:2 (June 1999): 293-322.

Mouffe, Chantal, ed. *Dimensions of Radical Democracy: Pluralism, Citizenship, Community.* New York: Verso, 1992.

Okamoto, Ariel Rubissow. *Golden Gate National Parks: Guide to the Parks.* 2nd ed. San Francisco: Golden Gate National Parks Conservancy, 2000.

Pateman, Carol. *Participation and Democratic Theory.* New York: Cambridge University Press, 1970.

Phillips, Anne. *Engendering Democracy.* University Park, PA: The Pennsylvania State University Press, 1991.

Podberscek, Anthony L., Elizabeth S. Paul, and James A. Serpell, eds. *Companion Animals and Us: Exploring the Relationship between People and Pets.* New York: Cambridge University Press, 2000.

Putnam, Robert. *Bowling Alone: The Collapse and Revival of American Community.* New York: Simon and Schuster, 2000.

Robinson, Eric W., ed. *Ancient Greek Democracy: Readings and Sources.* Malden, MA: Blackwell Publishing, Ltd, 2004.

Sanders, Clinton R. *Understanding Dogs: Living and Working with Canine Companions.* Philadelphia: Temple University Press, 1999.

Schaffer, Michael. *One Nation Under Dog: Adventures in the New World of Prozac-Popping Puppies, Dog-Park Politics, and Organic Pet Food.* New York: Henry Holt and Company, 2009.

Schwartz, Marion. *A History of Dogs in the Early Americas.* New Haven, CT: Yale University Press, 1997.

Serpell, James A., ed. *The Domestic Dog: Its Evolution, Behavior and Interactions with People.* New York: Cambridge University Press, 1995.

Shea, Daniel, ed. *Mass Politics: The Politics of Popular Culture.* New York: St. Martin's/Worth, 1999.

Sinclair, T. A. *A History of Greek Political Thought.* New York: Meridian Books— The World Publishing Company, 1967.

Sunstein, Cass R. *Democracy and the Problem of Free Speech.* New York: The Free Press, 1995.

———, and Martha C. Nussbaum. *Animal Rights: Current Debates and New Directions.* New York: Oxford University Press, 2004.

Terchek, Ronald J., and Thomas C. Conte, eds. *Theories of Democracy: A Reader.* New York: Rowman and Littlefield Publishers, Inc., 2001.

Thomas, Elizabeth Marshall. *The Hidden Life of Dogs.* Boston: A Peter Davison Book, Houghton Mifflin Company, 1993.

Thompson, Dennis F. *John Stuart Mill and Representative Government*. Princeton, New Jersey: Princeton University Press, 1976.

Truman, David. *The Governmental Process: Political Interests and Public Opinion*. Berkeley: University of California Press, 1993.

Wisch, Rebecca F. "Overview of State Dog Leash Laws." Michigan State University College of Law: Animal Legal and Historical Center, December 2004. http://www.animallaw.info/articles/ovusdogleashlaws.htm. Accessed July 7, 2005.

Woodruff, Paul. *First Democracy: The Challenge of an Ancient Idea*. New York: Oxford University Press, 2005.

# Notes

## NOTES FOR CHAPTER I

1   Ken Ayers, an attorney who assisted the dog walkers, described Michelle Parris as Mother Teresa. For the quote, see Peter Fimrite, "Presidio Dog Fight: Canine Crackdown unleashes the ire of S. F. Pooch Owners," *San Francisco Chronicle* 6 November 1997, A-1. For quote, see ibid.

2   Peter Fimrite, "Anger Unleashed: Dog Lovers Protest Pacifica's Woman's Leash law Citation in S.F.," *San Francisco Chronicle,* 13 November 1997, A-19.

3   See, for example, C. A. Sime, "Domestic Dogs in wildlife habitats," in Joslin G. Youmans, coordinator, *Effects of Recreation on Rocky Mountain Wildlife: A Review for Montana committee on effects of recreation on wildlife, Montana Chapter of the Wildlife Society* (Montana: Wildlife Society, 1999), 8.1-8.17; E. Fernandez-Juricic and J. L. Telleria, "Effects of human disturbance on spatial and temporal feeding patterns of blackbird *Turdus merula* in urban parks in Madrid, Spain," *Bird Study* 47 (2000): 13-21; and T. K. Fuller, "Dynamics of a declining white-tailed deer population in north central Minnesota," *Wildlife Monographs* 110 (1990): 37.

4   Andrew Forrest and Colleen Cassady St. Clair, "Effects of dog leash laws and habitat type on avian and small mammal communities in urban parks," *Urban Ecosyst* 9 (2006): 61. For other studies finding no impact, see Marc Bekoff and C. A. Meaney, "Interactions among dogs, people, and the environment in Boulder, Colorado," *Anthrozoos* 10 (1997): 23-31; and Megan Warren, "Recreation Disturbance Does Not Change Feeding Behavior of the Western Snowy Plover," University of California-Berkeley Environmental Sciences Study (May 2007).

5   Benjamin Lenth, Mark Brennan, and Richard Knight, "The Effects of Dogs on Wildlife Communities," Final research report submitted to Boulder County Open Space and Mountain Parks (2006). For examples of other studies that found an influence on flushing patterns, see R. A. MacArthur, R. H. Johnston, and V. Geist, "Factors influencing heart-rate

in free-ranging big horn sheep—physiological approach to the study of wildlife harassment," *Canadian Journal of Zoology* 57 (1979): 1020-2021; and B. Mainini, P. Neuhaus, and P. Ingold, "Behavior of marmots (*Marmota marmot)* under the influence of different hiking activities," *Biological Conservation* 64 (1993): 161-64.

6    Jennifer Gill, K. Norris, and W. J. Sutherland, "Why behavioural responses may not reflect the population consequences of human disturbance," *Biological Conservation* 97 (2001): 266.

7    One study of ringed plovers found that "Sites that are highly disturbed are not used by breeding birds, and therefore any increase in disturbance levels on these sites will not alter population size. By contrast, large increases in disturbance levels to previously undisturbed sites would adversely affect population size." See Durwyn Liley and William J. Sutherland, "Predicting the population consequences of human disturbance for ringed plovers *Charadrius hiaticula:* A Game Theory Approach," *Ibis* 149: Supplement 1 (2007): 90.

8    Alan Beck and Aaron Katcher, *Between Pets and People: The Importance of Animal Companionship,* Revised Edition (West Lafayette, IN: Purdue University Press, 1996), 209.

9    See New York City Department of Health and Mental Hygiene, "Notice of Adoption of an Amendment to Article 161 of New York City Health Code," 2006. http://www.nyc.gov/html/doh/downloads/pdf/public/notice-adoption-hc-art161.pdf, accessed October 28, 2009.

10    Beck and Katcher, *Between Pets and People,* 220.

11    Michael Brandow, *New York's Poop Scoop Law: Dogs, the Dirt, and Due Process* (West Lafayette, IN: Purdue University Press, 2008), 89. On this issue, also see Alan M. Beck, "The Impact of the Canine Clean-up Law," *Environment* 21:8 (October 1979): 28-31.

12    Raymond Bancroft, "NLC Research Report—America's Mayors and Councilmen: Their Problems and Frustrations," (Washington, DC: National League of Cities, 1974), 8.

13    Quoted in Ju-Don Marshall, "A New Niche in Paradise: Fenced Dog Park Receives High Barks," *Washington Post,* 19 November 1998.

14    Don Waye, *Bacteria Source Investigation in an Urban Watershed: DNA Sleuthing in Four Mile Run* (Northern Virginia Regional Commission, December 14, 2000). Waye found that waterfowl accounted for 37 percent of the coliform, humans 17 percent, raccoons 15 percent, deer 10 percent, and dogs 9 percent. The findings were as of September 30, 2000.

15    Charles Mahtesian, "The Trouble with Dogs," *Governing* (March 1999). http://www.governing.com/archive/1999/mar/dogs.txt, accessed August 5, 2003 (link discontinued).

16    James Serpell, "Introduction," in James Serpell, ed., *The Domestic Dog: Its Evolution, Behavior and Interactions with People* (New York: Cambridge University Press, 1995), 2.

17    Ibid.

18  Juliet Clutton-Brock, "Origins of the Dog: Domestication and Early History," in James Serpell, ed., *The Domestic Dog*, 10-12. On the newer study, see Nicholas Wade, "New Finding Puts Origins of Dogs in Middle East," *New York Times*, 18 March 2010, A8.

19  American Pet Association, "Fun Pet Statistics,"2004. http://www.apapets.com/petstats2.htm, accessed June 4, 2005 (link discontinued). Eighty-three percent cited companionship, and ninety percent cited someone with whom to play. People could cite more than one purpose.

20  Lynette A. Hart, "Dogs as Human Companions: A Review of the Relationship," in James Serpell, ed., *The Domestic Dog*, 164.

21  Jeffrey Moussaieff Masson, *Dogs Never Lie About Love* (New York: Three Rivers Press, 1997), 9-10.

22  Ibid., 39. For more on the nature of this relationship and the depth of the canine-human bond, see BARK Editors, eds., *Dog is My Co-Pilot: Great Writers on the World's Oldest Friendship* (New York: Three Rivers Press, 2003).

23  Clinton R. Sanders, *Understanding Dogs: Living and Working with Canine Companions* (Philadelphia: Temple University Press, 1999), 22.

24  American Veterinary Medical Association, *U.S. Pet Ownership and Demographics Sourcebook*, 2007 ed. (Schaumburg, IL: American Veterinary Medical Association, 2007), 105.

25  Beck and Katcher, *Between Pets and People*, 45.

26  Mahtesian, "The Trouble with Dogs," and Deborah Sharp, "Fur Flies in Fights over Four-Leggers: Off-Leash Recreation Areas are Both Playgrounds, Battlegrounds," *USA Today*, 29 June 2001. For studies, see Hart, "Dogs as Human Companions," 163; and Sanders, *Understanding Dogs*, 10 and 16. For more on this, see Sheila Bonas, June McNicholas, and Glyn M. Collis, "Pets in the Network of Family Relationships," in Anthony L. Podberscek, Elizabeth S. Paul, and James A. Serpell, eds., *Companion Animals and Us: Exploring the Relationship between People and Pets* (New York: Cambridge University Press, 2000), 209-36.

27  Michael Schaffer, *One Nation Under Dog: Adventures in the New World of Prozac-Popping Puppies, Dog-Park Politics, and Organic Pet Food* (New York: Henry Holt and Company, 2009), 86.

28  Ibid., 15.

29  P. Elizabeth Anderson, *The Powerful Bond between People and Pets: Our Boundless Connections to Companion Animals* (Westport, CT: Praeger, 2008), 82.

30  Schaffer, *One Nation Under Dog*, 89.

31  Ibid., 169.

32  Hart, "Dogs as Human Companions," 168 and 166 for a discussion of Messent's study.

33  Marc Bekoff, with a forward by Jane Goodall, *The Emotional Lives of Animals: A Leading Scientist Explores Animal Joy, Sorrow, and Empathy—and Why They Matter* (Novato, California: New World Library, 2007), 20.

34 Alan M. Beck and Aaron H. Katcher, "Future Directions in Human-Animal Bond Research," *American Behavioral Scientist* 47:1 (2003): 81. Beck and Katcher review the literature in this article and cite findings by European researchers on this point.

35 Anderson, *The Powerful Bond Between People and Pets*, 124.

36 See Beck and Katcher, *Between Pets and People*, 2-8.

37 Ibid., 105.

38 Ibid., 88 and 105.

39 Beck and Katcher, "Future Directions," 87. On need for additional measurements, see ibid., 82.

40 In fact, one study found that combined people-pet weight loss programs can be effective. See R. F. Kushner, D. J. Blatner, D. E. Jewell, and K. Rudloff, "The PPET Study: People and Pets Exercising Together," *Obesity* 14 (2006): 1762-70.

41 Hart, "Dogs as Human Companions," 171. For another study citing the benefits of dogs for humans, see Erika Friedmann, Sue A. Thomas, and Timothy J. Eddy, "Companion Animals and Human Health: Physical and Cardiovascular Influences," in Anthony L. Podberscek, Elizabeth S. Paul, and James A. Serpell, eds., *Companion Animals*, 125-42.

42 Sanders, *Understanding Dogs*, 11-12.

43 Bekoff, *The Emotional Lives of Animals*, 95.

44 Mary Battiata, "Lassie Go Home: Dogs and Humans have belonged to a Mutual Admiration Society for thousands of years. So why, suddenly, do dogs seem so annoying so much of the time?" *Washington Post*, 30 May 1999.

45 Associated Press, "Dog Parks New Meet-and-Greet Spots," *Azcentral.com*, 30 October 2007. http://dogblog.dogster.com/2007/11/08/dog-parks-fill-social-niche, accessed (September 17, 2010).

46 Robert Putnam, *Bowling Alone: The Collapse and Revival of American Community* (New York: Simon and Schuster, 2000), 100.

47 Herbert S. Klein, *A Population History of the United States* (New York: Cambridge University Press, 2004), Chapter 8.

48 In 2001, the total fertility rate was 2.1, which means that women would be expected to have two children, on average, by the time they reached the end of their childbearing years. In 1957, the total fertility rate was 3.8, a rate not seen since the early years of the twentieth century. In the 1960s, fertility rates resumed their decline and have remained at low levels. See Ameristat, "U.S. Fertility Trends: Boom and Bust and Leveling Off," Population Bureau. http://www.prb.org, accessed June 4, 2005. Also see Population Reference Bureau, "Diverging Mortality and Fertility Trends: Canada and the United States," January 2003. http://www.prb.org/search.aspx?q=u.s.%20fertility%20trends, accessed June 14, 2008.

49 American Veterinary Medical Association, *U.S. Pet Ownership and Demographics Sourcebook*, 2007 ed., 105.

50 Hart, "Dogs as Human Companions," 165.

51 Battiata, "Lassie Go Home." Here she cites Harriet Ritvo, an author, as a source.

52 Hart, "Dogs as Human Companions," 173.

53 American Veterinary Medical Association, *U.S. Pet Ownership and Demographics Sourcebook*, 2007 ed., 105.

54 Battiata, "Lassie Go Home."

55 Elizabeth Marshall Thomas, *The Hidden Life of Dogs* (Boston: A Peter Davison Book, Houghton Mifflin Company, 1993).

56 John W. S. Bradshaw and Helen M. R. Nott, "Social and Communication Behaviour of Companion Dogs," in James Serpell, ed., *The Domestic Dog*, 116-21. Quote is on 116.

## NOTES FOR CHAPTER II

1 For some historical background on laws about dogs, see Jordan Curnutt, *Animals and the Law: A Sourcebook* (Santa Barbara: ABC-CLIO, 2001), 114-16. For an overview of state leash laws and some background on dogs and the law, see Rebecca F. Wisch, "Overview of State Dog Leash Laws," Michigan State University College of Law: Animal Legal and Historical Center, December, 2004. http://www.animallaw.info/articles/ovusdogleashlaws.htm, accessed July 7, 2005.

2 Andres Duany, Elizabeth Plater-Zyberk, and Jeff Speck, *Suburban Nation: The Rise of Sprawl and the Decline of the American Dream* (New York: North Point Press, A Division of Farrar, Straus and Giroux, 2000), 7. For components, see ibid., 5. For importance of housing, see ibid., 39.

3 U.S. Department of Transportation, Federal Highway Administration, Office of Highway Policy Information, "Licensed Drivers." https://www.fhwa.dot.gov/ohim/onhoo/onh2p4.htm, accessed September 19, 2010.

4 Ibid., and Sierra Club, "Sprawl: The Dark Side of the American Dream," 1998. http://www.sierraclub.org/sprawl/report98/report.asp, accessed January 14, 2004.

5 Mary Battiata, "Lassie Go Home: Dogs and Humans have belonged to a mutual admiration society for thousands of years. So why, suddenly, do dogs seems so annoying so much of the time?" *Washington Post*, 30 May 1999.

6 Robert D. Putnam, *Bowling Alone: The Collapse and Revival of American Community* (New York: Simon and Schuster, 2000), 213.

7 Ibid., 43-44. On decline of community, also see an older but seminal work: Robert N. Bellah, Richard Madsen, William M. Sullivan, Ann Swidler, and Steven M. Tipton, *Habits of the Heart: Individualism and Commitment in American Life* (New York: Harper and Row Publishers, 1985).

8 Putnam, *Bowling Alone*, 72.

9 Ibid., 98.

10 Mary Pipher, "The Shelter of Each Other: One Big Town," in Daniel Shea, ed., *Mass Politics: The Politics of Popular Culture* (New York: St. Martin's/Worth, 1999), 149.

11 Putnam, *Bowling Alone*, 115.

12 Pipher, "The Shelter of Each Other," 149. She refers to these functional relationships as secondary ones and to those in which people know each other in a multiplicity of roles as primary.

13 Ibid., 153.

14 Michael Medved, "TV Vice? Sex and Violence Aren't the Problem," in Daniel Shea, ed., *Mass Politics*, 143.

15 See Barbara Garson, *The Electronic Sweatshop: How Computers are Transforming the Office of the Future* (New York: Penguin, 1989).

16 For some limited statistics on outdoor recreation, see American Recreation Coalition, "Roper Research—Outdoor Recreation in America," 1994-2003. http://www.funoutdoors.com/research, accessed August 4, 2005.

17 Frank Hobbs and Nicole Stoops, US Census Bureau, Census 2000 Special Reports, Series CENSR-4, *Demographic Trends in the Twentieth Century* (Washington, DC: US Government Printing Office, 2002), 14, 47.

18 Ibid., 28.

19 See the American Pet Products Manufacturers Association, Inc., "Industry Statistics and Trends," 2007-2008. http://www.appma.org/press_industrytrends.app, accessed June 3, 2008.

20 D. Caroline Coile, *Barron's Encyclopedia of Dog Breeds* (Hauppauge, New York: Barron's Educational Series, Inc., 1998), 19.

21 See American Kennel Club, "AKC Registration Statistics—Fact Sheet," 2007. http://www.akc.org/press_center/facts_stats.cfm?page=popular_pooches, accessed June 4, 2008. On the popularity of small dogs, also see Mark Derr, "The Little Dog Has His Day," *New York Times*, 5 May 2007, A13.

22 James Serpell, "From Paragon to Pariah: Some Reflections on Human Attitudes Towards Dogs," in James Serpell, ed., *The Domestic Dog: Its Evolution, Behavior and Interaction with People* (New York: Cambridge University Press, 1995), 254.

23 Steven M. Wise, "Animal Rights, One Step at a Time," in Cass R. Sunstein and Martha Nussbaum, eds., *Animal Rights: Current Debates and New Directions* (New York: Oxford University Press, 2004), 24.

24 Sanders, *Understanding Dogs*, 114.

25 Pipher, "The Shelter of Each Other," 150.

26 Alan Beck and Aaron Katcher, *Between Pets and People: The Importance of Animal Companionship* (West Lafayette, IN: Purdue University Press, 1996), 61.

27 Peter Maass, *Love Thy Neighbor: A Story of War* (New York: Vintage Books, A Divison of Random House, 1996), 3.

28 Organisation for Economic Co-operation and Development, "Employment Outlook 2004," 2. Also see Putnam, *Bowling Alone*, 194, 190. Putnam notes that there has been little change in work and leisure time in the last twenty-five years.

29  See Lance Bennett, *News: Politics of Illusion*, 7th ed., (New York: Longman, 2006) and James Fallows, *Breaking the News: How the Media Undermine American Democracy* (New York: Vintage, 1997).

## NOTES FOR CHAPTER III

1  There is dispute as to which is the first dog park in the United States. Ohlone is credited with the honor in some places, but there are other candidates in New York City and California. Importantly, though, dog parks were not common at this time in the 1970s.

2  Carolyn Jones, "A Magazine with A Bite: Activists Become Voice of Dog Culture," *San Francisco Chronicle*, 9 February 2000, A-15. The magazine remains very successful in 2010. For circulation number, see Michael Schaffer, *One Nation Under Dog: Adventures in the New World of Prozac-Popping Puppies, Dog-Park Politics, and Organic Pet Food* (New York: Henry Holt and Company, 2009), 18.

3  Citizens for Off-Leash Areas, "History of COLA." .http://www.coladog.org/history, accessed September 17, 2010.

4  City of Portland, Oregon—Portland Parks and Recreation, "History of the Off-Leash Program in Portland." http://www.portlandonline.com/parks/index.cfm?c=40212, accessed June 26, 2008.

5  JoAnna Downey with Christian Lau, *The Dog Lovers' Companion to New York City: The Inside Scoop on where to take your Dog* (Emeryville, CA: Avalon Travel Publications, 2002), 4.

6  Peter Harkin, *Inside City Parks* (Washington, DC: Urban Land Institute, 2000), 9.

7  Keith O'Brien, "Some fear Town's beach is going to the Dogs," *The Boston Globe*, 23 February 2008.

8  Rich Daly, "Arlington Parks' Dog Runs on Shaky Ground," *The Journal Newspapers*, 28 January 1998.

9  Jeff Bradley, "Trails for Dog-Walking can be easily located near Metropolitan Area," *Denver Post*, 24 April 1994.

10  Bill Briggs, "Dog Lovers, Foes in Battle over Park: Pooch Owners Take Complaints to the City," *Denver Post*, 3 October 1991, 5B.

11  See Eco-Animal, "Dog Fun Directory: The Original Dog Park Directory." http://www.ecoanimal.com/dogfun, accessed July 12, 2008.

12  For a national listing of dog parks and off-leash areas, see ibid. Even this listing is not necessarily comprehensive, as it relies on people to report the existence of these parks. It also does not always include timed-use areas.

13  Bruce Miroff, *Icons of Democracy: American Leaders as Heroes, Aristocrats, Dissenters and Democrats* (New York: Basic Books, 1994).

14  There are those who argue that three or more models exist. Such classifications make sense when one delves into the debates in democratic

theory. For my practical purpose of developing standards of evaluation, it makes sense to use two straightforward models.

15 For one description of the various schools of democratic thought, see David Held, *Models of Democracy*, 3rd ed., (Stanford, California: Stanford University Press, 2006).

16 On this point, see James Fishkin, *Democracy and Deliberation: New Directions for Democratic Reform* (New Haven: Yale University Press, 1991), 34; and Amy Gutmann and Dennis Thompson, *Democracy and Disagreement: Why Moral Conflict cannot be avoided in Politics, and What Should be Done about It* (Cambridge, MA: Belknap Press, Harvard University, 1998).

17 Winston Churchill, Speech to House of Commons, 11 November 1947. Bartelby.Com, Great Books Online. http://www.bartelby.com/73/417.html, accessed July 30, 2008.

## NOTES FOR CHAPTER IV

1 See Lisa Birnbach, *The Official Preppy Handbook* (New York: Workman Publishing, 1980). For the safety rating, see *Money.CNN*. http://money.cnn.com/magazines/moneymag/bplive/2005/topten/safest.html, accessed September 21, 2008.

2 Joel Lang, "The Dog Mess," *Northeast, The Hartford Courant Sunday Magazine,* 25 October 1998, 15.

3 Ibid., 10-16. This sentiment was also corroborated by interviews.

4 Income is stated in 1999 dollars. US Census Bureau, "Avon Town, Hartford County, Connecticut," *American Fact Finder* 2000. See "Profile of Selected Economic Characteristics, 2000." http://censtats.census.gov/data/ct/0600900302060.pdf, accessed September 18, 2010.

5 *Ibid.* For marriage statistics, see "Profile of Selected Social Characteristics, 2000."

6 M. H. Bartlett, "Avon," in *Memorial History of Hartford County, Connecticut,* J. Hammond Trumbull, ed., (Edward L. Osgood, 1886). http://history.rays-place.com/ct/avon-ct.htm, accessed September 18, 2010.

7 Town of Avon, "Town Newsletter," April 2006. http://www.town.avon.ct.us/Public_Documents/AvonCT_WebDocs/NewsApril2006, accessed May 14, 2007.

8 Ibid. On loss of 419 acres, see "Connecticut's Changing Landscape," A Project of the University of Connecticut's Center for Land Use Education and Research (CLEAR)—Avon, Connecticut. http://clear.uconn.edu/projects/landscape/your/town.asp, accessed May 14, 2007.

9 Nora Howard, "Avon, 1830-2005, A Brief History," (Town of Avon, Connecticut). http://www.town.avon.ct.us/Public_Documents/AvonCT_AvonInfo/brief_history?textpage, accessed May 14, 2007.

10 Deed of the Fisher Family Property to the Town of Avon, signed 23 December 1976 (Town Records 95: 816-17).

11 Diane Fisher Bell, Letter to Philip Schenck, Jr., Town Manager, Avon, 12 June 1998.

12 Per Avon Town Council Meeting Minutes, 6 April 1995 (Town Records 94: 606).

13 Lisa Chedekel, "Activism in the Particular Seeds Hope for Activism in General," *Hartford Courant,* 18 July 1995, A2.

14 Per Avon Town Council Meeting Minutes, 3 August 1995, 7 (Town Records 1994: 839).

15 Rita A. Niro, "Leash Law Passes with a Partial Exception," *Hartford Courant,* 8 August 1995, B4.

16 Hornaday joined the Council in 1994, while Shea joined in 1991. Jeter and Hines had been on the Council since 1981, and Woodford began his service in 1983.

17 US Census Bureau, "Avon Town, Hartford County, Connecticut," *American Fact Finder* 2000. For race, see "Profile of General Demographic Characteristics, 2000;"and for marriage statistics, see "Profile of Selected Social Characteristics, 2000." http://censtats.census.gov/data/CT/0600900302060.pdf, accessed September 18, 2010.

18 Per Avon Town Council Meeting Minutes, 6 April 1995, 11 (Town Records 1994: 608).

19 Woodford suggested fencing and Jeter proposed a leash law for weekends only, though he expressed concerns about its enforcement. See Avon Town Council Meeting Minutes, 6 July 1995, 12 (Town Records 1994: 769); and Avon Town Council Meeting Minutes, 1 June 1995, 12 (Town Records 1994: 698), respectively.

20 Per Avon Town Council Meeting Minutes, 6 July 1995, 10 (Town Records 1994: 767).

21 Ibid., 24 (Town Records 1994: 781).

22 Avon provided me copies of these letters in response to a Freedom of Information request. For the 1998 dispute, Avon had legally discarded most letters, retaining eleven or so in support of its position. Given that letters from 1998 were discarded legally, it is entirely possible that more letters were received in 1995.

23 Per Avon Town Council Meeting Minutes, 6 July 1995, 15 (Town Records 1994: 772).

24 Ibid., 13, 14, 21 (Town Records 1994: 770-71, 778).

25 Rita A. Niro, "Compromise Urged on Proposed Leash Law," *Hartford Courant,* 7 July 1995, B2.

26 Per Avon Town Council Meeting Minutes, 6 July 1995, 9, 12, 16, 20, 23 (Town Records 1994: 766, 769, 773, 777, 780). Three opponents of the law cited Fisher Meadows as an important reason for their acquisition of property.

27 Ibid., 8, 18 (Town Records 1994: 765, 775), for quotations, respectively.

28 Ibid., 18 (Town Records 1994: 775).

29  Ibid., 21 (Town Records 1994: 778).
30  Ibid., 24 (Town Records 1994: 781).
31  Ibid., 8 (Town Records 1994: 765).
32  Ibid., 13 (Town Records 1994: 770).
33  Ibid., 23 (Town Records 1994: 780).
34  Ibid., 8, 9, 11, 17 (Town Records 1994: 765-66, 768, 774).
35  See "Proposed Leash Law will be Hearing Topic—Avon News Notes," *Hartford Courant*, 4 July 1995, B2; and Chedekel, "Activism in the Particular," A2.
36  Per Avon Town Council Meeting Minutes, 6 July 1995, 23 (Town Records 1994: 780).
37  These letters were obtained from Avon.
38  For Hines's comments, see Avon Town Council Meeting Minutes, 6 April 1995, 12 (Town Records 1994: 609). For citizens' complaints about outsiders, see Avon Town Council Meeting Minutes, 4 May 1995, 2 (Town Records 1994: 638).
39  Steering Committee, Trails for Tails, the Dog Loving Friends of Fisher Meadows, Letter to Avon Town Council Members, Philip Schenck (Town Manager), Rudolf Fromm (Public Works), Glenn Marston (Recreation Director), and James Marino (Chief of Police), 30 May 1998.
40  Phil Lemos, "Objections to Town's Leash Law Raised," *Hartford Courant*, 9 May 1998, B3.
41  Avon provided these letters of complaint, one from 1996 and the other from 1997, in response to a Freedom of Information request. Avon did not tabulate phone or verbal complaints. It is also possible that the town has legally discarded of others.
42  At least, that is what a representative from the Nod Brook Committee said at an Avon Town Council Meeting. Dog trainers did not want other recreational users at Nod Brook. However, the area, obtained partly with federal money, must in fact be open to the public unless closed for sanctioned events. For comments at the meeting, see Avon Town Council Meeting Minutes, 4 June 1998, 21-22 (Town Records 1996: 933-34).
43  See Avon Town Council Meeting Minutes, 2 July 1998, 2 (Town Records 1996:1015); and Lang, "The Dog Mess," 14.
44  In a letter to Town Manager Philip Schenck, Jr., Town Attorney Dwight Johnson stated that "it is my opinion that the vote at the meeting [on July 27] to amend ordinance 49 had no force and effect." The letter is dated 31 July 1998. For the promise to patrol the park, see Elizabeth Hamilton, "Silenced Resident Blames Council, Complains Unfair Treatment at Meeting," *Hartford Courant*, 30 July 1998, B6.
45  Lang, "The Dog Mess," 15.
46  Ibid.
47  In fact, in his statement at the Special Meeting, which was read into the record because he could not attend, Hines stated, "It's just the intense use of the lake by unleashed dogs has eliminated the use of a very

desirable passive recreation area by other people." Per Avon Town Council Special Town Meeting Minutes, 27 July 1998, 3 (Town Records 1996: 1087).

48 Per Avon Town Council Meeting Minutes, 7 May 1998, 2 (Town Records 1996: 838).

49 Per Avon Town Council Meeting Minutes, 4 June 1998, 6-7 (Town Records 1996: 918-19).

50 Per Avon Town Council Meeting Minutes, 2 July 1998, 2-3 (Town Records 1996: 1015-16).

51 Ibid.

52 Ibid., 3-5, 7, 11 (Town Records 1996: 1016-18, 1020, 1024).

53 Per Avon Town Council Special Meeting Minutes, 10 July 1998, 3 (Town Records 1996: 1037).

54 Per Avon Town Council Special Meeting Minutes, 27 July 1998, 18 (Town Records 1996: 1102).

55 Elizabeth Hamilton, "Owners Speak out for their Dogs; More Than 400 Protest Leash Law Enforcement at Council Meeting," *Hartford Courant*, 5 June 1998, B1.

56 Per the Avon Town Council Meeting Minutes, 4 June 1998.

57 Ibid., 17, 27 (Town Records 1996: 929, 939).

58 Ibid., 18, 31 (Town Records 1996: 930, 943).

59 Ibid., 17 (Town Records 1996: 929).

60 Ibid., 15 (Town Records 1996: 927).

61 Ibid., 15, 20 (Town Records 1996: 927, 932).

62 Ibid., 19 (Town Records 1996: 931).

63 Ibid., 30 (Town Records 1996: 942).

64 Ibid., 14 (Town Records 1996: 926).

65 According to Scott Lewis of Trails for Tails, the vote rescinding the leash law at the July 27 Special Town Meeting was legal and therefore, the leash law would be rescinded ten days after the meeting, on August 6. The Town disagreed, declaring the vote illegal and Trails for Tails did not challenge the Town's interpretation in court.

66 Per Avon Town Council Special Meeting Minutes, 27 July 1998, 8-9 (Town Records 1996: 1092-93).

67 Ibid., 11 (Town Records 1996: 1095).

68 Ibid., 8 (Town Records 1996: 1092).

69 Ibid., 14 (Town Records 1996: 1098).

70 Ibid., 6 (Town Records 1996: 1090).

71 Elizabeth Hamilton, "Fisher Meadows Leash Law Draws Protest," *Hartford Courant*, 28 July 1998, A3.

72 Editors, "Time to Put a Leash on It," *Hartford Courant*, 6 August 1998, A18.

73 Denis Horgan, "Making Much Ado over Park for Dogs," *Hartford Courant*, 1 September 1998, A2.

74 Diane Carney, interview by Julie Walsh, July 23, 2007, Avon, Connecticut.

75 Carol Hauss, interview by Julie Walsh, July 6, 2007, Hartford, Connecticut.

76 Per written response of interview questions from Julie Walsh, received from Michael Tanguay in September 2007.

77 By the time of my research, Avon had legally disposed of letters. However, Lang, writing immediately after the controversy, referred to more than one hundred letters, with approximately half in support and half against the law. See Lang, "The Dog Mess," 13.

78 Elizabeth Hamilton, "Avon Denies Dogs Place to Roam," *Hartford Courant*, 15 September 1998, A3.

79 Per interview with Julie Walsh.

80 Per written response to interview questions from Julie Walsh.

## NOTES FOR CHAPTER V

1 Meredith May, "S.F.'s Best Friend: Where Pooches Outnumber Kids, Impassioned, Doting Owners and Hounds dressed to the Canines treat all Days like Dog Days," *San Francisco Chronicle*, 17 June 2007, A-1.

2 See Ilene Lelchuk, "S.F. Rated Top Spot to Hang your Leash: Despite Controversies, City called 'Far and Away the most Dog Friendly,'" *San Francisco Chronicle*, 8 September 2001, A-13. According to this article, *Dog Fancy* rated San Francisco the best city. For a time, it lost that status. In 2006 and 2007, for example, Portland, Oregon claimed the honor.

3 Mark Seppenfield, "In San Francisco, Pet Owners recast as 'Guardians,'" *The Christian Science Monitor*, December 2002, 1. On number of dogs, see May, "S.F.'s Best Friend," A-1. Others estimate a higher number of dogs, but this is the figure from the Animal Care and Control Department for this time period.

4 Erika Lenkert, *Frommer's San Francisco 2007* (Hoboken, New Jersey: Wiley Publishing, Inc., 2007), 321-28.

5 Ibid.,331.

6 See Seppenfield, "In San Francisco, Pet Owners Recast as 'Guardians,'" 1; and Lelchuk, "S.F. Rated Top Spot to Hang your Leash," A-13.

7 Ken Ayers, "Comments for Advanced Notice for Proposed Rulemaking," Ocean Beach Dog (2002); and Marion Schwartz, *A History of Dogs in the Early Americas* (New Haven: Yale University Press, 1997), 37.

8 Malcolm E. Barker, *Bummer and Lazarus, San Francisco's Famous Dogs: A True Story, as Reported in the Newspapers of 1861-1865* (San Francisco: Londonborn Publications, 2001), 10.

9 Ibid., v-xv, 1-14.

10 US Census Bureau, American Community Survey "San Francisco city, Fact Sheet, 2000." http://www.census.gov/acs/www.index.html,

accessed September 18, 2010. Because the leashing controversy broke out at the turn of the century, 2000 census data is used.

11 For percentage of renters, see ibid. For dog innovations and events, see Sappenfield, "In San Francisco," 1; Lelchuk, "S.F. Rated Top," A-13.

12 Peter Harnik, *Inside City Parks* (Washington, DC: The Urban Land Institute, 2000), 18.

13 Lenkert, *Frommer's*, 174-76.

14 Sue Adolphson, "Getting off the Leash: Dog Lovers and their Canine Companions Follow the Pack to Fort Funston," *San Francisco Chronicle*, 7 May 2000.

15 Linda McKay, phone interview with Julie Walsh, August 5, 2007.

16 Kathleen Manning and Jim Dickson, *Images of America: San Francisco's Ocean Beach* (San Francisco: Arcadia Publishing, 2003), 77.

17 *Fodor's San Francisco 2008*, Michael Nilepa and Jennifer Paull, eds., (New York: Random House, 2008), 118.

18 Ariel Rubissow Okamoto, *Golden Gate National Parks: Guide to the Parks* ed., (San Francisco: Golden Gate National Parks Conservancy, 2000), 47.

19 Harnik, *Inside City Parks,* 89.

20 Marcelo Rodriguez, "In S.F., Tree Huggers versus Sand Huggers: Bid to Return Areas to Original Dune and Shrub Habitat, partly by Felling Thousands of Cypresses and Pines, has Activists Bitterly Split," *Los Angeles Times*, 29 June 2003, B8.

21 On this controversy, there has been much coverage. For example, see Peter Fimrite, "Politicians protest Point Reyes Deer-Killing Program," *San Francisco Chronicle*, 22 December 2007, B-1.

22 "Golden Gate National Recreation Area—Nonnative Species," National Park Service, US Department of the Interior, January 12, 2007. http://www.nps.gov/goga/naturescience/nonnativespecies.htm, accessed August 14, 2007.

23 Manning and Dickson, *Images of America*, 10.

24 "Golden Gate National Recreation Area—Nonnative Species," National Park Service, US Department of the Interior, January 12, 2007. http://www.nps.gov/goga/naturescience/nonnativespecies.htm, accessed August 14, 2007.

25 "Our Mission," Center for Biological Diversity. http://www.biologicaldiversity.org/swcbd/aboutus/index.html, accessed September 10, 2007.

26 "Mission," National Park Service, US Department of the Interior. http://www.nps.gov, accessed August 17, 2007.

27 On this phenomenon, see Hugh M. Heclo, "Issue Networks and the Executive Establishment," in *The New American Political System,* Anthony King, ed., (Washington, DC: American Enterprise Institute, 1978), 87-124. Almost any textbook on American government provides a descrip-

tion of iron triangles or tight relationships between congressional committees, executive agencies, and interest groups.

28 For example, dog walkers use the studies of the National Park Service against the agency. Ayers cites studies done at Fort Funston and Ocean Beach that found 99.7 percent of dogs did not chase snowy plovers and 94 percent did not chase any wildlife. Dog walkers also cited a 1989 study by the Center for Environmental Studies at San Francisco State University and studies in Boulder, Colorado to support the conclusion that dogs have minimal impact on sea birds and wildlife. See Ayers, "Comments for Advanced."

29 Rodriguez, "In S.F., Tree Huggers versus Sand Huggers."

30 Arthur M. Shapiro, Letter to Supervisor Gavin Newsom, 7 May 2002. Posted on the Web at http://naprap.home.mindspring.com/id57.html, accessed August 14, 2007. He focused on butterfly collectors in his study, but the principle would apply to dog walkers as well.

31 Written response to questionnaire sent from Julie Walsh, received August 7, 2007. I sent a general inquiry to all subscribers of SFDog, asking if they would be interviewed or answer a questionnaire. This individual submitted written responses and indicated that s/he had been very involved in this issue. The phone conversations were also with people who had much involvement on this issue. Those phone conversations took place in August 2007.

32 Ilene Lelchuk, "Barking up that Same Old Tree: As New Set of Leash-law Fights heat up, even Those in Fray tire of seemingly Intractable Battles," *San Francisco Chronicle*, 6 July 2005, B-1.

33 Richard M. Nixon, "Presidential Statement: Gateway Recreation Areas—East and West," *Weekly Compilation of Presidential Documents* (8:44), 28 October 1972, 1583.

34 US Congress, House, Committee on Interior and Insular Affairs, "Establishing the Golden Gate National Urban Recreation Area in San Francisco and Marin Counties, Calif.," 1972, 92nd Congress, Second Session, 92-1391.

35 The expectations of the city are subject to dispute. There is reference to a memorandum of understanding (MOU) that cites the city's expectations. However, this document has not been located.

36 US Congress, "An Act to Establish the Golden Gate National Recreation Area in the State of California, and for other Purposes," Public Law 92-589, 1972.

37 Congressional Record, 1972, 92nd Congress, 2nd Session, vol.118, 35060.

38 Ibid., 35062.

39 US Congress, Senate, Committee on Interior and Insular Affairs, "For the Establishment of the Golden Gate National Recreation Area in the State of California, and for other Purposes," 1972, 92nd Congress, 2nd Session, S. Report 92-1271.

40 US Congress, House, Committee on Interior and Insular Affairs, "Establishing the Golden Gate."

41 Ibid.

42 Ibid.

43 In the hearings, dog walkers can point to a letter from a child asking for space for her mother to play with the dog. However, others from the Sierra Club testified for nature preservation. I place emphasis on the words of the legislators themselves and the committee reports. Testimony, whether it was for or against dog walking, does not necessarily mean that legislators bought that particular purpose. However, there was support for the continuation of recreational activities, and dogs were walked off-leash at the time that the GGNRA was created.

44 Congressional Record, 92$^{nd}$ Congress, 2nd Session, 1972, vol.118, 35062.

45 US Congress, Public Law 92-589, 1972.

46 US Department of the Interior, National Park Service, January 11, 2002. "Pet Management in Golden Gate National Recreation Area, San Francisco, California—Advanced Notice of Proposed Rulemaking," *Federal Register*, vol. 67, no. 8, 1424-30. http://www.nps.gov/goga/parkmgmt/loader. cfm?csModule=security/getfile&PageID=104485, accessed September 18, 2010.

47 "History," National Park Service, US Department of the Interior. http://www.nps.gov, accessed August 15, 2007.

48 *Fort Funston Dog Walkers, et al. versus Bruce Babbitt, et al., with Golden Gate Audubon Society as intervenor-defendant*, US District Court for the Northern District of California, 13 February 2001.

49 The SPCA Report is quoted in Peter Fimrite, "Swallows' Habitat Source of Parks Battle on US use of Fort Funston," *San Francisco Chronicle*, 25 October 2000, A-22.

50 Ken Garcia, "Move to Rein in Pooches/Free Run of Beaches Could be Cut Off," *San Francisco Chronicle*, 23 January 2001, A-15.

51 The San Francisco SPCA issued a nine-page study noting this fact and criticizing the NPS for ignoring the myriad other factors that could scare plovers. See Steve Rubensteing, "Fur Set to Fly over Leash Law: SPCA Chief Calls for Dog Lovers' Protest at Ocean Beach," *San Francisco Chronicle*, 10 January 1997, A-22.

52 Peter Fimrite, "Presidio Dog Fight: Canine Crackdown unleashes the Ire of S. F. Pooch Owners," *San Francisco Chronicle*, 6 November 1997, A-1.

53 Ibid.

54 Peter Fimrite, "Anger Unleashed: Dog Lovers Protest Pacifica's Woman's Leash-law Citation in S.F.," *San Francisco Chronicle*, 13 November 1997, A-19.

55 Peter Fimrite, "Dog Walkers' Case in Hands of Judge," *San Francisco Chronicle*, 17 November 1997, A-21.

56 Ibid.

57 Jaxon Van Derbeken, "Suspended sentence for Presidio Dog Walker: Case led to Opening up Park for Off-leash dogs," *San Francisco Chronicle,* 24 October 1998, A-15.

58 Peter Fimrite, "Paws Off Our E-Mail, S.F. Dog Lovers Warn: Park Staff Accused of Doing Some Spying," *San Francisco Chronicle,* 22 December 1998, A-1.

59 Transcript of the Meeting of the Advisory Commission for the Golden Gate National Recreation Area and Point Reyes National Seashore, Golden Gate Club, The Presidio of San Francisco, San Francisco, California, 23 January 2001, 14.

60 Ibid., 35, 62.

61 Ibid., 91-92.

62 Ibid., 35.

63 Ibid., 47.

64 Ibid., 88.

65 Ibid., 94.

66 Ibid., 100.

67 Ibid., 76. Another stated, "We feel like you guys are against us." See ibid., 84.

68 Minutes of the Advisory Commission Meeting, Golden Gate National Recreation Area and Point Reyes National Seashore, 23 January 2001.

69 Transcript of the Meeting of the Advisory Commission, 23 January 2001, 160.

70 Ibid., 154-55. The vote was 14-1, with Commissioner Meyer the lone dissenter.

71 Ibid., 45.

72 This murder conviction was reversed by the trial judge, then reinstated by an appeals court, and finally appealed to the California Supreme Court. In 2007, that Court ordered the trial court to reconsider the conviction in light of the standard that the defendant had been aware of engaging in conduct that endangered the life of another. In September 2008, Knoller was sentenced to fifteen years to life. Noel completed his sentence in September 2003.

73 See "The Diane Whipple Case," Dog Bite Law. http://dogbitelaw.com/Pages/Whipple.html, accessed August 3, 2007. For more on the case, see Aphrodite Jones, *Red Zone: The Behind-the-Scenes Story of the San Francisco Dog Mauling* (New York: Avon, 2004).

74 Dog Breed Information Center, http://www.dogbreedinfo.com, accessed August 25, 2007.

75 Tetsu Yamazaki and Toyoharu Kojima, *Legacy of the Dog: The Ultimate Illustrated Guide to Over 200 Breeds* (San Francisco: Chronicle Books, 1993), 162-63.

76 Ibid., 152.

77 *U.S. versus Barley,* 405 F. Supp.2d (Northern District California, 2005), 1124.

78 GGNRA spokesperson Sherwin Smith made this claim. See "Crissy Field Leash Rules Tossed: Federal Magistrate dismisses Recent Tickets to 3 Dog Walkers," *San Francisco Chronicle,* 4 December 2004, B-4.

79 *U.S. versus Barley,* 1124.

80 Ibid., 1125.

81 Ibid.

82 Ibid., 1123, 1125.

## NOTES FOR CHAPTER VI

1 On the extensive rulemaking authority of executive agencies, a classic work is Hugh Heclo, *A Government of Strangers: Executive Politics in Washington* (Washington, DC: Brookings Institution, 1977). For a discussion about how rulemaking works, see Cornelius M. Kerwin, *Rulemaking: How Government Agencies Write Law and Make Policy,* 3rd ed., (Washington, DC: Congressional Quarterly Press, 2003). For a discussion about the implications for democracy, see William T. Gormley, Jr. and Steven J. Balla, *Bureaucracy and Democracy: Accountability and Performance* (Washington, DC: Congressional Quarterly Press, 2003); and Joel D. Aberbach and Bert A. Rockman, *The Web of Politics* (Washington, DC: Brookings Institution, 2000).

2 US Department of the Interior, National Park Service, "Organization." http://www.nps.gov/aboutus/organization.htm, accessed July 4, 2007.

3 American Academy for Parks and Recreation Administration, Biography of Winners of Honorable Cornelius Amory Pugsley Award, "Brian O'Neill." http://www.rpts.tamu.edu/Pugsley/O'Neill.htm, accessed September 17, 2010.

4 Ken Garcia, "Move to Rein in Pooches: Free Run of Beaches could be cut off," *San Francisco Chronicle,* 23 January 2001, A-15.

5 US Department of the Interior, National Park Service, Golden Gate National Recreation Area. *Advance Notice of Proposed Rulemaking Pet Management in Golden Gate National Recreation Area: Questions and Answers* (February 2002). This document and the other documents and reports cited below in this section were obtained at the NPS's GGNRA Web site under the heading of "Dog Management." See http://www.nps.gov/goga/parkmgmt/dog-management.htm.

6 US Department of the Interior, National Park Service, January 11, 2002. "Pet Management in Golden Gate National Recreation Area, San Francisco, California—Advanced Notice of Proposed Rulemaking," *Federal Register,* vol. 67, no. 8, 1424-30. http://www.nps.gov/goga/parkmgmt/anpr-background.htm, accessed July 15, 2007.

7 Ibid., 1427.

8 Ibid., 1428.

9   Ken Ayers, "Comments for Advanced." In this well researched and comprehensive commentary, Ayers cites several scientific studies in support of dog walkers. For example, one found that dogs had little impact on seabirds residing on urban beaches. See M. Josselyn, M. Martindale, and J. Duffield, 1989, "Public Access and Wetlands: Impacts of Recreational Use," *Technical Report #9*, Romberg Tiberon Center, Centers for Environmental Studies, San Francisco State University, Tiberon, California. Ayers also cites Bekoff and Meaney's study, earlier discussed, which found that dogs on recreational trails had no impact on wildlife.

10  US Department of the Interior, National Park Service, January 11, 2002. "Pet Management in the Golden Gate National Recreational Area," 1430.

11  The preference for the remaining 1 percent could not be determined. See Frederic Solop, Kristi Hagen, James Bowie, et al., The Social Research Laboratory, Northern Arizona University, August 2002. *Golden Gate National Recreation Area Announced Notice of Proposed Rulemaking: Public Comment Analysis.*

12  Ibid., 13.

13  Ibid., 18.

14  Ibid., 19.

15  For details about the survey information, see Frederic I. Solop and Kristi Hagen, Social Research Laboratory, Northern Arizona University, August 15, 2002. *Golden Gate National Recreation Area: Public Opinion Research Telephone Survey and Public Comment Analysis.*

16  Brian O'Neill, Superintendent, Golden Gate National Recreation Area, November 19, 2002. *Letter to Director, National Park Service Through the Regional Director, Pacific West Regional Office Re: Federal Panel Recommendations on Proposed Rulemaking for Pet Management at Golden Gate National Recreation Area.*

17  Federal Panel Recommendation to the General Superintendent on Proposed Rulemaking for Pet Management at Golden Gate National Recreation Area, revised 7 November 2002.

18  Kathleen Sullivan, "Dogs' Life Revisited: Golden Gate National Recreation Area is trying to define an Off-Leash Policy," *San Francisco Chronicle*, 15 July 2005, F-1.

19  CDR Associates and the Center for Collaborative Policy, California State University-Sacramento, under contract to the US Institute for Environmental Conflict Resolution. September 14, 2004. *Situation Assessment Report: Proposed Negotiated Rulemaking on Dog Management in the Golden Gate National Recreation Area.*

20  Ibid., 8.

21  Negotiated Rulemaking Advisory Committee for Dog Management at Golden Gate National Recreation Area (GGNRA), "Meeting Summary," Meeting #4, 31 July 2006.

22  Ibid.

23 Negotiated Rulemaking Advisory Committee for Dog Management at Golden Gate National Recreation Area (GGNRA), "Meeting Summary," Meeting # 5, 21 September 2006.

24 US Department of the Interior, National Park Service, Golden Gate National Recreation Area. "Use of NEPA and Negotiated Rulemaking Act, Technique: Negotiated Rulemaking run concurrently with NEPA," Document is not dated.

25 US Department of the Interior, National Park Service, Golden Gate National Recreation Area, 2006. *Dog Management Plan/Environmental Impact Statement: Public Scoping Workshops.*

26 US Department of the Interior, National Park Service, February 22, 2006. "Dog Management Plan; Golden Gate National Recreation Area, Marin, San Francisco, and San Mateo Counties, California; Notice of Intent to Prepare an Environmental Impact Statement," *Federal Register,* vol. 71, no. 35, 9147-48.

27 Ibid.

28 Negotiated Rulemaking Advisory Committee for Dog Management at Golden Gate National Recreation Area (GGNRA), "Meeting Summary," Meeting #6, 5 April 2007.

29 Attachment B. Negotiated Rulemaking Advisory Committee for Dog Management at Golden Gate National Recreation Area (GGNRA), "Meeting Summary," Meeting #7, 27 October 2007.

30 Negotiated Rulemaking Advisory Committee for Dog Management at Golden Gate National Recreation Area (GGNRA ), "Meeting Summary," Meeting #7, 27 October 2007.

31 Ibid.

32 San Francisco Dog Owners Group, "Who We Are." http://www.sfdog.org/aboutus/aboutus.htm, accessed November 23, 2007.

33 Fort Funston Dog Walkers Association, "Mission Statement." http://www.fortfunstondog.org/mission.htm, accessed May 12, 2008.

34 Golden Gate Audubon Society, "About Us." http://www.goldengateaudubon.org/about-us/, accessed March 6, 2010.

35 Sierra Club, "Our Mission Statement." http://www.sierraclub.org/inside/, accessed May 12, 2008.

36 Sierra Club, San Francisco Bay Chapter, Local Groups—San Francisco. http://sanfranciscobay.sierraclub.org/chapter/aboutus/groups.htm#sfgroup, accessed September 18, 2010.

37 For the classic account of this theory, see David B. Truman, *The Governmental Process,* 2nd ed., (New York: Knopf, 1971). The theory certainly has its critics, some of whom note the elite bias in interest group representation, and others who advocate a stronger role for the government, which is charged with advancing a common good. That concept of a common good is not acknowledged in pluralist theory.

38 Sierra Club, San Francisco Bay Chapter, Local Groups—San Francisco.

39  For a full discussion of this concern, a classic work is Theodore J. Lowi, *The End of Liberalism: The Second Republic of the United States,* 2nd ed., (New York: W. W. Norton and Company, 1979).

## NOTES FOR CHAPTER VII

1  Per e-mail correspondence with Julie Walsh.

2  Editors, "A Candidate's Guide to San Francisco Political Life," *San Francisco Chronicle*, 10 September 2000, ED-8.

3  Peter Harnik, *Inside City Parks* (Washington, DC: The Urban Land Institute, 2000) 19-20.

4  Leslie Crawford, "What's Hounding San Francisco?" *San Francisco* March 2003. http://sanfranmag.com/story/whatrsquos-hounding-san-francisco, accessed September 18, 2010.

5  Erika Lenkert, *Frommer's San Francisco 2007* (Hoboken, NJ: Wiley Publishing, Inc., 2007), 44.

6  Hank Pellissier, "Dolores Park Dogs: A Group Dedicated to City Dogs," *San Francisco Chronicle* 3 February 2003.http://articles.sfgate.com/2003-02-03/bay-area/17475453_1_dog-park-park-cleanup-dolores-park-dogs, accessed September 18, 2010.

7  Rachel Gordon, "S.F. Supervisors Get Ready to Challenge Leash Law: They threaten to take back coastal land from National Park," *San Francisco Chronicle*, 23 January 2001, A-15.

8  Ray Delgado, "City Dog Showdown: 'Critical Mutt' Rally to protest tough leash law plan for parks," *San Francisco Chronicle*, 3 August 2001, A-1.

9  Leslie Crawford, "Dogs and Kids: Can't We all Just Get Along?" *Bay Area Parent*, June 2003. http://wwwparenthood.com/articles.html?article_id=4392, accessed July 13, 2007.

10  Harnik, *Inside City Parks*, 19. The city still battles the problem of homelessness and attempts to prevent people from setting up homesteads at Golden Gate Park. As of 2007, the homeless population in San Francisco was estimated at 6,377. For more on this issue, see Heather Knight, "Golden Gate Park Sweep: Can City Make it Stick?" *San Francisco Chronicle*, 2 August 2007; and Heather Knight, "Homeless Tally Open to Debate: Numbers on Street aren't Whole Picture, Advocates Contend," *San Francisco Chronicle*, 31 January 2007.

11  National Association of Counties. http://www.naco.org, accessed January 15, 2008.

12  Crawford, "What's Hounding San Francisco?"

13  San Francisco City Charter, Article IV, Executive Branch— Boards, Commissions and Departments, Section 4.102, Boards and Commissions—Powers and Duties.http://library.municode.com/HTML/14130/level1/AIV.html#AIV_s4.102, accessed September 18, 2010.

14  SFGov, Official San Francisco Web Site, Animal Care and Control, "Mission Statement." http://www.sfgov2.org/index.aspx?page=1335, accessed September 18, 2010.

15  SFGov, Official San Francisco Web Site, Commission of Animal Control and Welfare, "Considered/Addressed Issues." http://www.sfgov.org/site/awcc_index.asp?id=1342, accessed September 24, 2008.

16  Yumi Wilson, "S. F. Supervisor Urges Meeting on Leash Laws," *San Francisco Chronicle*, 18 February 1998, A-11.

17  Yumi Wilson, "S. F. Dogs would get more room to rove under New Plan: 19 Parks suggested for Off-leash Runs," *San Francisco Chronicle*, 29 March 1999, A-20.

18  San Francisco Recreation and Parks Department. Recreation and Parks Commission Minutes of Special Meeting, 8 May 2002. http://www.parks.sfgov.org/site/recpark_page.asp?id=2910, accessed July 27, 2007. Online version does not have page numbers.

19  Ilene Lelchuk, "S.F. to air New Dog Policy: Plan for New Parks, More Enforcement," *San Francisco Chronicle*, 12 June 2001, A-15.

20  Meredith May, "S.F. Dog Owners Unleash Anger: Critical Mutt Rally Demands Open Space," *San Francisco Chronicle*, 4 August 2001, A-1.

21  San Francisco Recreation and Parks Department. May 8, 2002. *Final Dog* Policy, 7.2 "Health Code," section 41.12.

22  Ibid., 3.6 "DPA Opportunities."

23  Ibid.

24  Ibid.

25  Ibid., 4.2 "RPD/Partner Responsibilities."

26  Ibid., 4.3 "Advisory Committee."

27  Heather Knight and Ray Delgado, "Canine Crackdown: Unleashed Dogs in Parks Limited to Fenced Runs," *San Francisco Chronicle*, 9 May 2002, A-1.

28  Ibid.

29  San Francisco Recreation and Parks Department. Recreation and Parks Commission Minutes of Special Meeting, 8 May 2002.

30  Ibid. All quotations are taken from the minutes.

31  Ibid.

32  Ibid.

33  Ibid.

34  Ibid.

35  George Orwell, *Animal Farm* (London: Penguin UK, 1994).

36  San Francisco Recreation and Parks Department. Recreation and Parks Commission Minutes of Special Meeting, 8 May 2002.

37  Ibid.

38  Ibid.

39  Ibid.

40  Ibid.

41  Ibid.

42 Knight and Delgado, "Canine Crackdown."

43 Crawford, "What's Hounding San Francisco?"

44 San Francisco Recreation and Parks Department. Recreation and Parks Commission, Minutes of Special Meeting, 8 May 2002.

45 Ibid.

46 Ibid.

47 San Francisco Recreation and Parks Department. Dog Advisory Committee Meeting Minutes, 22 July 2003.

48 Ilene Lelchuk, "Barking up that Same old Tree: A New Set of Leash-Law Fights heats up, even those in fray tire of seemingly intractable battles," *San Francisco Chronicle*, 6 July 2005, B-1.

49 Becky Bowman, "Dog Plan Dividing Duboce Park OKd: Little Opposition to 3-Way Usage Split: No Dogs, On-, Off-Leash," *San Francisco Chronicle*, 21 January 2006, B-1.

50 San Francisco Recreation and Parks Department. May 8. 2002. *Final Dog Policy*, 7.5 "Current RPD Off Leash Sites"; and Amber Evans, "Status Update on Implementation of Dog Policy," Recreation and Parks Commission, San Francisco Recreation and Parks Department, September 7 and 15, 2005. In addition to the nineteen sites, there were also two trial areas in the original policy.

51 San Francisco Recreation and Parks Department. Dog Advisory Committee Meeting Minutes, 8 March 2005.

52 San Francisco Recreation and Parks Department. Dog Advisory Committee Meeting Minutes, 10 October 2006.

53 Low attendance at the Dog Advisory Committee meeting made passage difficult. However, a discussion took place and the RPD made some changes to the plan as a result.

54 San Francisco Recreation and Parks Department. Dog Advisory Committee Meeting Minutes, 14 November 2006.

55 Bob Palacio, Neighborhood Services Manager, Area 6 Neighborhood Services, San Francisco Recreation and Parks Department. *Memorandum to San Francisco Dog Advisory Committee re: Report related to Timed Use for Off-Leash Areas*, 29 September 2006.

56 San Francisco Recreation and Parks Department. *Study Draft Dog Policy with Timed Used Concept Wording*.

57 San Francisco Recreation and Parks Department. Recreation and Parks Commission Minutes of Special Meeting, 8 May 2002.

# Index